Letterforms

Brimming with creative inspiration, how-to projects, and useful information to enrich your everyday life, Quarto Knows is a favorite destination for those pursuing their interests and passions. Visit our site and dig deeper with our books into your area of interest: Quarto Creates, Quarto Cooks, Quarto Homes, Quarto Lives, Quarto Drives, Quarto Explores, Quarto Gifts, or Quarto Kids.

First Published in 2018 by Rockport Publishers,
an imprint of The Quarto Group,
100 Cummings Center, Suite 265-D
Beverly, MA 01915, USA.
T (978) 282-9590 F (978) 283-2742
QuartoKnows.com

Rockport Publishers titles are also available at discount for retail, wholesale, promotional, and bulk purchase. For details, contact the Special Sales Manager by email at specialsales@quarto.com or by mail at

The Quarto Group
Attn: Special Sales Manager
401 Second Avenue North, Suite 310
Minneapolis, MN 55401, USA

10 9 8 7 6 5 4 3 2 1

ISBN: 978-1-63159-334-5

Digital edition published in 2018
eISBN: 978-1-63159-474-8

Library of Congress Cataloging-in-Publication Data is available.

Design: Timothy Samara
Printed in China

MIX
Paper from
responsible sources
FSC® C008047

TIMOTHY SAMARA

*Type design from
past to future*

Letterforms

ROCKPORT

Contents

PREFACE

From the time that I first showed interest in art, drawing letters was of great fascination to me. Alongside other subjects—dinosaurs, trains, and birds—my childhood explorations often focused on inventing type forms: by themselves, then as elements in birthday and holiday cards and, eventually, as titling for flyers or drama club posters in junior high school. I was ecstatic to find a copy of *The Type Specimen Book,* a huge 1970s tome of type-face styles, left in my father's photo studio by one of his art director clients. Before I even knew what design or typography was, I joyfully toiled to replicate the examples cataloged within its pages.

I think typography's appeal for designers derives from its specialized nature, not generally shared by other kinds of art-making; or, because letters embody the abstract, mystical fusion of beauty and utility that is fundamental to the design ethos; or, perhaps, that drawing alphabets links contemporary makers to those of ancient times along an uninterrupted continuum. It is most likely a combination of all these things.

Historically, type design was the purview of a privileged class of artisans who closely guarded their knowledge. The chance to enter into this secret club was one of the factors that determined where I would study after high school—at a design program in which "letterforms" was a core, year-long course, not merely a cursory elective. Creating new, custom typefaces became possible as a result but, more importantly, the course revealed type as an image, and its nuanced interaction of positive and negative shapes, details, and texture as the under-pinnings of typographic layout and the metaphorical qualities of a designed text.

The desktop computer appeared while I was in school during the 1980s, and membership in that secret club exploded a thousand-fold; pioneers like Zusanna Licko and Jeffrey Keedy demonstrated that anyone could make their own typeface. Despite this laudable demo-cratization—introducing a new diversity of overlooked aesthetic voices into what has been described as a window into the soul of a culture—type design has become nearly extinct in the majority of formal educa-tional programs. Some naïve endeavors have yielded beautiful results; but truly effective type design requires awareness of historical norms and the optical relation-ships that drive them to adequately reinvent an alphabet for future, real-world use. No one designs the next-generation car, for instance, without first being steeped in automotive design concepts of the past.

There exists a number of software applications that help speed up the type design process. The most powerful tool, however, won't help if one doesn't know what one is trying to achieve with it. Clearly, technology is indispens-able for modern font creation; still, the most code-savvy type designers will tell you that they start off drawing by hand. This book is not about how to use font-design soft-ware, nor even the mechanics of engineering individual characters, as presented in other books. Instead, the focus here is foundational: growing the ability to see complex visual relationships and building manual skills that contribute to a holistic understanding and feel for form—whether one wants to create utilitarian text faces or to extrapolate those skills to develop experimental and expressive display faces, titling applications, or letter-based brand symbols and wordmarks that nonethe-less respect the craft's heritage while reimagining it.

In my studio sits the remains of a sawed-off door that I found on the street—for me, a reminder of letterforms' concrete connection to the real world; of their potential to unexpectedly reveal themselves in the everyday; and of their power to capture the imagination in the most unexpected, and unlikely, of places.

G A Z Y R Z Y
4 Q t
W 2 & F

W ct 5 H LP O W q n æ

An assortment of vintage wood and metal type specimens from the 19th century, printed for this book by Gregory Paone of Papo Letterpress.

The modern alphabet's standardized shapes and nuanced details are the culmination of a 10,000-year progression from pure image-making for representation to a notational system of abstract symbols, or writing. Its roots lie in the day-to-day recording of market transactions and inventories of grains and livestock; over millenia it has evolved into a sophisticated medium whose visual character-istics, in the stylistic qualities of one typeface or another, capture the loftiest thoughts and transmit them from present to future—not only in the functional sense, but metaphorically coloring them for readers. Crafting an effective typeface by today's aesthetic standards first depends on knowing how those standards came to be, and why.

Heritage

A VERY LONG [YET SOMEWHAT ABRIDGED] INTRODUCTION TO THE HISTORY OF LETTERFORM DESIGN

Spoken language is said to have evolved among our ancestors 150,000 years ago, but writing evolved only relatively recently. Like all cultural adaptations, the impetus to represent spoken language in visual form required specific conditions: People stopped nomadically following food sources, learned to farm and herd animals, and settled in large groups. For organization and governance, protection, and sharing of resources—or civilization—more complex architecture, trading practices, material storage, and laws of social conduct initiated methods to inform, instruct, and record information more flexibly, permanently, and on a large, newly public, scale.

But it was commerce, rather than codifications of law or the desire to disseminate learning, that initially gave rise to writing: The first acknowledged civilization to formulate a system of marks for commercial purposes was that of the Sumerians (nestled between the Tigris and Euphrates rivers in present-day Iraq). Around 3200 BCE, they began to exchange small clay strips, impressed with pictures rolled from carved stone cylinders that identified the completion of a transaction and its participants—delivery notes to "seal the deal." Initially, these exchanges were between high-ranking officials and merchants who could afford the time and expertise needed to carve such an intricate recording device; as commerce popularized, a more efficient approach was needed: Small clay tokens, representing the kind and quantity of goods, were sealed inside a compact clay pocket, its surface directly inscribed with simplified, linear images to describe the transaction, and then baked. Eventually, the tokens were discarded and the pocket simply flattened into a small slab to make the process easier. More importantly, using images to represent objects opened the way to proto-writing, or pictographic communication.

EMPIRES OF THE WORD

The Origins of Western Writing /
Ca. 3300 BCE–500 CE

A cylinder seal (left), of the kind found in the Sumerian city of Ur, dates to around 3500 BCE. It was pressed into clay and rolled to produce a relief (right) that identified a particular actor in a transaction—a sort of early bill of lading.

The evolution of Cuneiform writing from pictographic (using images to represent ideas) to abstract and logographic (a system of nonpictorial marks to represent words) can be seen in the sequence of artifacts above. From the earliest slab (top, left, from around 3200 BCE) to the stone inscription immediately above (from around 1600 BCE), a process of simplification and standardization is clearly evident.

Business, as ever, demanded continual improvements in efficiency. It's not very efficient to memorize thousands of pictures—and to still be left wanting when unfamiliar ideas come up; neither can everyone draw equally well. Over the subsequent 1,200 years, the Sumerians solved these problems by streamlining, by evolving purely pictorial signs into more stylized ones and restricting the variety of their shapes. Eventually, they settled on a wedge-shaped stylus to create mostly triangular marks, aligning them into linear sequences to improve readability and avoid time-consuming guesswork when laying them out. This writing is known as *cuneiform*, after the Latin word for wedge, *cuneius.*

Second, the Sumerians changed the meaning of the marks from representational to linguistic—standing in for the sounds of short phrases and then words. Each step in that succession reduced the overall number of signs to be mastered and made the system modular, meaning that the signs were like building blocks, able to be combined in different ways to communicate new ideas as needed. By around 1500 BCE, the Sumerians had whittled their written language to roughly 200 word-signs, or logographs, written horizontally.

Along the way, people recognized writing as valuable for recording accumulated knowledge of the natural world, plans and instructions, and proclamations of law; important writing of this latter kind were committed to stone carving for durability—hence, the notion of inviolable rules as being "set in stone." People who could write formed a new class of laborer that was accorded some prestige; they became known as scribes.

At left is the character set of the Ugarits, greatly simplified from its Cuneiform inspiration. The characters are believed to have represented words and individual sounds. Below is a Phoenician inscription in stone from around 800 BCE—the first truly phonetic writing in the West.

The Sumerians weren't the only ones developing complex writing systems. The Egyptians, located along the Nile River and its delta on the northern coast of Africa, also had developed a pictographic approach beginning around 3100 BCE. Evidence suggests their *hieroglyphs* (Greek for *sacred carving* or *God's writing*) functioned in several ways: sometimes as *pictographs* or *ideographs;* as *logographs,** as were cuneiform's later versions; and occasionally, as grammatical aids called determinatives. In general, they remained picto- and ideographic. Still, Semitic people from the Sinai pensinsula, working and soldiering for the Egyptians, adapted some of their

employers' ideographic signs for their own language, used logographically. Around 1400 BCE, people of Ugarit, in western Syria, developed writing for their language based on cuneiform's wedges—and a highly reduced character set. A combination of these two, possibly related, experiments influenced the growing culture of Canaan, the city-state of the Phoenicians, located where Lebanon is today.

Once again, commerce helped push things along. The Phoenicians were formidable traders nicknamed *Phoinikia* ("the purple people") by the Greeks because they produced an expensive purple dye that was in demand by nearly all royalty in antiquity. Between 1100 and 800 BCE, they set up a shipping empire networking the major

Egyptian writing, seen here on a scroll fragment from 2000 BCE, remained primarily pictographic until the Egyptians merged their writing with a variation of Greek, called Coptic, in the 2nd century CE.

Along with other significant cultural innovations, the Egyptians introduced papyrus as a writing substrate—a precursor to paper. Papyrus is made from flattening wet flax reeds and beating their fibers into a continuous surface.

PICTOGRAPHIC *Depicts physical objects/places*

LOGOGRAPHIC *Stands in for sounds of words/ short phrases*

IDEOGRAPHIC *Represents complex concepts*

PHONETIC *Represents individual sounds*

The Greeks listed their letters in order of assigned importance, creating the first true abecedary, or alphabetic writing system. It was especially useful because the vowels made the language even more compatible with those of their varied trading partners, allowing the Greeks to become a dominant force in the Mediterranean. They evolved the use of papyrus scrolls, folding them into accordions and sandwiching them between boards for protection to create a *codex*, the early form of the book.

Mediterranean economic powers: the Egyptians, the Greeks, the Carthaginians, the Etruscans, the Mesopotamians (formerly, Sumerians). Their script became the backbone of intercultural communication, the language of business—unforgivingly pared to 20 characters that represented individual sounds, rather than words, and rigorously based on circles, triangles, and fletch marks. Phoenican was a modular, flexible kit of parts that was easy to learn, draw, and use.

The written version of Phoenician contained only consonants, however. Vowel sounds were considered connective tissue and not given symbols. When the Greeks—whose own cultural and trading empire was on the rise in the 800s BCE—acquired Phoenician writing, they modified it to include representations of seven vowels. Following a Phoenician custom, the characters (letters) were named for important things: the Phoenician *aleph,* for A, became the Greek *alpha,* originally a pictograph of a cow, the most critical commodity; Phoenician *beth,* for house, became *beta.*

A grave marker from around 700 BCE shows an example of early Greek writing—clearly influenced by Phoenician characters and, like other writing systems before continued development, exhibits a lot of variation in character shaping and arrangement.

A	Alpha	N	Nu
B	Beta	Ξ	Xi
Γ	Gamma	O	Omicron
Δ	Delta	Π	Pi
E	Epsilon	P	Rho
Z	Zeta	Σ	Sigma
H	Eta	T	Tau
Θ	Theta	Υ	Upsilon
I	Iota	Φ	Phi
K	Kappa	X	Chi
Λ	Lambda	Ψ	Psi
M	Mu	Ω	Omega

Compare the regularized Greek inscription at left, from around 500 BCE, to that of the grave marker shown above it. By this time, the structure of Greek writing had been standardized—as had its alphabet of 24 phonetic characters, above.

Greeks established colonies around the Mediterranean, bringing their alphabet—and such cultural innovations as democracy—to the Etruscans, a still-mysterious people on the upper Italian peninsula, who were neither Semitic nor Latin, like those in south-central Italy. The Etruscans had developed their own culture and writing, but absorbed much of what the Greeks introduced, as did most of Greece's colonies. The Greeks enjoyed a cultural and military hegemony in the area for several centuries.

By the 700s BCE, however, the Latins of the south had established a city-state called Rome; 200 years later, the democracy-based republic into which the city evolved overran the surrounding Italic city-states and spread outward during successive waves of conquest. By 400 BCE, the Roman Empire stretched northward to what is now England, westward into what is now Turkey, and south across the northern African continent. As brutal as were their military campaigns, the Romans yet were sensitive, if calculating, cultural strategists: They intermarried and assimilated the beneficial aspects of local cultures even while imposing their own religion, laws, and written language—adopted from those of the Etruscans and Greeks, as was their architecture and use of plumbing. Rome built an infrastructure of stone roads, ensuring rapid access to, and easy control of, their vast domain.

AGMR
ACMR
AGMR

Romans adopted the Greek method of lapidary (inscribed stone) writing, as well as several characters from their alphabet. This tablet dates from the time of the Roman Republic—around 400 BCE—just before the expansion of Rome's empire across Europe.

As Rome's empire grew and its culture became more sophisticated, the writing of Latin followed suit. Above is shown the evolution of selected characters, from simple, linear, lapidary carving (ca. 300 BCE) to highly refined forms painted by a scribe to plan a layout on stone before carving. Their uniform geometry, based on the proportion of a square, reached its culmination in the inscription of the Trajan column (113 CE), left.

The Romans further cemented cultural unity across their empire by standardizing their writing. A young culture when they first encountered and tried to emulate the Greeks' writing, the Romans first inscribed their language, Latin, onto stone tablets rather roughly, without preliminary planning. With an eye for beauty and, in the face of an increasingly complex bureaucracy in far-flung locales, the Romans saw a need for greater uniformity in their developing alphabet. It is no wonder that, within 200 years, these consummate organizers established a strict geometry for the proportions and stroke shaping of their letters, based on a square defined by the letter M and the circle that describes it, the O; secondary characters were proportioned on the half-square. All were spaced evenly by one class of scribes—who first planned and then painted texts onto the stone surface—and then chiselled into eternity by a second (less prestigious) class of scribes.

Painting letters with a flat brush introduced a new visual effect that the Romans found aesthetically pleasing: a rhythmic thinning and thickening of strokes, created by the brush angle's uneven distribution of pigment as it was dragged across the surface. Accompanying this shading among the characters were small, sharp marks created by scribes' easing their brushes into and out of the strokes; instead of editing them, carvers reinforced them. Scribes considered these marks—later to become serifs—not only as pleasing, but also functional, helping the reader to more fluidly proceed along the written line.

Together with their geometric, proportional regularity, serifs, and shading, the refined *Quadrata*, or *Square Capitals*, became the formal benchmark for Western typography for the next 2,000 years, despite a minor interruption in the arc of European history: the Middle Ages.

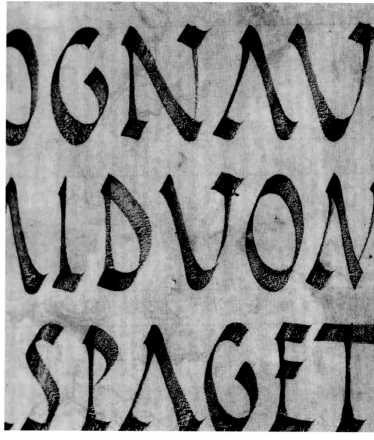

A variant of Roman capitals, shown here, were used for copying out literary works and, sometimes, for formal documents not requiring the permanence of stone carving. These so-called Rustic Capitals, or Rustica, were typically painted on parchment; a steeper brush angle resulted in a different distribution of weight among the strokes and a more condensed character width that economized space and, by extension, materials.

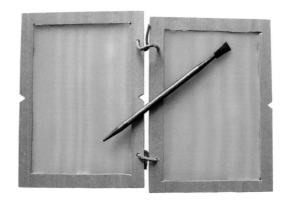

Stone carving was reserved for official Imperial inscription; letters and other day-to-day transactions used a rapidly-drawn casual form, called a cursive, that evolved after. The example at left is from around 100–300 CE.

Roman generals in the field used a wood frame filled with heavy wax— a slate—to convey orders to their troops. The wax was engraved with an iron stylus. When new orders were to be given out, the wax was heated and previous orders scraped away: hence, the idea of "starting with a clean slate."

Political partisanship, and a decadent, self-serving aristocracy who neglected to govern, eroded Roman imperial authority and the strength of its military. Between 100 BCE and 350 CE, a new religious faith devoted to a single deity and His resurrected Son gained ground among the lower classes, creating further disruption. Not surprisingly, the empire endured successive invasions by so-called "barbarians," Teutonic peoples emigrating west from the area east of the Alps. Huns, Visigoths, Ostragoths, Kazaks, and armies from a variety of other such tribes dismantled Roman infrastructure and spread Rome's defenses thin across the continent.

The empire crumbled in 476 CE. A free-for-all of warring factions, led by new regional kings, fragmented Europe. Isolated castles and manors, and the small territories they protected, provided refuge for peasants in exchange for servitude. Eking out a living in

MEROVINGIAN SCRIPT / 600 CE

EAST MEROVINGIAN / 700 CE

MEROVINGIAN TRANSITIONAL / 780 CE

POINTED ANGLO-SAXON / 700 CE

ITALIAN BOOK SCRIPT / 700 CE

IRISH HALF-UNCIAL / 700 CE

ROMANESQUE SEMI-CURSIVE / 600 CE

LOST AND FOUND

From the Fall of the Roman Empire to the End of the Middle Ages / Ca. 500–1300 CE

Above are a number of disparate script forms that proliferated across Europe after the Roman empire fell and standardized writing was lost. At left: the remains of a papyrus scroll showing one such new writing form—Pontifical Script from the 6th century—used by the upper hierarchy of the Catholic Church in Rome for Papal decrees.

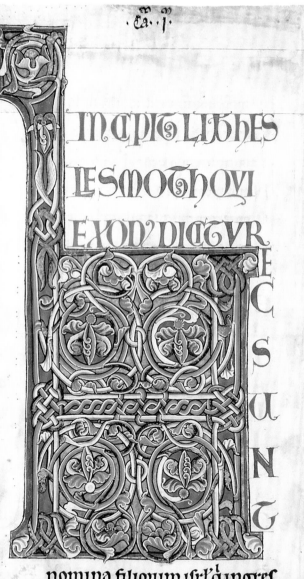

Warfare, strife, and pestilence notwithstanding— never mind ignorance of classical Roman writing—ecclesiastical scribes of the Middle Ages produced astoundingly beautiful manuscripts on vellum, sheets of dried sheepskin, using scripts with which they were familiar. Most, like the page detail from around 745 CE shown here, were elaborately painted and decorated with gold leaf, a treatment known as illumination.

The peoples who conquered Rome and disrupted the empire brought with them their own ideographic writing,

a runic form known as the Futharks. Its use was confined primarily to the areas that correspond to northern Germany,

the British Isles, and Scandinavia, where they primarily settled.

squalor and poverty left learning and philosophy to the nobility, and to the priests of the new religion—Christianity—protected from violence to some degree by fear of divine retribution and cloistered into abbeys. From there, they attempted to exert a moral influence aimed at curtailing the worst of feudal behavior and offering the relief of an eternal afterlife. It was the Christian church that saved much of Rome's accumulated knowledge, as well as their writing system. But they kept it under wraps as a now-sacred component of glorifying their deity through the careful copying of holy texts. Generation after generation of priests and monks wrote and rewrote the gospels of the faith's long-dead founders. And, generation after generation of copies of copies of copies spawned deviations in the letters' forms from region to isolated region— such that, by the early 700s, some fifty-odd

highly differentiated scripts proliferated across Europe. So disconnected were the abbeys by war and distance that the scripts were often illegible from one locale to the next. It didn't matter much; no one except for priests and a handful of nobility could read anyway. Literacy rates during the Middle Ages fell to around 5% of the population, who came to depend on pictures and spoken sermons for their understanding of the world and their place within it. Typography, in effect, became a gateway to power, and its distribution, as well as the teaching of reading, was closely guarded.

Above, a portrait of Alcuin, the Anglo-Saxon abbot credited with developing the emperor Charlemagne's standardized script in the early 800s.

ABDEFGHJ KLMNPST
amere accip gem cou olicu

CAROLINGIAN / 780 CE

ABDEFGHJ KLMNPST
remediu quere ad'o feralif comi

CAROLINGIAN / 1150 CE

From left to right, above, are examples of the Carolingian script, first in its original form and then subsequent iterations as it evolved over the course of four centuries. Split into three separate empires after Charlemagne's death in 814, the standard forms—which first show evidence of their rounded, Anglo-Irish heritage—began to undergo variations in different regions, becoming more

Between the late 600s and the mid-700s, the breadth of fighting diminished, and smaller monarchies steadily consolidated into larger ones. Among the more successful of these was Francia, the kindom of a Germanic tribe that had settled western Europe, ruled by the Merovingian family. In 749, after various intrigues, then Pope Zachary ended the Merovingian dynasty by installing Pepin, of Carolingian descent,as king; Pepin's son, Carolus, succeeded him in 768 and embarked on a series of military endeavors that reunited most of Europe. Carolus (or Charlemagne, as he is more commonly known) was crowned Emperor in 800 by Pope Leo III.

Charlemagne is believed to have been illiterate, but understood the value of learning and instituted a number of educational reforms during his tenure as emperor. Chief among them was his directive to create an imperial standard for writing, to assist in running his empire. He is said to have commissioned Alcuin of York, an Anglo-Saxon abbott who headed the palace school in Charlemagne's capital, Aachen, to devise a script combining Roman cursive and insular scripts in use in England and Ireland. The Carolingian script consisted of two forms for each letter: one of a larger scale (*majuscules*) and one of a smaller scale (*miniscules*), with rounded, uniform, yet clearly distinguishable shapes. The miniscules also exhibited strokes extending above and below the body, or ascenders and descenders. The use of majuscules to begin texts, spaces between words, and early instances of punctuation (such as the question mark) became standard.

The new script spread rapidly through western Europe and was far-reaching in its use: the 10th-century Freising manuscripts, which contain the oldest Slovene language, are written in Carolingian minuscule.

CAROLINGIAN, EARLY GOTHIC / 1200s CE

condensed and sharply drawn over time. Gothic scripts, or blackletter forms, derived from later Carolingian scripts as they became influenced by Visigothic writing and, most likely, the runic Futharks on which they were based.

This illustrated book from the 11th century, called an incunabulum, employed two new technologies discovered during the Crusades: paper and printing. In such books, both images and text were carved from page-sized blocks of wood and then inked. The process was still quite time-consuming; even so, it significantly sped up the process of reproducing publications.

Charlemagne died in 814 and the empire was split between his three sons. During the ensuing centuries, the Carolingian script would undergo variation, including becoming more condensed and formed from heavier, vertical, pointed strokes that suggest some influence from the Futharks; cultural interaction between the Carolingian empires and that of the Visigoths eventually began to evolve the script into the form known as blackletter, or Gothic script, around the 12th century.

In the meantime, however, yet another political and religious power arose east of the Mediterranean. The prophet Mohammed founded Islam and united much of the Arabian peninsula by the time of his death in 632. This influence spread to the northwest Indian subcontinent, across Central Asia, the Middle East, North Africa, southern Italy, the Iberian peninsula and the Pyrenees. Jerusalem, a city considered sacred by Christians, Muslims, and Jewish people, was taken during a siege in 637.

Beginning in the 8th century, European monarchs began campaigns to retake Jerusalem as the frontier between Christian and Arab territories became more and more hostile.

The short version of this story is that nine European campaigns over 300 years— the Crusades, or *Reconquista*—ultimately failed to accomplish that goal. Of far greater consequence are other results of those campaigns: New trade routes and access to Arabic and far-Eastern science and technologies like the astrolabe (a kind of compass for navigating); paper and printing; the introduction of spices and other food-preservation techniques; the rediscovery of numerous, intact Roman artifacts (with capital inscriptions) and the works of the Greek philosopher/naturalist, Aristotle; the notion of the university (the first in Europe was established in 1088, in Bologna, Italy); and the assimilation of algebra and Arabic numbers: a base-10 system using modular digits to represent the values between 1 and 9, and a mark to represent zero—a previously unknown mathematical concept.

I   V   X   L   C   D   M
1   5   10   50   100   500   1000

0 1 2 3 4 5 6 7 8 9

Roman numerals—letters assigned values—require complicated arrangements to convey middle values. The modular Arabic (in truth, Hindu) numbering system is far more efficient and flexible: compare the Arabic notation for the year 2018 with the Roman: MMXVIII. The diagram below reveals the clever basis for the Arabic numerals' shapes in the number of angles in each form.

The influx of new knowledge and goods encouraged exploration in science, art, and philosophy, engendering a cultural Renaissance—literally, a "rebirth" of intellectual activity—that celebrated Earthly life and its endeavors, a stark contrast to the Medieval worldview. A merchant class arose, establishing trading posts at crossroads that drew people from the countryside and grew into towns, adding to the stability of evolving nation-states.

Paper—first produced in Europe in Fabriano, Italy, in 1238—replaced vellum as an inexpensive substrate for writing; together with printing (both Chinese inventions), the dissemination of information expanded as broadsides and books became more readily available. Still, the library at the University of Oxford, in England (established in 1167), is said to have boasted a mere 140 volumes by the mid-1200s. Within 300 years, that number would multiply by the thousands.

During the 13th century, minuscules were incorporated with the rediscovered Roman capitals and Arabic numbers, and designed together as character sets following a consistent style—the modern Western

BY LEAPS AND BOUNDS

The Renaissance and the Enlightenment /
Ca. 1300–1790 CE

or Roman alphabet. A new kind of "middle-class" of artisans and laborers sought amusement and knowledge from pamphlets, books, playing cards, and other games. Printing was laborious and struggled to keep up: A single page of text and images had to be carved from a solid block of wood (in reverse), which could take weeks—and each time, the block would need to be inked for a single impression. Needless to say, people began looking for a more efficient way to produce publications.

The solution was movable type: Small blocks, each carrying the relief of a single character, to be arranged, inked, and then pressed all at once onto paper. The first movable type system is credited to Bi Sheng (990–1051) of China, around 1040; it used ceramic blocks, or slugs. Bi Sheng also is credited with evolving the use of wood blocks around the same time.

Whether anyone in Europe was aware of this system before Johannes Gutenberg, a German goldsmith, worked it out in 1450 using letters cast in lead is unknown. Being a goldsmith, Gutenberg would have been aware of coins and other artifacts from antiquity that were stamped with symbols, which were his likely inspiration.

Gutenberg designed a character set in the common Textura blackletter style, cutting each letter, in relief, from a block of steel, called a punch. The punches were pressed into a softer metal matrix to form individual moulds; lead, softer still, was poured into the moulds, casting individual slugs. A bit of antimony was added to the lead to help harden it when it cooled.

HANDWRITTEN TEXTURA / 1400 CE

Steel punch *Matrix*

Hand mould

Above, elements of the moveable type system as developed by Johannes Gutenberg in 1450. At left are individual letter slugs composed on the bed of a press.

The 42-line Bible that Gutenberg printed in 1455 is considered a watershed in the evolution of typography and print production. In one fell swoop, Gutenberg arrived at the visual characteristics for typesetting and print quality that are still held up as the ultimate exemplar today: uniform character proportion, unified style, uniform color, character crispness, even line spacing, and integrated proportional relationships among column widths, gutter, and margins.

GUTENBERG'S PRINTED TEXTURA / 1455 CE

By arranging the slugs in lines and stabilizing them with strips of lead between, and blocks of wood around them, a page of text could be composed within several minutes.

Gutenberg developed a press—derived from the kind used in cheesemaking—to apply even pressure across the entire area of a composed page, resulting in remarkably even color. Using his knowledge of alchemy and chemistry, he formulated an oil-based ink from lamp-black that adhered well to the slugs' surfaces. He printed an edition of 200 Bibles in about a month.

So regular in character shape, spacing, and color was Gutenberg's output—and produced so rapidly—that religious authorities accused him of dabbling in the occult. A costly trial to prove the process to be nonmagical—which grew to encompass a conflict over authorship with his assistants—vindicated him, but his fortunes declined afterward. Still, his legacy is profound: Uniformity in character proportion, weight, spacing, and texture are the guiding principles of type design to this day; and printed typography became ubiquitous—by 1530, there were 5,000 presses churning out publications across Europe.

ABCDEFGI KLNSNPT nípotens se ter œus bjꝼ

ROTUNDA BLACKLETTER / 1450s CE

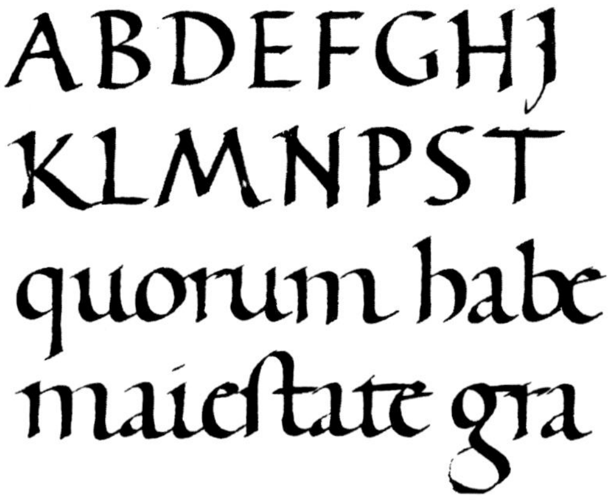

ABDEFGHJ KLMNPST quorum habe maiestate gra

HUMANIST SCRIPT / 1450s CE

The rounder, more open Rotunda variant of blackletter forms became more popular than its dense, pointed, northern counterparts like the Fraktur, Textura, and Bastarda—more for ideological reasons than for any intrinsically greater legibility, as has been argued in the past. Italian humanist scholars of the Renaissance gravitated toward more organically shaped writing that was closer in form to Roman examples.

Most of the type-design work that followed Gutenberg's focused on evolving the now-desirable qualities of regularity that his Bible had established, in tandem with refining the stylistic attributes of the letters. As the Renaissance unfolded in Italy, France, the Netherlands, and England, the needs of an increasing number of readers intersected with the aesthetic goals of type designers. New printing type designs initially followed Textura as a model, but Europeans outside German-speaking areas were more familiar with scripts of the rounder, Carolingian variety; further, humanist scholars privileged such scripts as embodying that philosophy because of their organic shaping and formal similarity to Roman type forms—classical culture was an ideological touchstone. By the 1470s, most type designers had transitioned to rounded, humanist script forms as a model.

The sample of humanist, Roman serif type shown here is from the 1470 publication De Evangelica Praeparatione. The type and the book were designed and printed by Nicolas Jenson, of France, working in Venice, Italy. It is considered remarkable for its consistent, comfortable rhythm and balanced proportions, raising the standard of typography to the level of fine art.

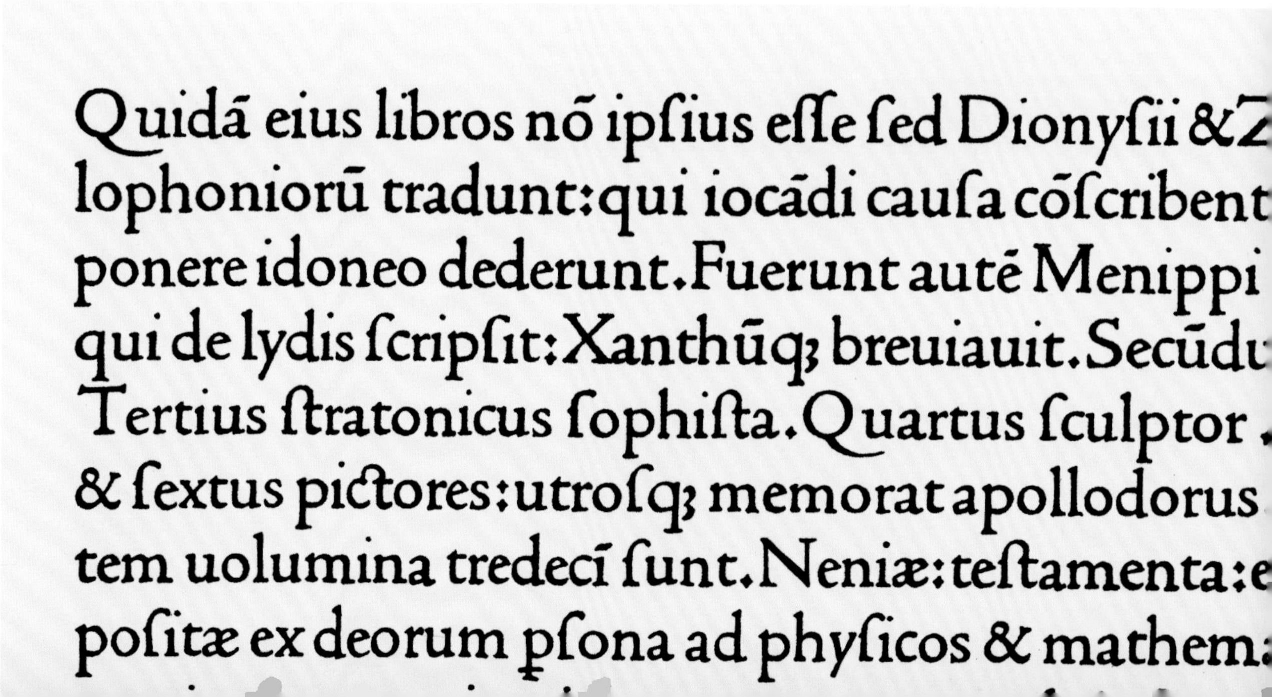

Quidā eius libros nō ipsius esse sed Dionysii &Z lophoniorū tradunt:qui iocādi causa cōscribent ponere idoneo dederunt.Fuerunt autē Menippi qui de lydis scripsit:Xanthūq; breuiauit.Secūdu Tertius stratonicus sophista.Quartus sculptor & sextus pictores:utrosq; memorat apollodorus tem uolumina tredecī sunt.Neniæ:testamenta: positæ ex deorum psona ad physicos & mathema

ABDEFGHJKLMST
et arge to: sub pena perden
igio armato, exceptis auro

HUMANIST CURSIVE / 1500s CE

Throughout the 1500s and into the 1600s, the way language was presented continued to change. Along with an increasingly consistent application of punctuation, publishers began to introduce visual differences between discontinuous text components to help readers navigate. Titles were distinguished by their size and presentation all in capitals; subtitles might be set smaller and more widely spaced; body text was set with the lowercase, with capitals to begin sentences. Type designers began to develop faces of heavier and lighter weights for greater variety in emphasis, although not yet as integrated families—printers would simply combine a bolder weight face and an unrelated regular-weight face. Added to the mix was a new class of Humanist font, based on the slant of handwriting, that came to be known as italic. Its slope and more condensed, forward rhythm imparted a pronouncedly organic quality and could be effective for emphasis, as well as for distinguishing a given portion of text as different from others.

As types used for extensive text evolved toward simplicity, others that could be used as decorative embellishments (like those of medieval illuminated manuscripts) also flourished. Above is a decorative capital designed in 1556 by Vespasiano Amphiareo, a Franciscan monk.

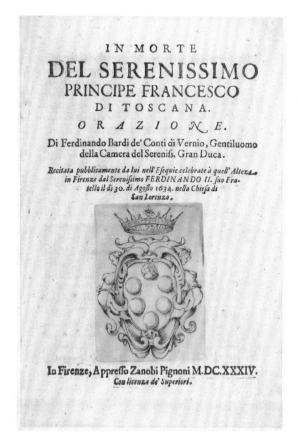

IN MORTE
DEL SERENISSIMO
PRINCIPE FRANCESCO
DI TOSCANA.
ORAZIONE.
Di Ferdinando Bardi de' Conti di Vernio, Gentiluomo della Camera del Serenifs, Gran Duca.

Recitata pubblicamente da lui nell' Efequie celebrate à quell' Alteza in Firenze dal Sereniſsimo FERDINANDO II. ſuo Fraſello il dì 30. di Agoſto 1634. nella Chieſa di San Lorenzo.

In Firenze, Appreſſo Zanobi Pignoni M.DC.XXXIV.
Con licenza de' Superiori.

This title page shows innovations in typographic layout that developed during the 16th century: visual differentiation to convey hierarchy or the relative importance and sense of different levels of text. New styles that integrated different weights and italics resulted in an effort to provide additional varieties of emphasis.

Santicum veteres urbis tia cunas, Illustresque tamque deus & qui vir

PRINTED HUMANIST ITALIC / 1600 CE

This elegantly typeset page is from a 17th-century treatise on insect biology and behavior, the Micrographia—an early instance of scientific writing from the Age of Enlightenment.

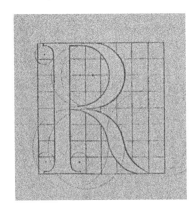

AGMR
adefgkrst

Above are the construction grid and a specimen of the Romain du Roi designed by Robert Grandjean and Louis Simmoneau in 1702.

The prevailing desire to better understand the natural world would be aided by several inventions during the 1600s and 1700s, like the microscope (revealing invisible aspects of physical reality) and spurred new investigative methods that drew conclusions from observed evidence—which often contradicted accepted notions about how the world worked. During the same time, new political and social philosophies suggested that existing class structures might bear some rethinking.

Much to the consternation of monarchs and clergy, such information was circulating freely through extensive proliferation of printed matter. In more than one instance, monarchies came to require that all prospective publications be reviewed and ideologically cleansed before being produced—under threat of death. King Louis XIII of France went a step further, decreeing that approved texts be set in official types provided by the court. Several prominent type designers were commissioned to produce such types—named *Romain du Roi* (the king's book type)—including Claude Garamond and Robert Grandjean. To impart a quality of regal authority, they designed character sets constructed on elaborate geometric grids, with exaggerated shading, that evoked the majesty of the Roman Imperium.

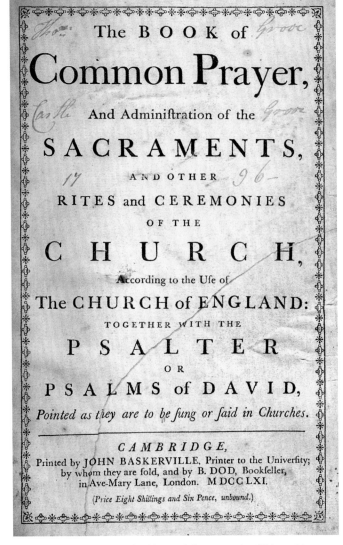

This title page is from a publication designed by John Baskerville, using the transitional serif form for which he is renowned. It is considered the first clear evolution of serif faces away from Oldstyle Romans toward a more rational form.

In addition to his typographic innovations, Baskerville is also known for improving the quality of paper by introducing sizing—a mixture of starch and clay—into its formation, resulting in a tighter fiber structure that allows for finer detail when printing.

These publishing sanctions were eventually lifted. Typographers, however, became fascinated with the *Romain du Roi*'s elegance, precision and contrast, perceiving its steadfast geometry and sharpness of detail as refuting the primitive heritage of the brush, potentially expressing the rationalism of the evolving scientific age. Individual letter proportions narrowed and were made more consistent in overall width; serifs changed from round to angular and thinned; thick strokes became thicker, and thins, thinner. The height of the lowercase, relative to their accompanying caps, was enlarged (opening the spaces inside the letters); and the heaviest weights of the curved strokes—heretofore situated lower on the left and higher on the right of a circular character, evidence of the brush angle—were oriented horizontally across the vertical 90° axis.

Types of this kind evolved first in England, through the work of John Baskerville and William Caslon, and culminated in types of extreme contrast and sharpness designed by Giambattista Bodoni in Italy and François Didot in France, who each arrived at these "modern" or "rationalist" styles independently in the 1780s—just in time for the next big thing.

AGMR
adefgkrst

DIDOT / 1785 CE

ACMR
adefgkrst

WALBAUM / 1803 CE

Comparison of changes in curved-form axis from oblique (top) to upright (bottom), from the 1500s to the late 1700s.

A page spread from Giambattista Bodoni's Manuale Tipografico (Manual of Typography) from 1818, showing specimens of his namesake character style and its usage in titling.

In 1778, James Watt of Scotland perfected a steam engine that could power a rotary device at high speed, with great force, and with little human intervention. Advances in metallurgy, chemistry and, eventually, electrical power generation, initiated the mass production of goods. People left their agrarian lives to work in factories. Despite horrific conditions and long work days, many workers could yet enjoy a bit of leisure time and disposable income—which they used to buy products; they were now *consumers*. Manufacturers worked hard to attract consumers' attention (and their money) away from competitors' products; they hired artists and printers to create leaflets and posters, pamphlets and signs, all geared to be as enticing as possible.

The 1800s saw the birth of advertising, and artists who produced promotions used every visual trick in the book to get their audiences to take notice. Alongside attractive illustrations, one of the most effective means of doing so was through typography.

LPF
Gloster

Examples of so-called "fat faces" of super bold weight and exaggerated thin/thick contrast, derived from Rationalist serifs and designed to grab viewers' attention in the context of a new kind of medium: advertising. These specimens were printed by Gregory Paone of Papo Letterpress.

CANON ORNAMENTED.
TYPOGRAPHY.
TWO LINES ENGLISH EGYPTIAN.
W CASLON JUNR   LETTERFOUNDER
TWO LINES ENGLISH OPEN.
SALISBURY SQUARE.

A BRAVE NEW WORLD

Innovations of Industrialization and the Transition to the Modern Era / 1790–1950 CE

Building on the extreme contrasts of the modern serifs, typographers began first to create super-exaggerated versions of exceptional boldness, then to decorate fonts and introduce illustrative elements into their structures. In 1816, William Caslon IV (following in his ancestors' footsteps) offered a specimen of fonts for advertising display that included something wholly unexpected: a font with no serifs, in which all the letters' strokes were uniformly bold in weight.

ACMRQS
adefgkmprst

FRENCH ANTIQUE (DESIGNER UNKNOWN) / 1862 CE

This apparently unassuming specimen produced by the Caslon foundry in 1816 includes an earth-shattering innovation in letter-form design: the sans serif, named "Two Lines English Egyptian," in the center. Sans serif faces would not become accepted as valid forms until the latter part of the 19th century.

ACMR
adefgkrst

LATIN (DESIGNER UNKNOWN) / 1870 CE

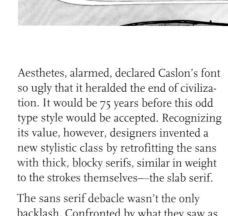

A signage type form, designed by Hector Guimard (famous for the French Metro [subway] station gates, exemplifies the organic Art Nouveau style of the 1880s.

Aesthetes, alarmed, declared Caslon's font so ugly that it heralded the end of civilization. It would be 75 years before this odd type style would be accepted. Recognizing its value, however, designers invented a new stylistic class by retrofitting the sans with thick, blocky serifs, similar in weight to the strokes themselves—the slab serif.

The sans serif debacle wasn't the only backlash. Confronted by what they saw as visual pollution (crowded advertising billboards defacing architecture) and aesthetic confusion (a mish-mash of unrelated, overworked decorative styles), English artists and philosophers like John Ruskin, William Morris, and Edward Burne-Jones called for a stylistically pure approach in which

form followed function, and followed a unified visual language—whether the design in question was a piece of furniture, wallpaper, or typography. This approach, given the name Arts & Crafts, also sought to close a rift between designer and manufacturer widened by industrialization and to reintroduce a reverence for nature into the filthy, mechanized, urban environment. The English looked to medieval art as a model for this approach; in France, the pronature rebuke of industrialism gave rise to a fluid, organic style of image and typography based on curling plant forms called *l'Art Nouveau* (New Art).

Industrial-era, Victorian advertising, such as the poster shown at top, deployed exceptionally ornamental letter styles— typically mixing several in one layout. The two specimens immediately above date from the same era, around the 1860s.

German engineer Peter Mitterhoffer's Schreibmaschine (or writing machine) of 1864 is one of the precursors of the modern typewriter (left). Such writing apparatus with a keyboard, each printing a specific character, allowed for other innovations like the Linotype (right).

The Linotype was invented by Otto Merganthaler in 1886. As its operator types on a keyboard, the machine organizes matrixes on the fly, into which lead is poured to cast a single line of lead type.

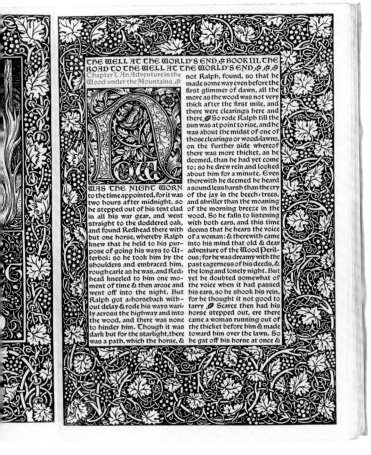

The true visionary of the Arts & Crafts movement, William Morris was the most prolific and wide-ranging of practitioners in his output; his namesake company produced his designs for wallpaper, glass, furniture, and other objects, and remains extant to this day. In the 1890s, he turned his attention to typography and the book arts, seeing that the quality of book design had become degraded in similar ways as had other kinds of design. In doing so, Morris led the way for a revival in book and text-face design, basing his work on the 15th-century faces of Nicolas Jenson.

The notion of uniting form and function, and closely integrated stylistic gestures, took hold across Europe in the last decade of the 19th century. Designers—typographic or otherwise—slowly adapted to, and embraced, the implications of industrialization. They warmed to the qualities of the mechanical, positing that mass production could, in fact, be a vehicle for introducing beauty and quality into everyday life.

An art colony in Darmstadt, Germany, (funded by the Grand Duke of Hesse) brought together a group of like-minded modernists keen to explore the intersection of art and industry. Among its leading aspirants was Peter Behrens, an architect and painter from Berlin who had begun his career in the *Art Nouveau* oeuvre, but whose work rapidly transitioned toward a more geometric form language to express

Layout (top) and page detail from The Story of the Glittering Plain, *designed and published by William Morris's Kelmscott Press in 1891. Morris sought to close a rift between design and production engendered by the Industrial Revolution; he advocated for designers to be craftsmen; to use visual style to fit a given purpose, rather than to decorate; and to unify the visual language of a work, rather than mix them. His inspiration was the Middle Ages, but the results formed the basis of Modernism.*

AGMR
adefgkrst

**AGMR
adefgkrst**

**AGMR
adefgkrst**

AKZIDENZ GROTESK FAMILY / 1896 CE

A page from Peter Behrens's 1901 book, Lebens in Kunst (Living with Art), *the first use of sans serif type (Bertholdt's Akzidenz Grotesk) as text, accompanied by initials and page borders of his own design.*

AGMR
adefgkmrst

BERENSCHRIFT (PETER BEHRENS) / 1902 CE

the desirability and transcendence of the industrial. The machine, together with the idea of systems that it implied, became a spiritual avatar for designers.

In 1896, the Berthold type foundry released the first font family consisting of multiple weights, as well as italic versions of each, designed with this kind of systematic idea. The sans serif Akzidenz font was labeled *grotesque*—the legacy of Caslon's attempts died slowly—but it came into relatively wide use once Behrens used it to set the text of a well-received art-philosophy book.

Behrens would continue to play a major role in the evolution of graphic design over the next half century, but his work, and that of Morris, immediately influenced art and design in Austria, where malcontents left the stuffy Viennese academy to pursue a revolutionary, geometric expression in imagery, as well as typography. The output of the Vienna Secession, as it was called, would set a new standard for avant-garde experimentation and systematic form, influencing the information design work of Edward Johnston for the London Underground subway and the typographic designs of Eric Gill, both in England.

Two posters designed by Hungarian designer Koloman Moser of the Viennese Secession show the radical, avant-garde approach to imagery and type design—following a strict, highly stylized geometry—that would set the stage for the Modern movement in the 20th century.

AGMR
adefgkrst

HOFFMANN BLOCK (JOSEF HOFFMANN) / 1908 CE

AGMRacfg
AGMRacfg

UNDERGROUND (EDWARD JOHNSTON), TOP / 1916 CE
GILL SANS (ERIC GILL), BOTTOM / 1928 CE

The quest for modern expression continued into the 20th century. Cubism, an approach to painting that fractured reality, was the first of many experimental movements (Futurism, De Stijl, Constructivism, and Vorticism, to name a few). Each pursued its own philosophy, but all shared an emphasis on geometry in one way or another. Book types, intended for extensive reading—even those that were based closely on classical Roman archetypes—exhibited the influence of this formal purity, albeit somewhat tempered for usability. Designers of display types, on the other hand, went for geometry whole hog.

The exuberance of early Modernism was interrupted by World War I, but it came roaring back afterward, as Europe got down to rebuilding (and partying really hard) during the 1920s. The United States joined Europe in celebration; city dwellers emulated Berlin's and Paris's raucous

This catalog cover for an exhibition devoted to Cubism features a custom, almost modular, geometric typeface designed by the Dutch De Stijl architect and artist, Theo van Doesburg, in 1916.

AGMR
adefgkrst

CITY (GEORG TRUMP) / 1930 CE

AGMR
adefgkrst

STYMIE (MORRIS FULLER BENTON) / 1931 CE

cabaret culture, adding to the fun with outlandish acrobatic feats, air shows, magic acts, and comedians—and a new genre of music called jazz.

Type design of the 1920s was bold and stylishly geometric. Posters, ads, and magazine titling presented forms decorated with exotic patterns and traced with geometric inlines, often taking on the quality of streamlined, mechanical surfaces and

AGMRS
adefgkmrst

CENTAUR (BRUCE ROGERS) / 1914 CE

AGMRS
adefgkrst

KOMBINATION (JOSEF ALBERS) / 1923 CE

AGMRS

The highly geometric, decorated capitals above are characteristic of type designs popular during the 1920s; they are derivatives of Broadway (small specimen), designed by Morris Fuller Benton, of American Type Founders, in 1928.

Qualities of luxury, elegance, and modernity emanate from the titling face in this car ad from the 1920s (right).

architectural detailing seen in household products, vehicles, and buildings designed in the Art Déco aesthetic.

Even after the global economic depression that began in 1929 put a dent in the festivities, type design continued to explore qualities of elegance. Condensed faces, with sharp detailing and exaggerated proportions, and sleek, sturdy slab serifs, offered escape to a (hopefully) future world where comfort, luxury, and style would once again become the norm. Type designers also made attempts at suggestively introducing

a mindset of order—a response to the cultural disarray of the time. They investigated stricter geometry in sans serifs of increasingly uniform weight and classical proportion, as well as modular fonts, built with parts that could be flexibly rearranged. Of the former, Futura, designed by Paul Renner in Germany in 1930, captured cultural imagination, becoming a standard for geometric sans serif faces, thereafter.

Unfortunately, things got worse before they got better. Poverty and social unrest in Germany and Italy set the stage for the

rise of Fascism, and a second world war promptly followed. Type designers' output during WWII fell off, especially in Europe. In the United States, typefaces retained their streamline characteristics until after the country entered the war in 1941; new display faces designed during that period reflected the war effort mindset, with forms that riffed on industrial stamping and stenciling of a military quality.

A poster produced by an artist of the Works Progress Adminsitration during the Great Depression.

AGMR
adefgkmst

FUTURA (PAUL RENNER) / 1930 CE

AGMR

PRISMA (RUDOLPH KOCH) / 1931 CE

MECHANO (DESIGNER UNKNOWN) / 1930s CE

Continued fascination with geometry during the 1930s found expression in Paul Renner's sans serif (top), which spawned derivatives like the line-shaded Prisma (middle). Another kind of experiment, Mechano (bottom), yielded an early modular typeface.

AGMR
adefgkrſt

ELEMENT (MAX BITTROF) / 1934 CE

AGMR

STENCIL (VERNACULAR) / 1940s CE

SIGNBOARD GOTHIC (DESIGNER UNKNOWN) / 1940s CE

From 1945 into the 60s, Europe and the United States were each reckoning with WWII's aftermath. America, emerging from war and the Depression as a military and economic powerhouse, perceived its cultural values validated. Wartime industry had invented a slew of new products that could be marketed in peacetime. TV dinners, toy chemistry sets, synthetic textiles for carpets, and the like brought prices down and comfort home. Business peddled aspiration to the good life's status quo; cocktails, conformity, and keeping up with the Joneses were paramount concerns. The visual landscape was awash with paternalistic, illustrative pastiche and text-heavy advertising. That state of affairs turned out well for type designers, who were in demand for new faces—especially ones that would capture the dreamy postwar happiness that everyone wanted.

UP FOR FUN, DOWN TO BUSINESS

Reenvisioning the Future After World War II / 1950–1980 CE

Post-WWII advertising made use of corny illustrations and stylish faces, especially scripts, to create a narrative of pleasure and conformity in American culture.

ACMR adefgkrst
CHOC (ROGER EXCOFFON) / 1955 CE

AGMR adefgkrst
BRUSH SCRIPT (ROBERT E. SMITH) / 1942 CE

ABEGRMS aadefgkr
AL-BRO (ALEXEY BRODOVITCH) / 1950 CE

ABCEG MROSTZ
BANCO (ROGER EXCOFFON) / 1951 CE

AGMR adefgs
ROCKET SCRIPT (DESIGNER UNKNOWN) / 1950s CE

AGMR adefgkrst
AD LIB (FREEMAN CRAW) / 1961 CE

Much of the imagery produced for advertising in this context focused on illustration, often drawing on references to cartooning and both Abstract Expressionism and Surrealism, two prevalent visual gestures of the time. Type designers responded with faces that would capture both the freer, visual qualities of these visual languages, in particular script forms. Scripts offered a carefree, spontaneous quality; some kept their references to the brush—a nod to vernacular languages like supermaket-promotion sign painting—while others veered toward the industrial and more tightly controlled, characteristic of detailing and nameplates on automobiles.

Along with scripts, there also appeared during the late 1940s–1950s other playful faces based on sans serifs, which offered bolder and more muscular options for display while adding the playful element in the form of irregularly shaped counter-forms, stroke contours that escaped the confines of being parallel or more classically modulated, and graphical details appended to stroke terminals.

Of course, there still was a need for subtler, more restrained faces that could be used for text. Very often, graphic designers would turn to existing, well-worn fonts—so-called "workhorses" like Garamond or Caslon, Franklin Gothic or Akzidenz or Futura—but a number of new serifs, in particular, attempted to cross the boundary between fun and function by playing with rhythmic elements and stroke details. The heavier strokes in the serif Vendome, for example, are slightly irregular in their contours and shift the weight within them into a slightly forward-leaning emphasis, creating a kind of pronounced "loopiness."

AGMR adefgkrst
VENDOME (FRANÇOIS GANEAU) / 1951 CE

AGMR adefgkrst
MELIOR (HERMANN ZAPF) / 1952 CE

The IBM Selectric II type-writer, icon of the office secretary and American corporate culture in the 1950s and 60s.

A page detail from Haas Type Foundry director Eduard Hoffmann's notebook, showing preliminary tests of what would become Helvetica (accompanied by Hoffmann's notations for further development).

AGMR adefgkrst

HELVETICA (MAX MIEDINGER) / 1957 CE

AGMR adefgkrst

EUROSTYLE (ALDO NOVARESE) / 1962 CE

AGMR adefgkrst

UNIVERS (ADRIAN FRUTIGER) / 1957 CE

AGMR adefgkrst

ANTIQUE OLIVE (ROGER EXCOFFON) / 1962 CE

This poster, designed in Switzerland in 1954, exemplifies the reductive, refined approach to imagery and type that came to be so characteristic of the European International Style.

Europe, on the other hand, was rebuilding. Design and business were both seen as Utopian, benevolent forces working to elevate the quality of life, not merely as commodifying influences. European designers—in particular, the Swiss—came to favor neutral, diligently structured messaging through meticulously finessed form—a visual rebuke to the regionalism and exclusionary narratives that had given rise to the war itself. Communicating clearly, with respect for the audience's intelligence and sociocultural interconnection, was paramount.

The so-called International Style that embodied these ideals initially evolved in Switzerland, but quickly gained adherents in Germany, Italy, Spain, and the Netherlands. Its approach was heavily typographic; at its outset, designers gravitated toward Akzidenz Grotesk—until Max Miedinger, a freelance designer, and Eduard Hoffmann, the president of Haas Type Foundry (in Münchenstein, Switzerland), set about to create a font with no intrinsic meaning in its form. Haas Type Foundry released the result, based on Akzidenz, as *Neue Haas Grotesk* (later renamed *Helvetica*) in 1957.

That same year, a second neo-grotesque family appeared—Univers, designed by Adrian Frutiger for Deberny & Peignot, in Paris. Like Helvetica, it was also based on Akzidenz Grotesk and neutral in its form, suggesting no meaningful associations. These two sans serifs became the juggernauts of the International Style.

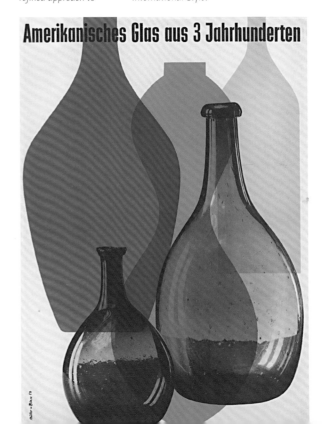

As the American and European economic markets became increasingly intertwined, American business took note of the powerful example set by Europeans; American executives saw Swiss companies like Geigy, a chemical and pharmaceutical operation, succeed through a monolithic, strikingly visual, branded presence. Both Helvetica and Univers were deployed ubiquitously in the development of corporate branding systems throughout the 1960s and 70s.

Not all of the design establishment was wrapped up in neutralism. Jan Tschichold, a Swiss designer who—while working in Germany in the 1920s and 30s, almost single-handedly established the basis for asymmetrical design and sans serif typography—fomented controversy by renounc-

Geigy, a Swiss pharmaceutical and chemical company, was instrumental in disseminating the International Style and sans serif typography through its monolithic corporate branding program, which reached every continent where it did business. Shown here are packaging (left) and a promotional brochure, both designed by Steff Geissbuhler in the late 1960s, using Univers and Helvetica Compressed.

ing that approach as Fascist. In tandem with returning to classically symmetrical layouts, he also designed Sabon, a serif based on the work of Claude Garamond in the 1600s. Hermann Zapf, a German designer working for the Hallmark Greeting Card company in the U.S. introduced a number of calligraphic faces, among them: a script, Chancery; a serif, Palatino, derived from the work of Francesco Griffo in the 1500s; and Optima, a sans serif with strokes that thickened and thinned as though drawn with a pen. Typographic voices such as these, in counterpoint to the aesthetic austerity of the International Style, suggested there might be unacknowledged cultural undercurrents with which to be reckoned.

NEU ALPHABET (WIM CROUWEL) / 1967 CE

SABON (JAN TSCHICHOLD) / 1967 CE

VROMGEVERS (WIM CROUWEL) / 1968 CE

OPTIMA (HERMANN ZAPF) / 1958 CE

International Style designers, like Wim Crouwel of the Netherlands, were enthralled by the precepts of reduction and neutralism that were pervasive throughout Europe in the 1950s and 60s. Above are two of his experimental typefaces that carry these ideas to their extremes.

At the same time, a return to more classically derived forms surfaced as a counterpoint to strict Modernism.

a∃GK mɔrs

EPPS EVANS (TIMOTHY EPPS) / 1969 CE

AGHMR aefgkpvwx

SINTEX (ALDO NOVARESE) / 1973 CE

ABDEGLM NQSTUVZ

ITC MACHINE (RONNE BONDER, TOM CARNASE) / 1970 CE

ADEG HMRS

BABY TEETH (MILTON GLASER) / 1968 CE

ADGMR adegkrst

ARTONE (SEYMOUR CHWAST) / 1968 CE

ABDEGi MQRST

STOP (ALDO NOVARESE) / 1970 CE

At left is an assortment of quirky, stylized typefaces that were in wide circulation as a rebuke to Modernism during the 1960s and 70s. Below, a magazine ad from the era showcases a headline drawn in another of these expressive styles.

There ensued, during the late 1960s and 70s, the inevitable backlash. The veneer of the "good life" began to fracture under a variety of pressures: an escalating Cold War; class and racial tensions; and assassinations of political and cultural figures. All of these, and more, fed the anxiety of a disaffected youth culture and a rift between the generations. The visceral beat of rock 'n roll, helped by a certain set of gyrating hips from Tupelo, Mississippi, crossed racial boundaries and instigated a sexual revolution. Taboos fell and irony ruled as art-world images of tomato soup cans, car crashes, and gender benders critiqued long-held values while sordidly celebrating them.

To paraphrase designer Paula Scher in Gary Hustwit's documentary, *Helvetica* (2008), International Style Modernism equated with "the Man." Younger designers began to seek alternatives everywhere—especially in the design of type.

Font design went everywhere in a quest to acknowledge marginalized subcultures and neglected aesthetics; the notion of "taste" underwent heavy scrutiny. New typefaces drew from the vernacular of car-graphic detailing, computer punch cards, varsity sweater lettering, cartooning, science fiction, Art Nouveau, Art Déco, the Viennese Secession, and industrial Victoriana. In defiance of "neutral" came narrative, metaphor, and idiosyncracy. Type design experienced its own version of free love.

[2] [E35]

Lugano   8 km
Chiasso   32 km
Milano   75 km

AGMR
adefgkrst

AVANT GARDE (HERB LUBALIN) / 1970 CE

AGWR
adefgkrst

ERAS (EDWARD BENGUIAT) / 1976 CE

AGMR
adefgkrst

BELL CENTENNIAL (MATTHEW CARTER) / 1976 CE

AGMR
adefgkrst

BENGUIAT GOTHIC (EDWARD BENGUIAT) / 1979 CE

Although flashier, idiosyncratic fonts were in high demand for popular advertising, seriously well-crafted ones still were necessary for utilitarian purposes, like information design. Adrian Frutiger, the originator of Univers, first developed the sans serif seen here as a design proposal for the Charles de Gaulle airport in Roissy, France. Like Univers, it is based on the forms of a Neo-Grotesque, but exhibits greater modulation in its strokes and rounder curves, shifting it toward a classification known as a humanist sans serif. The font was rejected by the airport's administration, but was used by the Swiss National Roadway authority for highway signage—and a huge number of corporate branding designers ever since.

Still, the Modernist impulse toward clarity and usability continued with the development of typefaces that addressed issues of legibility in specific contexts—such as for road signs and printed telephone directories, as well as for more day-to-day text applications like editorial work. A number of type designers, like Edward Benguiat, in New York, worked at bridging that divide, merging idiosyncratic and expressive elements with more rigorous structuring, as can be seen in a variety of his typefaces that became exceptionally popular during the 1970s.

All along the way, technology was keeping step with, and often opening up, new possibilities, for type designers' aspirations. Most typesetting was still accomplished with lead, limited to a size of 72 points, or about 1 inch (2.5 cm) in height; achieving larger sizes meant enlarging settings of that size photographically and then cleaning up the results by hand, with paint or marker. Phototypesetting—in which type was "cast" as film negatives and exposed onto photographic printing paper—allowed for larger sizes to be set, as well as for some interesting manipulations in their exposure.

That, however, was about to change.

During the 1960s, typesetting production began to shift from lead-based letterpress methods to photographic and electronic ones. The advent of phototypesetting allowed for setting sizes above 72 points. The Mergenthaler Company that had introduced the Linotype in 1886 also introduced the CRT typesetting station. In essence, an operator input codes into a keyboard terminal that instructed an imagesetter to expose photographic paper with characters of a particular style—via glass templates like the one shown at far right.

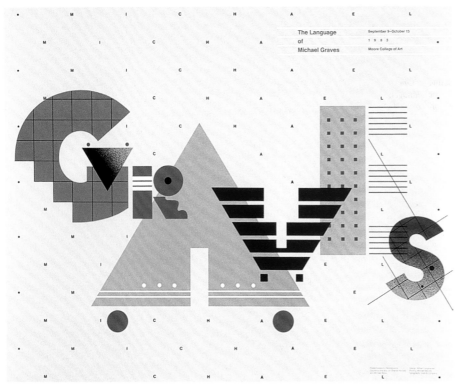

This iconic poster by William Longhauser exemplifies the Postmodern typographic approach known as

Deconstructivism—taking apart, layering, and pictorializing its type forms to communicate narrative ideas.

In short order, conceptual experiments of the 1970s colored the thinking of even the staunchest of Modernists. Grid-based sans serif layouts (famously denigrated by Katherine McCoy as "mere housekeeping") were replaced by multilayered ones in which type and imagery traded identities, reshaped in ambiguous spaces—a mannered, *Post*modern process termed *deconstruction*. Typical only of display uses, pictorialized type forms suggested new possibilities, maybe even for text faces—building on, yet abstracting, their classical Roman understructures.

Enter: the Macintosh personal computer in 1984. Decades of tech company work had moved computing from huge mainframes to the desktop with varied commercial success—the Olivetti *Programma 101* (1965); the IBM *SCAMP* (1973); the Tandy *TRS-80* (1977); and the *Commodore 64* (1982).

The critical difference was that the Macintosh (or *Mac*) displayed what computer code described in a modular field of *pixels* that a user could manipulate directly; designers rapidly took advantage of its potential. Most important in this new environment, perhaps, was typography—fonts of differing styles could actually be seen onscreen

PARADIGM SHIFTS
New Technologies and Postmodernism / 1980s to the Present

To the far left, a typical DOS-code computer terminal showing command lines of program code—the standard before the graphical user interface (GUI) introduced by the Apple Macintosh in 1984 (near left).

AGMR
adefgkrst

OAKLAND (ZUZANA LICKO) / 1984 CE

AGMR
adefgkrst

EMPEROR (ZUZANA LICKO) / 1985 CE

TRIPLEX SERIF (ZUZANA LICKO) / 1989 CE

AGMR adefgkrst

REMEDY (FRANK HEINE) / 1991 CE

AGMR adefgkrst

DOGMA (ZUZANA LICKO) / 1994 CE

The Postscript language and improved display technology led to rapid advances in the complexity of typefaces. The ones shown here are second-generation, exploiting that technology for both greater precision and more decorative possibilities.

ATM Control Panel

Adobe *Type Manager.*

Version: 1.15

ATM
● O**n**
○ O**ff**

Installed ATM Fonts:
Arial MT
BrushScript,ITALIC
GillSans
LetterGothic
NewsGothic
Perpetua
Perpetua,BOLD
Symbol
TimesNewRomanPS
TimesNewRomanPS,BOLD
TimesNewRomanPS,BOLDITALIC

Add...
Remove

Font C**a**che
96K

Exit

☒ **U**se Pre-built or Resident Bitmap Fonts

© 1983-1991 Adobe Systems Incorporated.
All Rights Reserved. Patents Pending.

In the early Mac operating systems, control panels coordinated various functions (much like system preferences in its current OS)—including those of third-party software. One of these was Type Manager, which turned fonts on and off and enabled the anti-aliasing feature.

Bitmap vs. vector (exaggerated)   *Anti-aliasing*

AEGKM AEGKM
abcefg abcefg

CHICAGO (SUSAN KARE), BITMAP AND POSTSCRIPT / 1984 CE

Onscreen type suffered from poor resolution and bitmap construction until Adobe Systems introduced the Postscript page-description language in the late 1980s. Postscript is based on vector points whose coordinates and attributes hint at, and direct, the shape of line segments that connect them. It allowed for fonts to be drawn and displayed more accurately, using less information. A further development was that of "anti-aliasing," a new feature for screen display that softened the boundary between font area and page space, using a progression of gray pixels to create smooth curves and details.

and altered. Early adopters like Zuzana Licko, a Slovakian-born designer educated at Berkeley, in California, experimented with creating fonts that specifically addressed the Mac's display and output capabilities—or, its limitations. "The challenge," Licko recalled once, "was that…you really had to design something special…It was physically impossible to adapt 8-point Goudy Old Style to 72 dots to the inch. In the end you couldn't tell Goudy Old Style from Times Roman." Licko's bitmap fonts led the way to an independent font foundry, Emigré (which she formed with her husband, Rudy VanderLans), and a lasting, critical influence on the design of typefaces. During the late 1980s and early 90s, it was nearly impossible to find a work of graphic design that didn't include an Emigré font.

Aside from the obvious—defining a new language of construction for the form of typefaces—the work of Licko and other early digital typographers liberated font design from established foundries and put it in the hands of…well, anyone. Of course, classically trained, professional type designers assimilated the technology into

their working process. But now designers could independently create bespoke faces to enhance their projects—as could those who were self-taught, or who were not even designers by trade at all. Free from the constraints of formal type education, type designs that pushed the boundaries of accepted form and taste multiplied like wildfire. Compared to the roughly 2,000 fonts available through traditional foundries in the early 1980s, more than 50,000 were in circulation by the mid-1990s.

Design tools and display quality increased with the Adobe Systems introduction of the Postscript® page- and font-description programming language. The vector-based, line-segment "hinting" it incorporated allowed for the crisp rendering of smooth curves and more accurate stroke and counter control without showing the evidence of the square pixel.

Throughout the 1990s, the proliferation of new font designs continued unabated. In the independent, Postmodern quarter, work by Emigré and like-minded font adventurers unabashedly explored narrative and conceptual terrain that derived from diverse inspirations: quilting and embroidery; medieval architecture; highway signage; disturbed psychological states; scientific diagramming; photographic processes; and ethnographic appropriations (these latter, in particular, fueled by a rising, popular concern for multiculturalism). Aided by early desktop-platform font design software like Fontographer, new foundries appeared on a regular basis; the number of available typefaces quadrupled.

Improvements in imaging and font design software during the 1990s helped designers visualize new kinds of forms (as in the poster by Rick Valicenti, at left, from 1993).

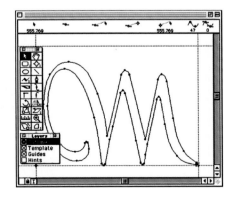

Desktop font-design software became popularly available in 1996, giving access to high-quality editing techniques to just about anyone who was interested.

AGMR adefgkrst
BLUR (NEVILLE BRODY) / 1991 CE

abDefgJK MQRStuvx
HOUSE GOTHIC (HOUSE INDUSTRIES) / 1993 CE

AGMR adefgkrst
TEMPLATE GOTHIC (BARRY DECK) / 1991 CE

ABEJKMR abefgiprst
PLATELET (CONOR MANGAT) / 1993 CE

AGIMQR adefgijkmpst
SUBURBAN (RUDY VAN DERLANS) / 1993 CE

AGMR adefgkrst
INTERSTATE (TOBIAS FRERE-JONES) / 1993 CE

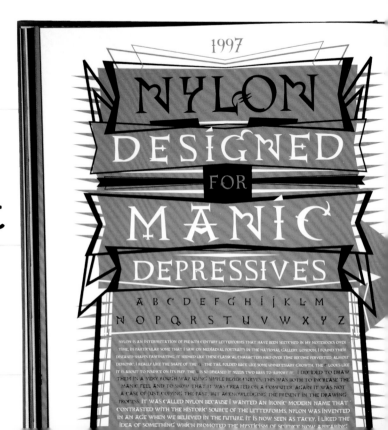

In the establishment type design quarter, high-resolution scanning technology and powerful software tools allowed for detailed analysis, comparison, and reinterpretation of classical sources. Designers like Kris Holmes, Robert Slimbach, Carol Twombly, Sumner Stone, and Erik Spiekermann presided over these new offerings from monolithic foundries like Adobe and Linotype: updated Roman capitals and drawings by Jenson, Garamond, Baskerville, and Caslon—as well as fonts that hybridized serif and sans serif characteristics.

In the mid-1980s, Adobe Systems began exploration of a new technology (first developed by the German company URW++) by which two or more design variations, or "axes" (for instance, weight and width),

Below, a page spread from type designer Jonathan Barnbrook's monograph, The Barnbrook Bible (2007), *which catalogs his visionary output from the late 1980s onward.*

could be interpolated to derive a number of "in-between" states, very much like image morphing (readers will recognize this idea in recalling the 1991 sci-fi film, *Terminator 2: Judgement Day*).

Its development was spearheaded by Sumner Stone (then Director of Typography at Adobe), who deployed it to expand his Stone Typeface Family in 1987; it also figured significantly in creating the Adobe Originals type library as the 1980s transitioned into the 1990s. Another early application came in 1994 with Penumbra (created by Lance Hidy, a freelance graphic artist and member of Adobe's Type Advisory Board), blending traits from classical forms like the Trajan inscription and Paul Renner's geometric sans serif, Futura.

The experiment above by Lance Hidy, from the development process of Penumbra, demonstrates the power of Multiple Master technology: the interpolation of four master drawings (in red) to efficiently generate an expansive family of weight and serif variants.

ABEGKJ MQRST

TRAJAN (CAROL TWOMBLY) / 1989 CE

AGMR adefgkrst

META (ERIK SPIEKERMANN) / 1991 CE

ABEGKJ MQRST

PENUMBRA (LANCE HIDY) / 1994 CE

The technology, named *Multiple Master,* was short-lived, but profoundly far-reaching. Along with helping generate comprehensive families more rapidly, it facilitated the return of optical sizing, whereby fonts are redrawn with alternate traits for use at different sizes (less contrast and larger counters, for captions, or greater contrast and finer details, for display). Most importantly, it was the source of the later TrueType and, eventually, OpenType protocols and related programming languages, like Python, with which fonts are developed today.

The year 1994 was also significant for the appearance of a little bit of technological innovation called the internet.

AGMR
adefgkrst

HOEFLER TEXT (JONATHAN HOEFLER) / 1991 CE

AGMR
adefgkrst

GEORGIA (MATTHEW CARTER) / 1996 CE

AGMR
adefgkrst

VERDANA (MATTHEW CARTER) / 1996 CE

AGMR
adefgkrst

DOLLY (UNDERWARE) / 2001 CE

AGMQR
adefgikrsty

FEDRA (PETER BI'LAK) / 2001 CE

AGMR
adefgkrst

ARCHER (JONATHAN HOEFLER, TOBIAS FRERE-JONES) / 2003 CE

AGMR
adefgkrst

GUARDIAN EGYPTIAN (PAUL BARNES, CHRISTIAN SCHWARTZ) / 2005 CE

Ah, the internet. Today, we take the idea of globally networked (and now, wirelessly portable) computer connectivity for granted. The fact of web- and cloud-based computing is not so important, other than that access to fonts that were well-designed specifically for screen use in web contexts became a priority. The model for screen-conscious typeface detailing was defined by an old-style serif, Hoefler Text, that Apple incorporated into their Mac operating system in 1991. Matthew Carter, of Bell Centennial fame, was tapped by Microsoft in 1993 to create a serif font (Georgia) and a sans serif (Verdana), to be bundled with its Windows® operating system, both released in 1996. Hoefler Text provided many of the OpenType features (before OpenType existed) that contemporary font designers accept as de rigeur: alternate character designs, ligatures, and small capitals.

A test layout for The Guardian newspaper, using the bespoke superfamily designed by Commercial Type.

AGMR AGMR AGMR
AGMR *AGMR* *AGMR*
AGMR AGMR **AGMR**
AGMR *AGMR* *AGMR*
AGMR AGMR **AGMR**
AGMR *AGMR* *AGMR*
AGMR **AGMR** **AGMR**
AGMR *AGMR* *AGMR*
AGMR **AGMR** **AGMR**
AGMR **AGMR** **AGMR**
AGMR **AGMR** **AGMR**
AGMR **AGMR** **AGMR**
AGMR **AGMR** AGMR

Stag, by Christian Schwartz, exemplifies the "superfamily," an extensive array of variants, inspired by Adrian Frutiger's Univers (in theory) and made more practical by advances in character interpolation.

Indeed, the OpenType format, and its capacity to allow fonts to respond "smartly" to text conditions as they are generated on the fly—for instance, automatically selecting different alternate characters, or ligatures between characters, depending on their sequence in text—is one of the hallmarks of font designs created in the subsequent twenty years. It has proven exceptionally useful for designers of script fonts, which have enjoyed a resurgence in popularity in recent years, to overcome the recognizable artificiality of identical, repeating characters. The OpenType paradigm has also

AGMR
adefgkrst

AKKURAT (LAURENZ BRUNNER) / 2004 CE

ΛᎠᎪᏏᎡᏴᏴ
ᏴＣᏟᏟᎠᏗᏴ

LŸNO (KARL NAWROT, RADIM PEŠKO) / 2010 CE

AGRW
abefgnpst

LE SONIA MONOCHROME (PIERRE DI SCIULLO) / 2008 CE

AGMR
adefgkrst

KADE (DAVID QUAY) / 2011 CE

AGMR
adefgkrst

BRANDON GROTESQUE (HANNES VAN DÖHREN) / 2010 CE

AGMR
adefgkrst

INFINI (SANDRINE NUGUE) / 2014 CE

Contemporary designers have embraced the OpenType format for its "smart" features, like the ability to choose from different, alternate characters depending on their context—as in the case of the script specimen here, designed by Alejandro Paul of the foundry Sudtipos.

PRISMASET (JAMES GOGGIN) / 2010 CE

given rise to "superfamilies," extensive arrays of variation in weight, width, posture, and detailing. These are ideal for intricate distinctions in informational hierarchy demanded by such complex editorial applications as newspapers and magazines—whether of the traditional print or purely digital variety.

As of this writing, approaches to the design of letterforms continues its pluralistic journey, much as it always has. Today's typographers are as fascinated by the precedents established thoughout history as they are with opportunies afforded by changing aesthetic notions and new technologies. But, all approaches—from rigorously utilitarian to irreverently expressive, for text or display application—owe a debt to the thousands of years of evolution that have led to each kind of creative possibility to be considered. Type designers of any ilk ignore that history at great risk of their work being sidelined to the bin of irrelevance. And all, from the aspiring beginner to the most accomplished master, can only benefit from the lessons of that history as they work to move their craft forward, wherever that may lead, into the future.

Over time, like any other discipline with a long history, typeface design has developed a set of conventions. Some of these are related to how characters—letters, numerals, punctuation, and glyphs—are structured for clear recognition and legibility; others have to do with cultural expectations of what makes a comfortable, readable style, or how a particular style conveys emotions or feelings or even appears "beautiful," based on historical context. And, of course, all of the parts of a typeface, from character shapes to individual components in each form, have had names given to them over the centuries—type designers are consummate wonks for their jargon. Designers who want to walk the walk must talk the talk (so to speak) and school themselves on the basics of their chosen craft.

Legacies

**NOMENCLATURE
AND CURRENT AESTHETIC
DESIGN CONVENTIONS**

THE VERY BASICS

THE STROKE

The shape of a character or other letter is defined by lines, called strokes, each with a particular gestural movement, arranged in a specific combination: an H is made of two vertical strokes, joined by a horizontal stroke; a D consists, in essence, of a vertical and a curved stroke. Every stroke is itself a shape, consisting of a beginning, middle, and end. The visual quality of a stroke derives from how it is formed: the kind of tool used; its thickness, or weight, relative to the height of the drawn form; the angle at which the tool is dragged across the surface; and the degree of pressure applied, from the beginning of the stroke to its finish. The stroke is the positive form that establishes a character's archetypal shape, for recognition, and its general texture.

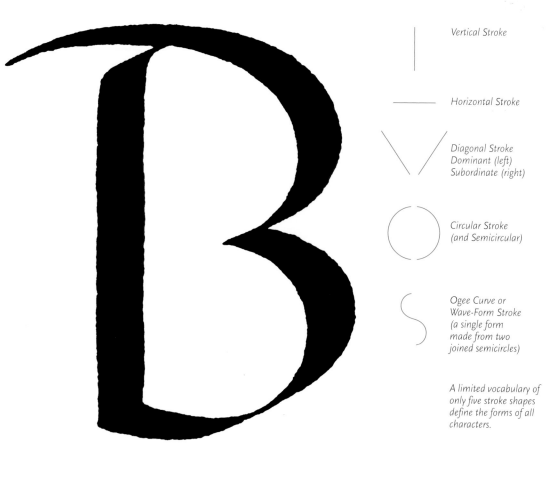

Vertical Stroke

Horizontal Stroke

*Diagonal Stroke
Dominant (left)
Subordinate (right)*

*Circular Stroke
(and Semicircular)*

*Ogee Curve or
Wave-Form Stroke
(a single form
made from two
joined semicircles)*

*A limited vocabulary of
only five stroke shapes
define the forms of all
characters.*

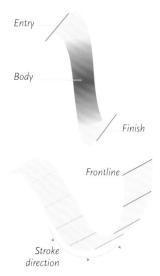

Entry

Body

Finish

Frontline

Stroke direction

A stroke comprises two basic parts: the body, its main component; and the terminals, its ends. The beginning terminal is called the entry or the attack; the terminal at which the stroke ends is called the finish.

The frontline is the leading edge of the stroke as it's being formed by the drawing tool, whose dimensions define the paths of the stroke's outer contours. The contours follow each other as the frontline moves through the gesture.

Consistent, or uniform, weight

Modulated (inconsistent weight)

An individual stroke may be consistent in its thickness or weight (A); or it may be modulated, changing in weight from beginning to end (B). The relative rapidity of change in thickness is described as ductus.

The strokes of well-formed characters are designed to flow into and out of each other to appear inseparable—even when they join abruptly.

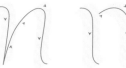

Continuous   Interrupted

Stroke formation may be continuous—made without lifting the tool from the surface—or it may be interrupted, where the tool is lifted and repositioned after each stroke is made.

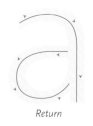

Return

Drawing direction is typically from left to right and top to bottom, but it sometimes reverses, as it does in the lower lobe of this lowercase a. The portion of a stroke that resumes "normal" direction is called a return.

THE COUNTER

Equally, or perhaps, more important for a character's definition are the spaces created between and around the strokes as they're formed: the negative areas or *counterforms* (typically called *counters*, for short). While strokes establish a character's shapes, counters define its overall proportion—width versus height—and, therefore, its density and rhythm: how much dark versus light it exhibits; how compressed or open it appears; and how much space will be appreciated as the eye traverses from left to right. In general, the more counter that exists, the easier it is to rapidly identify the shapes and arrangement of strokes and, so, read the character efficiently.

The counters separate strokes at recognizable intervals. Their ratio is reciprocal: The more stroke information present, the less counter—and vice versa.

The internal counters in a well-crafted typeface are systematically designed to be similar to each other in apparent volume, despite the variety of stroke shaping.

H R O N

Differences in stroke/counter ratio dramatically affect character density and rhythm—and, ultimately, the spacing within continuous text.

dorem tuis vexure summa est

To create even "color" or texture, a font's default spacing responds proportionally by tightening (top) or loosening (bottom) to optically match that of the counters inside the letters.

dorem tuis vexu

THE VERY BASICS

STRUCTURAL GROUPS

Characters of like structure—those consisting only of vertical and horizontal strokes, for instance—can be grouped for consideration of their shared visual qualities during the design process.

The majority of the capitals, or uppercase forms, are bilaterally symmetrical: that is, their stroke formations mirror each other across a central axis from top to bottom. Other characters are asymmetrical from left to right, but most often are symmetrical from top to bottom.

Some characters are composed of structures that repeat from top to bottom, and are described as having two storys, like a building: the capital B, E, K, and P, for example, as well as the lowercase a and e. The lowercase a is sometimes drawn with a single story—a circular stroke combined with a vertical one, both of the same general height. It's not the only one that appears in several structural variations; the uppercase G, M, Q, and W may be made in several ways that all conform to their respective, general structures.

The term *character set* describes the selection of characters—and which kinds—that are included in a typeface's design.

* The modern capital R is formed with a diagonal (the leg) that was originally built as a quarter circle—hence, its appearance in this category.

** Although the modern capital J is drawn with a curved hook to better differentiate it from the capital I, its original form was a single vertical stroke that descended below the baseline.

Archetype Groups

EFHLT
Verticals and horizontals

VWX
Diagonals only

MNKY
Verticals and diagonals

ZA
Diagonals and horizontals

COQS
Circular strokes only

DGBPRU
Circular strokes and verticals

IJ
Vertical strokes only

Symmetrical Characters

A M H I M O S T U V W X Y 0 1 8

Asymmetrical Characters

B C D E F G J K L N Q R Z

2 3 4 5 6 7 9

Two-Story Characters

B E F H K P R S X Y a e x

3 4 5 6 8 9

Common Structural Variations

G
Straight or Archaic

G
Crossed

G
Crossed and Spurred

M
Canted or Angled

M
Modern or Vertical

M
High Vertex

Q
Linked Tail

Q
Crossed Tail

Q
Appended Tail

Q
Open or Script Form

U
Running

U
Interrupted

W
Running

W
Interrupted, crossed, or "Germanic" form

a
Single story

a
Two story

t
Tailed or Conventional

†
Cruciform

g
Oldstyle or Serif Style

g
Modern or Sans Serif Style

4
Closed

4
Open and Angled

4
Open and Vertical

3
Curvilinear

3
Angle/Curve Hybrid

Character Set

Alphabetic Characters (including accented alternates)

ABCDEFGHIJKLMNOPQRSTUVWXYZ
ÀÁÂÃÄÅÆÇÇÐÈÉÊÊËÌÍÎÏŁÑÒÓÔÕÖØŒ
ŠÙÚÛÜÝŸŽ

Uppercase (or Capitals)

abcdefghijklmnopqrstuvwxyz
àáâãäåæçèéêëìíîïðłñòóôõöøœùúûü
šýÿžſƒ   fi ffi fl ffl

Lowercase   *Ligatures*

Numerals

0123456789 M   0123456789 M

Modern, or Lining, figures   *Oldstyle, or Text, figures*

¼ ½ ¾ ⅖ ⅗ ⅘ ⅛ ⅜ ⅝ ⅞

Fractions

Punctuation

:;.,!!??_-–—()[]{}/|\'' ""…" ~´`··

Glyphs or Analphabetic Characters

& # $ ¢ £ ¥ € № % § ℔ * < > ¶ ≠ ±

BODY

Type designers refer to the overall pro-portion of characters—their width/height proportion—as their body, a term that derives from the general size of a letter's slug, as cast in lead. The body includes the aggregate of the width and height of the uppercase and the lowercase (miniscules or small letters). Even in digital fonts, a character's body includes a little space on either side of the character that, in lead form, helped space each character evenly, relative to others, in a line of set text— the sidebearing.

A typeface's body, in totality, can be de-scribed as wide or narrow (relative to that of other faces); individually, each character in a typeface also exhibits its own body proportion.

The characters in any given font may be designed with variable bodies, changing based on the individual character's width; or they may all be designed to fit within a single body measure. Such faces are referred to as *fixed width* or *monospaced*.

Lead type slug

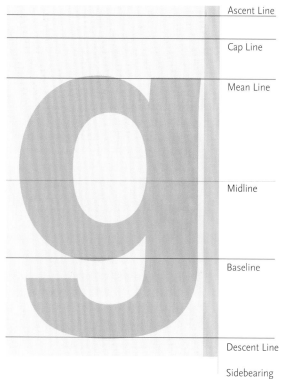

Ascent Line

Cap Line

Mean Line

Midline

Baseline

Descent Line

Sidebearing

The body of most fonts flexes in width from char-acter to character, designed to ensure even spacing within text—what is called optical, or variable-width, body. Some fonts have a fixed body width for all the characters; these are sometimes referred to as monospaced fonts.

AfMgQ

AfMgQ

FONT, FACE, AND FAMILY

These three terms usually confuse designers because they are often used interchangeably, and because they've been used to mean different things at different times.

For the record: The word *font* refers to the design of a single character set, all sharing the same proportional and stylistic qualities. The word *face* means the same thing, although it's often used to refer to all the variations of a character set's style—meaning, the light, bold, italic versions. This latter usage is best described as a *family*, meaning the group of varied character sets that all share the same proportions and stylistic details.

Type designers will often refer to what they call the *cut* of a font or face—the specific interpretation of a font style as created by one designer or foundry or another. For example, one might speak about the Stempel foundry's cut of Garamond in comparison to that cut by Claude Garamond himself, or that produced by some other foundry. The word *cut* (not surprisingly) is a reference to the steel master punch that created the typeface's moulds for casting in lead.

Each cut of a face or font is usually distinguished by its designer's specific focus on aspects of the font's structure, proportion, and detailing that he or she found interesting, or on some external desire that informed how they went about reinterpreting the form—for example, an exceptionally large lowercase and increased contrast between thin and thick strokes is characteristic of the ITC (International Typeface Corporation) cut of Garamond.

AaHhGg *AaHhGg*
Regular or Roman   Italic

AaHhGg ***AaHhGg***
Bold   Bold Italic

Most font families consist of four basic variants to provide options for styling text of different function or of different levels of importance within a hierarchy.

The original Univers family

Some font families comprise an extensive number of variants—those that vary in weight and posture, as well as width. The typical number of family variants has increased dramatically in recent years, aided by automated functions in font design software; many contemporary font designs comprise these so-called superfamilies.

AaHhGgPpSsQqX
Adobe Garamond Pro

AaHhGgPpSsQqX
ITC Garamond

AaHhGgPpSsQqX
Stempel Garamond

The three typefaces shown here are all based on the form known as Garamond, and all are set in the Roman, or regular, weight at the same point size. Even a quick comparison reveals significant differences between each of these three cuts, released by different foundries: heavier or lighter weight; larger or smaller lowercase; and relative sharpness or softness in the shape of the terminals, among others.

THE PARTS OF LETTERS

All of the individual components of letters (as well as of numerals) have names, given to them over the past 2,000 years. The terms for these parts are general and apply to instances in every character that incorporates them into its structure.

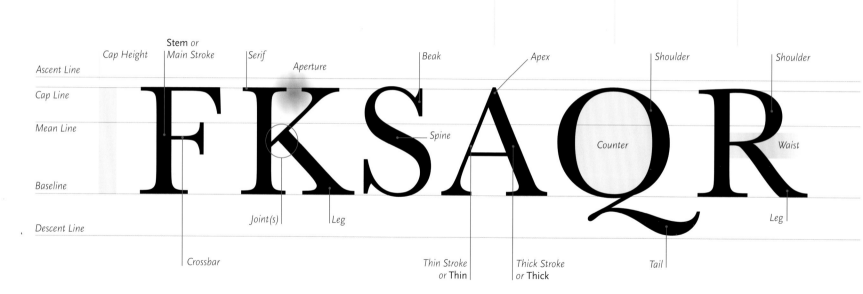

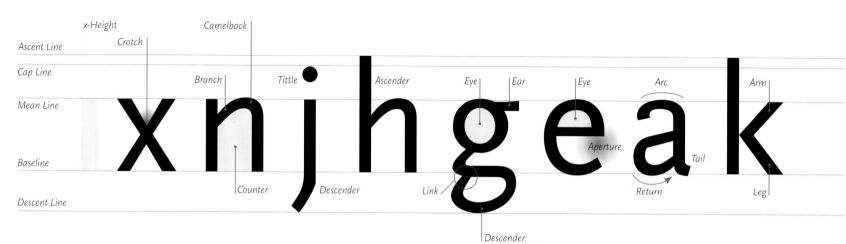

To compensate for weight buildup in joints, strokes at these locations are often minutely tapered, or have a tiny notch "carved" out.

Ostensibly, the notch helps absorb ink when the letter is printed (hence, *ink trap*), but it's really about optical lightening of the joint.

The weights of strokes are situated differently, left to right, in the curved forms of a given typeface—establishing an axis for those forms. The axis may be perpendicular (90° to the baseline), or oblique (slanted off vertical, usually to the left: evidence of drawing with brush or pen).

Ink Trap

Swash

MYOTGUB

Crotch
Arm or Crossbar
Shoulder
Shoulder
Upper Lobe
Waist
Stem
Lower Lobe
Bowl
Vertex
Stem
Axis
Bowl

Throat
Spur

btysefina

Serif
Shear or cut
Terminal: Brush serif
Pothook
Tail
Return
Descender: Tail
Axis
Taper
Ligature
Font Slope (Italics)
Tail
Terminal: Teardrop serif
Vertical Midline

ANATOMY & NOMENCLATURE

TERMINAL SHAPING

Stroke terminals from face to face exhibit a huge range of shaping possibilities. Especially in older typefaces, these differences express evidence of the tool used to draw them. As technologies changed, designers could decide on terminal attributes independent of the tool. The shaping of stroke terminals is one of the most pronounced stylistic characteristics of a typeface—despite how small a detail it may seem.

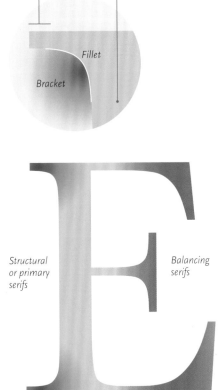

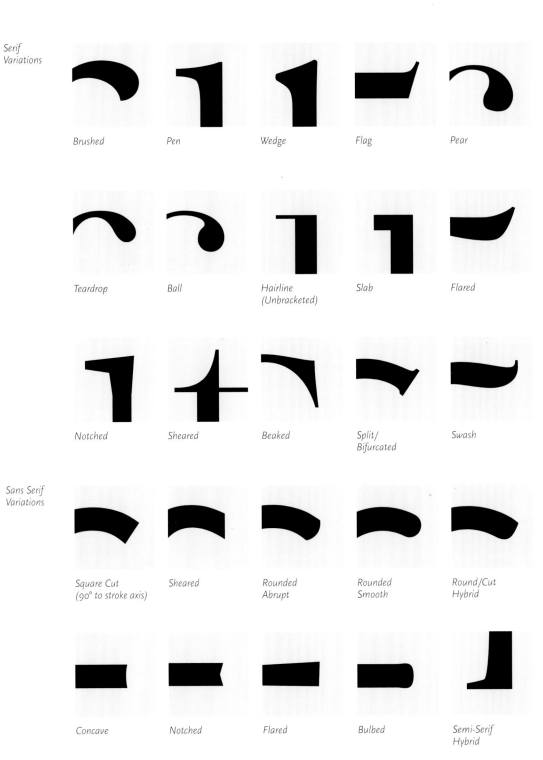

Serif Variations

Brushed

Pen

Wedge

Flag

Pear

Teardrop

Ball

Hairline (Unbracketed)

Slab

Flared

Notched

Sheared

Beaked

Split/ Bifurcated

Swash

Sans Serif Variations

Square Cut (90° to stroke axis)

Sheared

Rounded Abrupt

Rounded Smooth

Round/Cut Hybrid

Concave

Notched

Flared

Bulbed

Semi-Serif Hybrid

Terminal

Stem

Fillet

Bracket

Structural or primary serifs

Balancing serifs

JOINT FORMATION

Similar to terminal shaping, the way that strokes come together within the characters of a particular face—how they are joined—can also vary tremendously. The attributes of the joints among different characters within an alphabet contribute as profound an influence on that typeface's overall style as do its terminal shapes; and these two elements must usually be visually related to support characters' stylistic cohesion within the set.

Strokes join at particular places in different characters and, in each—in the A, for instance, as opposed to in the K or B or R—the kinds of strokes that are merging may be very different (a diagonal and a vertical, for example, versus a vertical and horizontal, or a vertical and a curve). When designing, it's important to compare each instance of a joint from character to character to consider how the formation of these junctures will be able to share some attributes, as different in general structure as they may be.

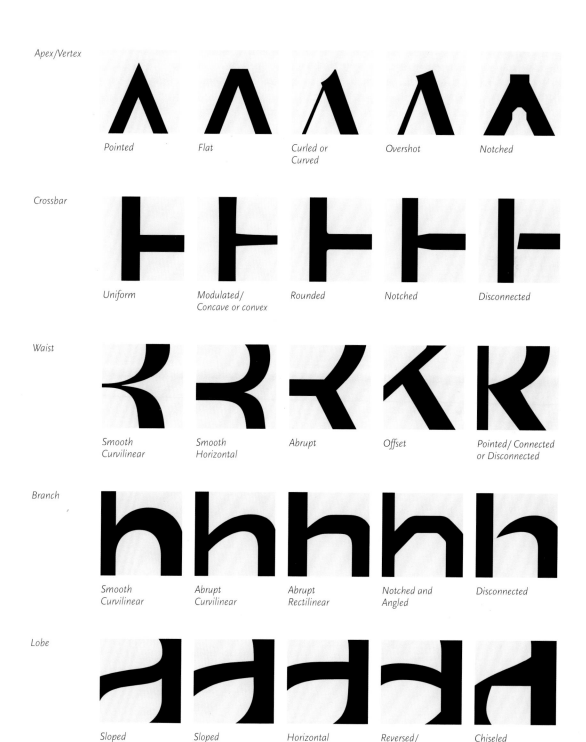

Apex/Vertex

| Pointed | Flat | Curled or Curved | Overshot | Notched |

Crossbar

| Uniform | Modulated/ Concave or convex | Rounded | Notched | Disconnected |

Waist

| Smooth Curvilinear | Smooth Horizontal | Abrupt | Offset | Pointed/ Connected or Disconnected |

Branch

| Smooth Curvilinear | Abrupt Curvilinear | Abrupt Rectilinear | Notched and Angled | Disconnected |

Lobe

| Sloped Smooth | Sloped Abrupt | Horizontal | Reversed/ Returned | Chiseled |

DESIGN VARIABLES

STYLE

This broad term can describe several different aspects of a typeface: whether it has serifs or not; its historical or formal characteristics; how reserved or expressive its qualities are; and its intended use, whether for extensive reading or short display applications.

WEIGHT

The strokes of a face's characters can be thick or thin overall, relative to their height. The design of most typefaces begins with developing a medium, or regular, weight—one whose stroke thickness results in an even alternation between stroke and counter that produces the appearance of a uniform gray value when set in text.

CONTRAST

The strokes within a given typeface may all be drawn to appear the same weight, or thickness; or they may vary in weight within each character. The degree of weight difference between the thin strokes (or thins) and the thick strokes (or thicks) defines the face's internal contrast. The more extreme a typeface's contrast, the less even will be its color when set in text.

01 / Style: Structural Class

Serif   *Sans Serif*   *Script*

02 / Style: Historical Class

Oldstyle   *Transitional*   *Neoclassical*

03 / Style: Relative Neutrality

Neutral   *Stylized*

04 / Style: Functional Use

Text   *Display*

Thin   *Extra Light*   *Light*

Book   *Regular or Medium*   *Bold*

Black or Heavy   *Extra Black, Super, or Ultra*

Historically, regular, or medium, stroke weight is one in which the stroke's thickness is $1/7$ the height of the capital I. Some faces establish a medium that is lighter or heavier in weight.

The characters in a face of uniform weight are designed to appear all the same thickness, whether the face is overall light or bold.

Contrasting stroke weights, or shading, is typical of serif faces. Thin strokes may be relatively similar in weight to thicks (diminished contrast) or far lighter than the thicks (extreme contrast).

As noted earlier, individual strokes may also exhibit contrast in weight, called *modulation*. The rapidity of change from heavier to lighter weight in the stroke body is called *ductus*, which may be slow and fluid, or quick and abrupt.

WIDTH

The characters of a specific face exhibit an overall width, relative to their height. This width may be regular—historically defined as a square of the height of the capital M—or, it may be narrower (*condensed*) or wider (*extended*) than that proportion. Contemporary faces are typically designed based on the M's width being about 80 to 90% of its height.

POSTURE

A typeface may be structured such that the stems of its characters are perpendicular to the baseline (or of Roman posture); alternatively, the characters may slant to the right (Italic posture), usually at an angle of 10 to 15° off vertical. The characters of most italic serif faces are drawn with their own forms; sans serif italics are most often created by simply slanting the Romans, creating a posture called *oblique*.

CASE

Following the Renaissance model, most fonts are designed with two forms for each letter—a majuscule, capital, or uppercase form; and a miniscule or lowercase form. Sometimes, a font includes a set of small capitals (uppercase forms that are similar in height and weight to the lowercase); some fonts are designed as "unicase," mixing uppercase and lowercase structures within a single character set.

Condensed | *Regular* | *Extended*

Roman

Fundamental stem structure perpendicular to baseline

Italic

Fundamental stem structure slanted, 12–15° to the right

MGA

Uppercase or Capital [Majuscule]

mfga

Lowercase [Miniscule]

Roman Proportion

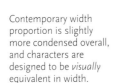

Modern Proportion

In the classical Roman model, characters are designed to be of either square or half square proportion.

Contemporary width proportion is slightly more condensed overall, and characters are designed to be *visually* equivalent in width.

Oblique

Fundamental stem structure mechanically slanted

MA Fm

Small Capital (compared to capital and lowercase)

Reverse Oblique or *Backslanted*

Slant is to the left, rather than to the right. In this case, the slope angle is far greater than the norm of 12–15°

a B D e
f J n R t

Unicase

STYLE CLASSIFICATION

SERIF

The serif form is the first major stylistic classification for typefaces—first, because it is the oldest form of Western writing. Its chief characteristic is that of small, horizontal, linear details at the terminals of its strokes, sometimes referred to as "feet."

Various serif styles are typically categorized by their characteristics based on when those attributes appeared historically, as they represent the definitive evolution of type forms from primitive to more advanced. Subcategories have been established to describe regional differences in serifs' visual characteristics as well.

In general, serif faces display the evidence of the brush or pen originally used to make them, especially in the shaping of stroke terminals and joints; the height of the lowercase, relative to that of the uppercase, is smaller the older the face, and increases in height over time. Most serif faces present an uneven, offset distribution of weight in the curved forms, like the O, resulting in the rotation of their internal counters off the 90° vertical axis—again, a characteristic of their drawing with brush or pen.

Contemporary serif designs often merge stylistic qualities of prior classes, together with those of sans serifs, simplifying them for a cleaner, less organic quality.

Throughout this section, guide lines and curve axes for each specimen are diagrammed in light gray, where appropriate; callouts in red isolate elements of interest for comparison.

Oldstyle / Garalde

Minimal stroke contrast

Rounded serifs with generous brackets

Smoothed joints

Small x-height, relative to cap height

Deep ascent/descent measures

Most extreme, oblique axis in curved forms

Oldstyle / Venetian

Minimal stroke contrast

Slightly sharpened, as well as rounded, serifs with restrained brackets

More abrupt joints

Small, but slightly taller, x-height than Garaldes

Deep ascent/descent measures

Oblique curve axis

Transitional

Pronounced stroke contrast

Sharply cut, angular serifs with rapid ductus in the brackets

Increased x-height

Reduced ascent/descent measures

More upright curve axis

Rationalist (also: Modern, Neoclassical, or Didone)

Extreme stroke contrast

Unbracketed, hairline serifs and occasional ball serifs

Markedly increased x-height

Reduced ascent/descent measures

Perpendicular curve axis

Inscribed *or* **Glyphic**

Minimal stroke contrast and instances of uniform stroke weight

Minimal, wedge-like serifs with minimal bracketing

Relatively large x-height

Reduced ascent/descent measures

Abrupt joints and visible angularity in curves, as though chiseled

Oblique curve axis

Contemporary

Minimal stroke contrast

Small, less varied serifs with rapid ductus in the brackets

Abrupt joints

Very large x-height

Shallow ascent/descent measures

Generally upright axis in the curved forms

SANS SERIF

The sans serif form is the second, major class of typeface style. They are principally characterised by their lack of serifs ("sans", in French, means "without) and an overall uniform stroke weight. As discussed in the first chapter, sans serifs were first developed in the early 1800s, but didn't gain wide acceptance until the early part of the 20th century.

Subcategories of the sans serif classification, developed within the past 100 years or so, generally are defined by visual attributes of their formation—how rigorously geometric they are, for instance—although such characteristics are usually also related to specific time periods: the Humanist sans serif form, for example, first came about in the 1910s.

Because sans serifs came to be after the evolution of the serif, they tend to exhibit characteristics of the later serif variants, like those of Rationalist style: a large x-height and a 90° curve axis.

RxmEgf

Grotesque

Relatively bold weight	Curved joints with abrupt ductus
Moderately condensed body and compressed counters	Reduced ascent/descent measures
Noticeable stroke contrast	Instances of serif forms, as in the lowercase g

RxmEgf

Gothic

Slightly bolder than historically regular weight	More abrupt joints
Medium body width	Reduced ascent/descent measures
Greater stroke weight uniformity	Instances of serif form, as in the lowercase g

RxmEgf

Geometric

Conventionally medium weight in the regular	Moderate ascent/descent measures
Slightly extended width	Pronounced circularity in curves and nearly isometric (45°) angles in the diagonals
Greater regularity in width among characters	
Fluid branch joints	Modern g form

RxmEgf

Neo-Grotesque

Conventionally medium weight in the regular	Very large x-height and further reduced ascent/descent measures
Slightly extended width	Less purely circular curved forms than in a Geometric sans
Further increased regularity in width among characters	

RxmEgf

Humanist

Slightly lighter than typical weight in the regular or Roman	Slight modulation in stroke weights
Slightly condensed body widths	Greater variation in curve formation
	Instances of serif forms

RxmEgf

Rectilinear *or* Machined

Constructed solely of angular strokes and, sometimes, from a repeated module shape	Slightly condensed width
	Abrupt joints
	Reduced ascent/descent measures

STYLE CLASSIFICATION

SLAB SERIF

Technically, most slab-serif typefaces—an invention of the Industrial Revolution when sans serifs were declared unacceptable—are sans serif faces with serifs stuck back onto them. Like their serifless counterparts, their lowercase characters tend to be quite large, relative to the height of the uppercase, and their curved forms most often show weight distributed evenly left to right across the characters' 90° axis.

Following their initial appearance in the early 1800s—when their form was new and not yet well-resolved—slab serifs increasingly came to follow the characteristics of sans serif styles; subclassifications are also described as being Geometric, Neo-Grotesque, or Humanist, depending on which sans serif style they're based.

A somewhat recent development in slab serif designs is an exaggerated rectilinearity in their curves, coupled with abrupt joints between vertical and curved elements.

RxmEgf

Grotesque *or* **Antique**

Heavy slabs, oftentimes awkwardly so, without bracketing

Generally bold or extra-bold weight

Compressed counters

Large x-height and diminished ascent/descent measures

RxmEgf

Scotch *or* **Clarendon**

Overall lighter weight

Extended width

Serifs are of the weight of the thins, with restrained bracketing of rapid ductus

Greater stroke contrast

Includes serif characteristics

The term *Scotch* refers to a style of transitional serif faces with heavier serifs than are typical

RxmEgf

Modern *or* **Geometric**

Conventionally medium weight in the regular

Slightly extended width

Greater regularity in width among characters

Fluid or abrupt branch joints

Pronounced circularity in curves and nearly isometric (45°) angles in the diagonals

RxmEgf

Neo-Grotesque *and* **Humanist**

Members of this subcategory tend to follow the characteristics of their sans serif counterparts in most respects. The serifs in Neo-Grotesque forms, as well as their joints, tend to be unbracketed and abrupt; those in Humanist forms tend to be bracketed and more curvacious.

RxmEgfAs

Italienne (also called French Clarendon)

Pronounced reversal of weight between vertical stems and horizontals (generally, the serifs, rather than among crossbars or waists).

Typically abrupt, unbracketed serifs

Generally condensed width

RxmEgf

Rectilinear

Emphasis on vertical stems

Squared-off curves of tight radius and rapid ductus

Slightly condensed width

Abrupt joints

Reduced ascent/descent measures

SCRIPT

The script form derives from informal writing, as made on the fly, rather than from formal inscription models. Its origin lies in Roman cursives used on a daily basis for notes, letters, and invitations, as opposed to other writing structures that were meant for permanance. In essence, a script is about handwriting.

Historical nomenclature notwistanding, the term *cursive* describes a script with fluid, interconnective strokes between letters—as would occur if writing spontaneously with a pen. The chancery style is a formalized version of the cursive, distinguished by clear separation of its characters, an evoution that dates to the Middle Ages. The remaining subclassifications have more to do with characteristics of style, referring to the English Spencerian period or, later, post-Industrial periods.

The most freeform of the scripts is that which is designed to emulate natural handwriting—which, surprisingly, is the most contemporary of script concepts. These fall into the category known as "casuals," scripts that are less regimented in their form (and often derived from vernacular, or "undesigned" sources); their freshness relies on the creation of alternate versions of characters to prevent easily noticed repetitions of recurring characters—and, so, avoid an artificial quality.

Cursive / Spencerian

Deep, horizontally inclined slope	Exaggerated ascent/descent measures
Relatively condensed body width	Relatively light weight and pronounced stroke contrast
Small x-height	Fluid, extended finishing strokes for connection

Chancery

Pronounced pen-shaping in terminals	Exaggerated ascent/descent measures
More upright slope	More conventional medium weight
Medium stroke contrast	Abrupt stroke finishes that do not connect characters
Larger x-height	

Upright

Pronounced lack of slope (perpendicularity)	Exaggerated ascent measure falling below the capline
Unusually small x-height	Near-vertical axis in curved forms
Pronounced stroke contrast	Fluid, extended finishing strokes for connection

Industrial

More upright slope	Minimal stroke contrast
Curves of tight, squared-off radius and rapid ductus	More contrived, less spontaneous/organic terminal shaping
Strong horizontal emphasis	Generally smaller x-height
	Pronounced descent measure

Casual (includes Handwritten and Graffiti forms)

Strokes drawn with brush, pen, marker, or spray paint	Great variety in stroke terminal and joint characteristics
Generally noticeable (at a minimum) to extremely dramatic variation in character height, width, and overall shaping	Moderate to large x-height, when lowercase are present
	May be mixed case or unicase

STYLE CLASSIFICATION

DISPLAY OR 'GRAPHIC': EMBELLISHED

Display faces are those that are designed with expressive, even ostentatious, visual characteristics for titling, callouts, and other accentuating typographic applications— not for continuous reading, for which their distracting optical qualities would make them unuseful.

Display faces can be divided into two major categories; the first might be said to include those that are, in essence, straightforward serif, sans serif, or slab serif forms that are somehow decorated or embellished. This kind of display face typically follows the rules for character proportion, stroke weight and contrast, curve logic and diagonal architecture that apply to text faces—it's just that they also integrate graphical elements that supersede their fundamental construction. These elements may be as simple as an outlining of the core structure; they may involve decoration of characters' internal surface area.

The subcategories shown here describe general distinctions; as always, there are plenty of hybrids and deviations to be found in this, as well as other, stylistic classification categories.

Stenciled

These faces are, self-explicitly, drawn as if made using a stencil— major stroke formations are separated by a small space, even including open and apertured forms (as opposed to closed ones, like the D and O). Any basic style may be stenciled.

Outline / Inline

An *outline* face is one that essentially appears "white" or "transparent," its contours described by relatively lightweight lines.

When the contours become thick enough that the strokes appear solid—but retain an interior linear counter— they are called *inline* faces.

Chiseled / Engraved

The terms *chiseling* and *engraving* refer to linear embellishments that appear to be drawn on the surfaces of the characters. Such chiseled or engraved detailing may run vertically along the stems (and so, may also be characterized as an inline face), or horizontally, creating a linear pattern.

Decorated

A tremendous variety of fonts is embellished with complex, detailed ornamentation across their surfaces. These may be florid, calligraphic, and even pictorial in nature, or extremely geometric in their patterning. Such decoration is typical of serif display fonts created during the 16th–19th centuries.

Shadowed

A shadowed font is one in which the characters' primary stroke information appears "white," or invisible against the background—defined by the appearance of a cast shadow underneath. When set in a page environment, the primary stroke material is transparent.

Two-Toned / Chromatic

These are faces that integrate positive and negative strokes within each character. They can appear flat or dimensional, giving the appearance of being cast or extruded from solid material, and sometimes incorporate chiseled or engraved details.

DISPLAY OR 'GRAPHIC': ABSTRACTED

At the other extreme of the display classification are forms that fundamentally violate established structural norms—that is, they're not really like a basic serif, sans serif, slab serif, or script that has been decorated or embellished.

Instead, typefaces in this class of display forms flout conventions of construction through a variety of means, from distortion of expected character contours to construction based on modular or illustrative components; or drawing styles based on reference to forms that aren't fundamentally classical in their derivation, like those based on embroidery.

It's an unfortunate state of affairs that most historical forms, like the blackletter or ancient Greek Boustrophedon, must be relegated to this category—because their stylistic qualities are no longer familiar enough to qualify them for easy reading, and because they carry a significant amount of narrative baggage.

As wild as the form of any display face becomes, however, the same considerations one must resolve to ensure rhythmic and stylistic logic for text faces apply here.

Distorted / Textural

Thousands of display faces fall into this category, which is chiefly characterized by irregular contouring (whether organic or geometric in quality) and textural deformations.

Constructed: Modular

These are faces whose character formation is clearly contrived and built from combinations of one, two, or more basic shapes. The shapes themselves may be geometric or organic in their quality.

Constructed: Nonmodular

This kind of face also calls attention to the fact of its structure, but in contrast to those of the modular variety, the shapes used to form the strokes are typically not based on the same building blocks. As a result, their internal language appears more highly varied and less mechanical.

Illustrated

Any typeface in which the characters are formed using pictorial images of objects—which may consist of plant matter, machine parts, and animal or human figures—or anything else, for that matter (sometimes in combination).

Vernacular

Typefaces whose strokes are formed from graphical languages that are associated with specific technologies (like typewriter fonts), naïve methods (like signpainting), or purely nontypographic sources (like stitch patterns in sewing or embroidery) are called *vernacular*, meaning "from the common or everyday."

Archaic

Most of the older forms that consitute the evolution of writing and typographic design may now be considered display faces, simply because their forms are so decorative, narrative, and unfamiliar to contemporary eyes.

IDEAL MECHANICS / THE CAPITALS

A hefty portion of this book—the following chapter, especially—is devoted to seeing how the optical qualities of letters' strokes and counters must be judged on a case-by-case basis, because they do things to our eyes in such a way that defies relying on measured, mathematical construction.

The reality, though, is that the master structure governing alphabetic form boils down to a simple, geometric framework: the letter body is a space broken into four quadrants. Each quadrant contains a portion of a letter's structure, and these portions more or less mirror each other, top to bottom and left to right. It's one of the hallmarks of the Western alphabet that its letters are so modular—varied enough for distinction between characters, but easy to memorize as a set because they're so closely related in structure.

A quick review of early Phoenician, Greek, and Roman writing in the previous chapter will reveal that primitve letter structure was formed mostly of angles—primarily because they're easier to carve into stone than curves. Once curves came into the picture, and as proportional logic began to change, the same basic idea remained as a standard to achieve.

The optical manipulations discussed later on, therefore, are all aimed at making sure the letters appear, or feel like, they uphold this symmetrical quadrant structure, even though they mathematically can not.

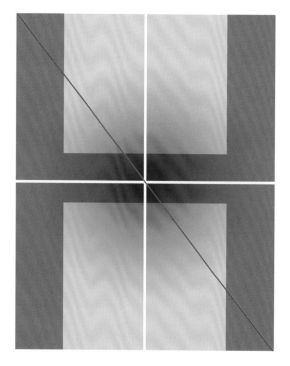

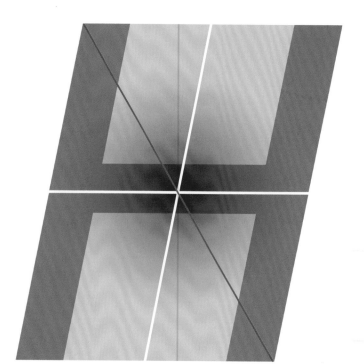

The ideal Roman super-structure is a rectangle whose dimensions are defined by the capital H.

This master rectangle is divided in half, along the form's vertical axis, and again, along the horizontal axis—creating four quadrants of equal proportion. The stroke information of letters is distributed more or less evenly among the quadrants. In serif forms, the base rectangle is defined by the outer sides of the stems, not including the serifs.

An ideal italic form is based on the same quadrant formation, but the base rectangle is skewed to the right, forming a parallelogram. Interestingly, the 12° slant typical of most italics derives from a number sacred to Christian numerology.

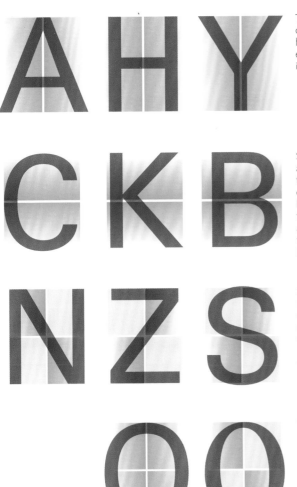

The majority of upper-case characters are bilaterally symmetrical, evidence of their earlier invention.

Several characters are symmetrical from top to bottom. Stroke elements in their right-hand quadrant areas are typically extended further and given extra weight to help them seem more bilaterally symmetrical.

Some characters are rotationally symmetrical, meaning that their stroke formations and densities are mirrored between the corner quadrants.

The capital O in geometric and neo-grotesque sans serif fonts, as well as in Rationalist serifs, tends to be bilaterally symmetrical (left); in fonts with oblique curve axis, the O tends to be rotationally symmetrical.

The aspect ratio of the base rectangle (how wide it is compared to its height) is described by a diagonal from upper left corner to lower right corner. This diagonal axis is the source of the primary diagonal language in the font—as defined by the diagonal stem in the N.

The diagonals in other letters, such as the A, V, M, and R cannot usually be drawn at the same angle and still maintain optically consistent width in these characters—still, they are often adjusted in different ways to feel more closely related to that of the N.

Joints between strokes are designed to appear at the same height and to mimic each other in angularity and shaping.

In angled forms with repeating structures, the downstroke (dominant) angles are parallel, as are the upstroke (sub-oridnate) diagonals.

The counters in such forms, as with all the letters, are designed to mirror each in shape and volume. In the crossed-form W at far right, the smaller and larger of the crossed counters "add up" in their combined volume to match that of the counters at left and right.

FORMAL CONVENTIONS

IDEAL MECHANICS / THE LOWERCASE

The construction of lowercase forms, being a late addition to the official alphabet, follows a different kind of logic. Some of the characters—a, e, k, m, o, v, x, s—do still refer to the symmetrical, quadrant relationships of the capitals (and it might stand out that these sometimes are simply reduced versions of their uppercase parents, and they also tend to represent the most basic sounds of speech).

The visual ideals to which designs for the lowercase forms aspire are more holistically about their relationship to each other than they are to a fixed structural model; the bulk of typographic design is made up of lowercase text that must facilitate extensive reading. Even so, the lowercase exist in relation to the capitals, and so must be designed to correspond to them.

Most specifically, the body of the lowercase must share proportion with that of the uppercase, having a similar height/width aspect ratio, so that the capitals don't seem to pop out as different when they occasionally appear. The height of the lowercase must accommodate greater density in stroke information, yet still allow enough room above to fit the ascending strokes within the capital body, ensuring easy horizontal flow. The descent measure should mirror that of the ascent so that descenders hug the line and avoid conflict with ascenders in a line of text below.

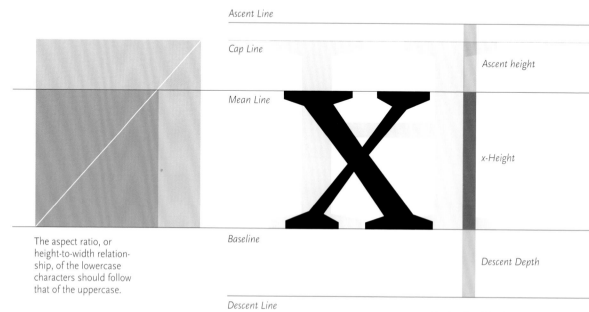

The aspect ratio, or height-to-width relationship, of the lowercase characters should follow that of the uppercase.

The height of the lowercase is defined by that of the letter x, which is the only character that comprises flat-topped stroke terminals at its left-most and right-most boundaries.

The ascent and descent measures are, in essence, defined by the x-height. Ideally, these two measures should be identical so that ascenders and descenders seem proportional in relation to each other, and to the capitals; and so that they remain as close to the line of text as possible to minimize their sometimes distracting qualities.

Between these three faces, compare the effects of their varied x-heights, aspect ratios, and ascent/descent measures. In each case, this confluence of interrelated variables in their respective structures results in radically different densities and spacing rhythm that is, each time, characteristic of the given font.

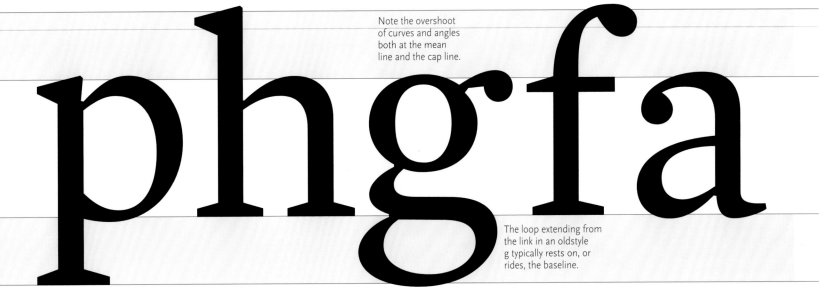

Note the overshoot of curves and angles both at the mean line and the cap line.

The loop extending from the link in an oldstyle g typically rests on, or rides, the baseline.

The majority of the lowercase characters' structures is contained within the area of the x-height. The area above the mean line, extending to the cap line, is the basic measure to be used for ascending strokes. If the x-height is somewhat large (to accommodate dense characters like the a and e), the ascent line is sometimes pushed higher than the capline to provide more room for the f's shoulder. In any event, the depth of descending characters is the same as (or very slightly less than) that of ascending characters.

As in the design of the uppercase, major joint structures in the lowercase are designed to be identical in position and shaping.

Most of the lowercase characters exhibit an emphasis on the circular component of the structure. Those with more completely circular elements, or lobes, that join with vertical stems—like the b, d, p, and q—are directly derivative of the O in their curvature and outer widths. Those like the n, m, and r (in which the curves branch from a stem and then join a subsequent stem) compress the o's curve to maintain a consistent counter shape and interval.

Lowercase forms are rhythmically more regular than their uppercase counterparts, but also are more greatly differentiated—the result of their heritage in miniscule forms of the Middle Ages.

Several lowercase forms are simply reduced versions of their capitals with minor detail changes.

FORMAL CONVENTIONS

STANDARD WEIGHT DISTRIBUTION

In every typeface—even in display fonts—each kind of stroke in a letter is charactersitically heavier or lighter in weight, regardless of style. The standard for which kinds of strokes are heavier, and which are lighter, originates in their drawing by brush and pen: the flat edges of these tools, deposit more ink or paint in very specific places along a stroke, depending on the angle at which the tool is held, and the direction the stroke is being drawn.

The conventional distribution of heavier, thickly weighted strokes (or thicks) and those that are of lighter weight (thins) in certain places is so heavily ingrained in our asethetic appreciation of type that deviations appear awkward or illformed. This is true even in those faces that are designed to appear as though their characters' strokes are uniform in weight throughout.

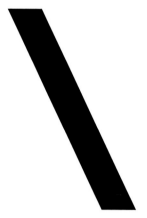

Vertical strokes are always heavy in weight. They form the basis of most letters, and so this weight defines that of other dominant strokes in characters made up of diagonals or curves.

Horizontal strokes are always lighter in weight, relative to any given vertical. How much lighter they are depends on the relative weight contrast among strokes within a particular style.

Dominant, or downward directional, diagonal strokes are always heavy in weight.

HAXEWKiJO

H A

N M

N M

Reversing established weight immediately makes a letter appear awkward and wrong (like the H), or that it is backward, like the A.

Two important exceptions are the capital N and M. If drawn following the logic noted above, the results would deviate significantly from surrounding forms—all of the strokes in the N would appear heavy, as would all but one in the M. The source for this logic is in these characters' archaic forms, which were both drawn as sets of diagonals.

Z
7
U

Other exceptions include the Z, the U, and the numeral 7. In the case of both Z and 7, the reasoning behind the weight reversal is that it accentuates the character's dominant stroke. In the U, it's about maintaining consistent heavy/light alternation in the form that is prevalent in other characters; it also follows from the logic of the V, with which the U shares a linguistic, as well as visual, relationship.

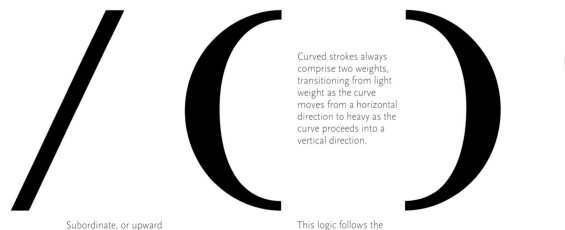

Curved strokes always comprise two weights, transitioning from light weight as the curve moves from a horizontal direction to heavy as the curve proceeds into a vertical direction.

In the wave-form, or joined half circle, stroke—the kind that forms the S—the weight within the stroke transitions from light to heavy to light, following the same logic as seen in the formation of simple, semi-circular curved strokes.

Subordinate, or upward directional, diagonal strokes are always lighter in weight; in a given typeface, the subordinate diagonals are the same optical weight as the horizontal strokes.

This logic follows the weight relationship established by vertical and horizopntal straight strokes, respectively.

R G F Q P L 2 Y 3 4 5 S 8 K ?

H R G

It's easy to see how weight differences are distibuted within a serif style (because there are thicks and thins) but less so in a sans serif of purportedly uniform stroke weight. These enlarged sans serif characters show that the historical legacy of a brush-drawn form still governs the design of modern faces. Each is accompanied by a small point-size version for comparison.

FORMAL CONVENTIONS

PROPORTIONAL REGULARITY

The chief goal in any typeface design is the appearance that all the characters are the same height, the same width (or, more accurately, that the strokes seem all the same distance apart, separated by spaces that all appear the same dimension). In the lowercase, ascenders and descenders, as previously noted, should appear equivalent in their respective height and depth.

VISUAL STABILITY

Despite variation in the kinds of shapes and structures that make up each letter, they must feel stable: upper stories should appear centered over lower stories, and seem top-heavy; from left to right, characters should feel evenly weighted, even when they're asymmetrical.

HOA
exmr

All of the uppercase characters should appear to be the same height—as should all of the lowercase characters that don't incorporate ascenders or descenders

ABCDEFGHI
JKLMNOPQ

As different in form as they are, all of the characters in a font should seem as though they're the same width; strokes should appear separated by the same amount of counter throughout.

kgfyp

The height of the ascenders should match the depth of the descenders

HRXB
exgsa

Characters that comprise an upper and lower half should appear symmetrically divided along the horizontal axis. The upper story should be centered visually over the lower one.

AXSK
mfyta

Asymmetrical, as well as symmetrical, characters should appear evenly weighted from left to right, and establish a similar sense of overall width as compared to characters that are defined by strokes on both left and right.

GESTURAL CONTINUITY

Within each letter, the strokes move into and out of each other with continuous and related kinds of thrust, appearing interdependent and inseparable. As each kind of stroke pushes or pulls inward or outward in one location, threatening instability, strokes in other locations must correspondingly pull or push back to restabilize the form. Joint and terminal shapes should relate to gestural thrust and be similar among all the forms.

CONSISTENT COUNTER PRESENCE

The counters among different characters should appear to be of the same volume; each of the two or more counters within a single character should appear equivalent; and the volume of counter, relative to the amount of stroke density, in each character should appear the same. This similarity in stroke/counter ratio should be optically equivalent between uppercase and lowercase forms, as well.

The little directional arrows on top of the characters, above, describe the thrust direction of individual strokes and their contours in particular places. Note how the outward push of a curve, or the way it raises and lowers along an axis in one location on a character finds an opposing counterpoint in another location. This gestural correspondence also is expressed in terminal and joint details, identified by the small circles.

Strokes that meet in joints should fluidly appear to merge into each other, as though each is growing from, or is a continuation of, the other stroke.

The counters in these uppercase and lowercase forms have been isolated and disconnected to better compare how overall similar each is to the others in terms of relative visual volume, despite how different in shape they all are.

Within an individual character, internal counter components are relatively similar in volume or visual mass; the same is true, in aggregate, between the counter(s) in one character and the others; and, between the two cases, the ratio of counter presence (compared to character body and stroke material) is also roughly equivalent.

CONSISTENT ANGULARITY

The diagonal strokes among angled letters should appear, or feel, as though they are of the same angle, relative to the vertical axis—even though this condition is physically impossible if the characters are also to appear the same width. The angularity of the diagonals should be reflected in the cut, or shear, of the terminals and in the relative pointiness or flatness of joints between angled strokes.

CONSISTENT CURVE SHAPING

All of the curves in a character set should look as though they are of the same radius, no matter where they appear, or how relatively larger or smaller they are—again, a physical impossibility, given how the curves will have to interact with other kinds of stroke structures in different forms. Curves along an interior counter always "track" those of the exterior of the stroke, widening steadily as the stroke moves from horizontal orientation to vertical and back again.

The stroke angles among the diagonal characters are designed to mimic each other in angularity, relative to the master body, as closely as possible.

The relative circularity of the curves among forms—not their mathematically measured radii—is the critical factor in creating unity within a given face.

The O defines a "master" curve, which is (in essence) scaled to different proportions to define other curves.

In asymmetrical characters, the curves tend to mirror each other from top to bottom.

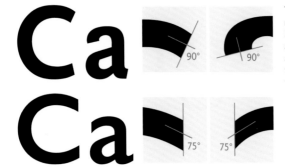

The terminals in most fonts are finished in such a way that the angle at which they are cut corresponds to the kind of angularity found among the diagonals' strokes.

The interior curves of strokes abutting counters track those of outer contours.

Similarly, joints between straight and angled strokes refer to overall angularity, and are consistent from character to character.

Large, structural curves are typically mirrored in radius and ductus by smaller curves that appear in details (such as one finds in joints and serif brackets).

CONSISTENT WEIGHT AND CONTRAST

All of the characters in a font should appear to be the same weight, whether the characters are without contrast (of uniform stroke weight) or show variation in weight (shading, or the presence of thicks and thins)—in which case, the gestalt, or visual aggregate, of thicks and thins in one character, should appear the same as that in any other. Thicks should be the same thickness—and thins the same thinness—throughout.

CONSISTENT MODULATION AND DUCTUS

In typefaces whose strokes modulate, or taper in thickness from one end to the other (as opposed to being parallel), the degree or "speed" of change from thick to thin, or vice versa—the ductus—should appear the same in every character. Curvilinear forms in every typeface show modulation, even if the stems don't; in such cases, the ductus should reflect the relative lack of change that the stems exhibit.

ABHa

ABHa

All of the characters in a given typeface should appear to be the same weight—none lighter or darker overall. This is true of fonts that are uniform in weight, as well as in those with strokes of contrasting weight (thins and thicks).

ABH

Thick
Thin

In a typeface with contrasting stroke weights, the thin strokes should be equivalent in weight (wherever they appear), as should the thick strokes.

ABH

Serifs should all appear the same size and weight; in general, they are designed to match the weight of the thins, although sometimes they are designed to be slightly lighter.

RMG
adgh

Slow or fluid ductus

RMG
adgh

Rapid or abrupt ductus

FORMAL CONVENTIONS

CORRESPONDENCE BETWEEN CASES

The lowercase forms should appear to be of the same proportion as their corresponding uppercase—neither more extended nor condensed. Uppercase and lowercase forms within a single character set should appear to be the same weight (whether uniform or contrasting). The stroke/counter ratio, again, should be similar between the two cases—in both forms of a single letter, and from letter to letter.

SIMILARITY OF VARIATIONS

Within families that include variants in weight (light, medium, and bold versions, for example) or width (condensed, medium, and extended)—or both—the differences between each variant should be not only appreciable, but similar in degree—that is, for instance, that the difference in weight between the light and medium should be equivalent to that between the medium and bold.

As weight changes from light to bold, the overall width of the forms should remain optically consistent; as width changes from condensed to extended, the weights of the characters from width to width should be the same.

Italic variants should appear the same width as their Roman counterparts.

In general and, as closely as possible, the aspect ratio of the uppercase and lowercase should strive to be identical.

It's worth noting again that the weight(s) of the lowercase forms should appear identical to those in the uppercase forms. Because there's more stroke information compressed into a smaller area in the lowercase, this usually means their strokes must be mathematically a tiny bit lighter.

Appreciated in aggregate, the relative ratio between stroke in counter should be the same in the lowercase as in the uppercase.

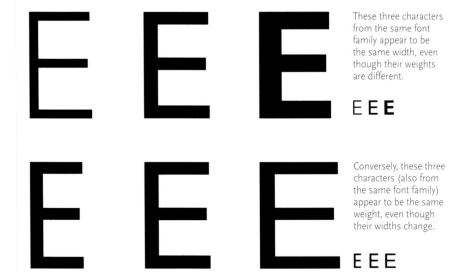

These three characters from the same font family appear to be the same width, even though their weights are different.

Conversely, these three characters (also from the same font family) appear to be the same weight, even though their widths change.

Although clearly physically wider than their Roman counterparts because they slant, the apparent width of the italic examples is the same as that of the Roman. This appearance, as noted on page 66, is the result of optical similarity in stroke separation, rather than of measuring of any kind.

WELL-MADE ITALICS AND SCRIPTS

Needless to say, the apparent heights, widths, weights, curvatures, angularity, and stroke/counter intervals among italic characters in a set should be consistent throughout. Further, the apparent slant, or slope, of all the characters should appear identical.

Script forms, intended to mimic the fluidity of handwriting, are typically designed with extended finishing strokes to connect characters in sequence, and usually benefit from the inclusion of alternate characters to prevent noticeable repetitions that might be appreciated as artificial or mechanical in feeling.

MODULAR AND FIXED-WIDTH FORMS

Although typically designed for industrial or electronic application (typewriters, text-reading software, and digital billboards), these rigidly constructed faces offer narrative potential and pose several challenges to type designers because of their mechanical limitations. Of chief concern are character recognition and overall color consistency, given the constraints such faces impose.

AaGgMm SsXx

All of the characters in an italic font should appear to slope at the same angle.

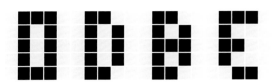

Special care must be taken in structuring characters made from modular forms (whether pixel-based or not) to ensure that each is readily identifiable, and not easily confused with, other similar forms.

duisautemvel duisautemvel **duisautemvel**

A script is generally considered well made when it includes finishing strokes that mimic the fluid continuity of handwriting to some degree.

AGMS agms

Lorem ipsum dolor sit amet consectituer adipscing

Fixed-width, or monospaced, typefaces present challenges with regard to achieving consistent stroke/ counter rhythm and, therefore, color. In most such faces, dense characters like the m (of both cases) always appear condensed and somewhat bolder than other characters. Word spaces, on the other hand, usually appear far bigger and more open.

MACRO/MICRO STYLE LOGIC

Consistent character structure, proportion, weight, contrast, and posture within any typeface define the minimum conditions for stylistically integrating all the members of a character set…but perfection is in the details. It's when the big picture of gestural movement and shaping are reflected in the smaller elements—the shear of terminals, the turning radius of brackets in serifs, even the shape of a tittle—that the holistic interrelationship of the forms within a font comes to life and unifies them as a totality of expression.

A well-resolved typeface expresses analogous logic between macro and micro levels of form, as well as among the tiny details as a subset of the overall idea. Depending on a font's relative neutrality of style, this analogous logic may be more strictly limited in its variation (the parts are more similar), or show a wider range of different kinds of logic details that intermix in different combinations. The nature of consistency in formal logic, as in any system, is flexible: It may be simpler and more regimented or more complex and organic.

This contemporary serif face includes a lot of stylistic variation in detailing for a text face, but notice how they appear in different combinations among the letters to create more cohesion among them overall.

EgA

EgAajG

Most scripts incorporate a staggering range of variation in their structural and stylistic details—it's the nature of the beast, an attempt to impart the form with the organic spontaneity of natural handwriting.

Looking closely, however, will reveal remarkable similarity among decisions. The designer has made an effort in the opposing direction: that of ensuring the forms feel related anyway.

Eg

Like the serif shown at top, this sans serif exhibits a wide array of details that aim to give it a more expressive personality—unlike the neutral sans serif above

ALI SCIANDRA / USA
PURCHASE COLLEGE SUNY
Timothy Samara, instructor

EgAaj

ajGnNtPk

nNtPk

This sans serif face, in contrast to the serif above, exhibits greater regularity in its detailing, which is one of the reasons it feels exceptionally clean and neutral.

AajGnNtPk

GnNtPk

FORMAL CONVENTIONS

RHYTHMIC REGULARITY AND COLOR

As far as fonts that are intended for in-depth, extended reading are concerned, the ultimate goal of all the consistency in proportion, stroke interval, and detailing under discussion is a relentlessly even texture that won't distract readers from reading—given how intellectually labor-intensive reading is, the brain will look for any way to get out of it that it can. This texture, or "color," should resolve itself, at a glance, as a middle-value gray without interruption: no big bright spots, created by counters that are too large, nor dark clusters of strokes being too close together or mistmatched in weight.

Lorem ipsum dolor sit amet consectetur adisce iscind evit fisce quam nisi dapibus at sem pulvi nar aliquam suscipit maurit. Aenean ac orciver justo tempor sceleriqe curabitur non rutru felis pentes.

VESTIBULURET SEMPER NULLA NEC NI SI MATSIT AMET DEI BLANDIT EROS.

Lorem ipsum dolor sit amet consectetur adisce iscind evit fisce quam nisi dapibus at sem pulvi nar aliquam suscipit maurit. Aenean ac orciver justo tempor sceleriqe curabitur non rutru felis pentesque.

VESTIBULURET SEMPER NULLA NEC NI SI MATSIT AMET DEI BLANDIT EROS.

At left, the text shown above is shown again, but reduced to a conventional text size. The gray rectangles below approximate this text's visual effect—that of an uninterrupted texture.

The evenness of color that the text specimen at top produces is considered ideal, the goal to be achieved when designing a font for extended reading.

The effect is the result of tinkering with the minutiae of character structure such that every heavy stroke—those within characters, and between characters when the text is properly spaced—appears equidistant.

In the bottom example, the repeated, lightly tinted instance of the specimen shows the heavy strokes called out in red to illustrate this condition emphatically.

Horbi donec maximus consebir
LOREM IPSUM DUIS AUTEM VELURE

Text color in sans serif faces tends to be of greater density and darkness than that of serifs: the body of the lowercase is larger, filling more of the line; and there are no thins.

Sans serifs usually benefit from being spaced a little more loosely in text to help alleviate this density, which can seem a little aggressive.

Horbi donec maximus consebir
LOREM IPSUM DUIS AUTEM VELURE

Horbi donec maximus consebir sunt felis semper nulla tempor vestibulur

Fonts with extreme contrast in their characters' stroke weights create spotty, uneven color— what is often called *strobing* or *flicker*.

While they're excellent for headlines or callouts, text set in such fonts usually suffers from appearing overly active. Rationalist serifs and many scripts fall into this category.

Very often, the distraction produced by flicker or strobing can be significantly reduced by increasing interline space (more leading) between lines of text.

Horbi donec maximus consebir
LOREM IPSUM DUIS AUTEM VELURE

In similar need of attention when setting them in text are geometric sans serifs, especially those based on Roman proportion. Their uneven color results from characters being much

different in width—making counters in curved forms appear as large holes, and creating situations where vertical strokes are sometimes close together and sometimes far apart.

Horbi donec maximus consebir su
LOREM IPSUM DUIS AUTEM VELURE

Super condensed fonts, especially ones of bold weight, create an extremely dense color in lines of text. Usually, loosening the spacing a little helps make such faces a little more

comfortable to read for extended periods. When used at large sizes in titling or headlines, tightening their spacing helps improve the dynamism of their appearance.

Horbi donec maximus con sebir felimanul tempor

Even display faces with unusual proportions and a variety of gestural movements may exhibit a recognizably consistent rhythm, as does the

specimen at left—which is great for stylistic unity, but not so much for continuous reading.

One might assume that familiarity with the basic standards and conventions of typeface construction would be sufficient to start designing a font. What those conventions don't reveal, however, are the challenges they impose in achieving them: Designing a font for extensive reading that requires a consistent gray texture, in which all the letters appear to have the same proportion and strokes of the same weight, for instance, is not an exercise in measuring. The variety of stroke shapes and their individual kinds of movement, of joints between them, and of the counters that glue them all together, necessitate throwing out the ruler. Ultimately, letterform design is a game of optical illusions that compensates for these differences to ensure the *perception* of consistency—what *is* and what *appears to be* are almost never the same.

Foundation

FUNDAMENTALS OF CHARACTER STRUCTURE AND OPTICS

FORM PERCEPTION

SHAPE, MASS, AND SPACE

Form is optically deceptive. Every kind of shape affects our perception of it differently than does another: it intrinsically embodies a particular heaviness, or mass; its specific contours produce individual kinds of movement to track; it pushes into, recedes from, or reshapes adjacent spaces in its own way. Much of type design revolves around taming these differences to achieve the appearance of similarity—assuming the goal is to make sure all the different kinds of parts among characters look like they belong to each other.

That means having to relearn how to see— and, more critically, how *to accept what is seen, rather than measured, as true:* If two shapes are intended to be the same size, but don't look the same size, they're not. It's extremely challenging to ignore mathematical facts when we're aware of them; worse, the differences to be evaluated are usually tiny. One might think these would be inconsequential when type forms are reduced to a small size, but the opposite is true: they become exaggerated. As one develops a character set, regularly testing their appearance at a common text size (10 or 12 points, for instance) is critical.

Shown here are some basic optical relationships among shapes and spaces to consider as a starting point.

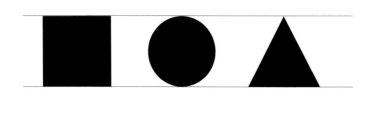

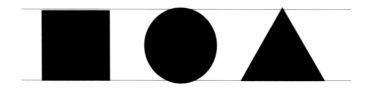

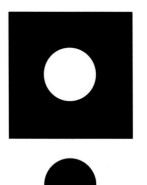

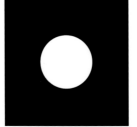

The square, circle, and triangle in the grouping at the top of the page are mathematically the same height (check the guide lines). You'll notice, however, that the square appears larger than both the circle and the triangle. Rectangular forms appear larger than other kinds because all their sides are clearly defined. Circular forms appear to contract because the eye can't fix on a specific location anywhere on its continuous curve. The diagonal sides of the triangle, similarly, pull the eyes away from the form's apex, causing it to appear shorter than the square; even though its sides are equilateral in measure, the triangle also appears somewhat narrower in width than does the square.

In the grouping closer to the bottom of the page, the sizes of the circle and triangle have been adjusted—and the base of the triangle widened—so that all three forms appear to be the same size.

A negative, or reversed form (the white circle), looks larger than the same positive form (the black circle), even though they are mathematically equivalent in size (top). In the lower example, the black circle has been slightly enlarged so both appear to be the same size.

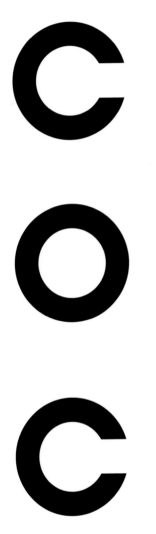

In a form with an aperture (top), the interior counter will appear larger than one of the same dimension that is completely enclosed (middle). The enclosing form itself will also appear more extended. The lower example has been adjusted to correct for this illusion.

Forms that are mathematically centered within a larger form (as is the white square within the black square at top) will appear lower than center. In the lower example, the white square has been raised very slightly so that it will appear centered within the black square.

The semicircle at top is precisely half the width and mass of the full circle in the middle—but appears slightly condensed. In the example at bottom, a little bit more of the original circle has been revealed, resulting in a semicircle that appears to be an actual semicircle.

In the top grouping of three lines, the middle one is mathematically centered between the upper and lower ones. Similar to the example with the square (at left), it appears lower than center. In the bottom example, the middle line has been raised slightly so that it will appear to be centered.

When two equivalent forms are positioned directly above and below each other, the upper one will appear larger and heavier than the one below it (top). In the lower example, the top circle has been slighlty reduced so that both will appear to be the same size.

FORM PERCEPTION

LINE IDENTITY AND PERCEIVED WEIGHT

Issues of mass and shape are generally important with regard to overall character proportion (and within exceptionally bold characters) but, for the most part, the design of type forms focuses on strokes— it's really all about lines.

Just like planar masses, the identity or character of a line affects how we perceive it. A vertical line, for instance, does things to our eyes that are different than what a horizontal, diagonal, or curved line does. The primary difference that we perceive among lines of differing character is that of weight change—which happens to be the most important thing to consider.

The fact that all of the characters' strokes within are the same thickness (or the same combination of thicknesses) is what makes that character set overall bold or light; further, visual consistency in the color, or density, of a type's strokes as they repeat sequentially is paramount in a text face, to ensure uninterrupted eye movement across a line of characters.

In a display face, or within a limited set of characters in a logotype or an ad's head-line, even pronounced weight variation among strokes may be desirable; still, the specific relative stroke weights will need to be evaluated to ensure clear, unified rhyth-mic and stylistic logic in that grouping.

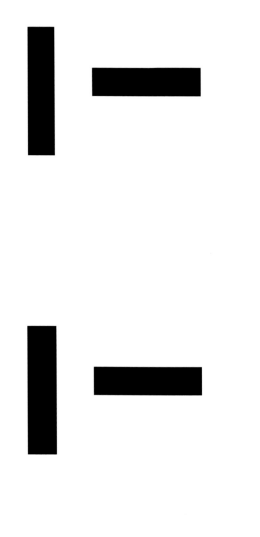

The vertical stroke and the horizontal one are exactly the same weight, mathematically speaking (top). Yet, the horizontal stroke appears heavier than the vertical one. This illusion results from our perception of horizontal forms as related to the horizon of the Earth—that they are affected by the force of gravity. (This misperception is the same kind that affects the centered square and line examples on the previous page.) The horizontal stroke in the lower example has been lightened in weight so that it appears to be the same thickness, or weight, as the vertical.

Diagonal lines are tricky. Compared to a vertical line, they will seem slightly heavier in weight; compared to a horizontal line, they will seem lighter. The angle of a diagonal affects how its weight is perceived in comparison to a vertical or horizontal line. As a diagonal's angle becomes more acute, or upright, it will be perceived as lighter; conversely, the closer its angle is to true horizonal, the heavier it will appear. The two diagonals at top are the same mathematical weight as the horizontal and vertical to the left; in the lower pair, their weights have been adjusted to make them appear equivalent.

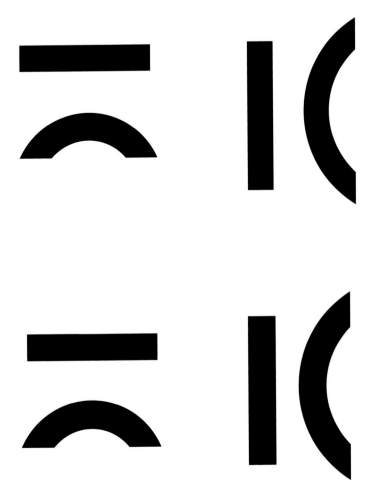

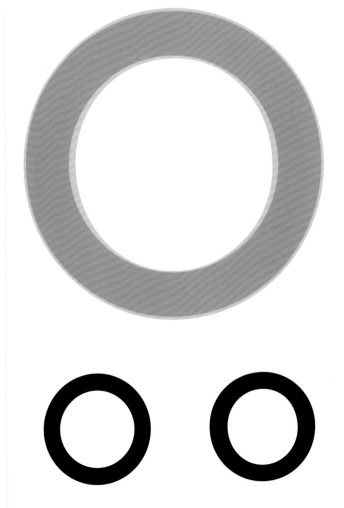

In the same way that a circular form appears smaller than a same-sized square form, a circular stroke will generally appear lighter than either a horizontal or vertical stroke—but again, the direction of its arc will affect how its weight is perceived relative to that of vertical and horizontal strokes. A circular or curved stroke that is moving horizontally will appear heavier than a similarly-weighted vertical, and a vertically moving stroke will appear lighter.

In the grouping at top, all of the strokes are of the same mathematical thickness or weight.

In the grouping below that, the weights of the various strokes have been adjusted so that all appear the same weight.

Following the logic described at left, the weight of a circular stroke must be thinned where it moves horizontally (at cap line and baseline, essentially), otherwise the stroke will appear heavier at these locations than it will in the lateral, vertically-moving portions of the curve.

At top is an enlarged diagram of the two circular forms immediately above, overlapped to show this difference. The circle at left is uniform in weight all the way around, while the one at right has been thinned at top and bottom.

OPTICAL EFFECTS OF STROKE INTERACTION

Once strokes combine to form structures, their individual characteristics begin to influence each other—making things just a little more complicated. Comparing any two kinds of strokes in close proximity calls attention to their individual characteristics and the contrast between them, which causes those differences to appear more exaggerated than if they're separated from one another. The more strokes (and the more kinds of strokes) that appear within a single character, the more challenging it will be to resolve the effects produced by their interaction.

In addition to their relative weights, the direction each stroke is moving will change perception of their relative lengths. In the case of two diagonals appearing near each other, not only will the apparent length of each come into question, but also the similarity of their angles—a downstroke and an upstroke diagonal, for example, will appear to be of different angle even if they are the same, mirroring each other. In a sequence of parallel, vertical strokes, the first two will look closer than will the second and third; a stroke that crosses another may appear broken or discontinuous and of different length on either side of the stroke it's crossing; the inventory of optical effects goes on and on, as you'll see here and on the following page spread.

Vertical strokes tend to appear shorter than horizontal ones of the same length (top); in order to appear the same length, a vertical stroke must usually be lengthened slightly (bottom).

In comparison to a horizontal stroke of the same mathematical length, a diagonal stroke will look shorter, especially if its terminals are sheared to match those of the horizontal. This effect is somewhat alleviated if the diagonal's terminal edges are perpendicular to the angle of the stroke, but not much.

The same effect occurs among diagonals with respect to verticals of identical height.

All three strokes (a horizontal and two diagonals) toward the top of the page are identical in length, as are the vertical stroke and its accompanying diagonals to the right.

In both of the repeated examples lower on the page, the lengths of the diagonals have been extended to appear equivalent to those of the horizontal and vertical, respectively.

Curved strokes—relative to orthogonal (vertical or horizontal) strokes—exhibit much the same kinds of effect as shown among the diagonals on the opposite page, left. In the lower grouping, the lengths of the curved strokes have been adjusted to appear equivalent to each other, as well as to the straight strokes.

More diagonal trickiness: strokes of opposing, or mirrored, angle appear to be of different angle. The left diagonal, or downstroke, in the pair at top appears to be slightly less acute, or vertical in its angle, than does the right diagonal, or upstroke. In addition to being identical in angle, these two diagonals are also identical in weight. However, the downstroke appears just the slightest bit heavier in weight. These illusions will hold true no matter the order of the strokes.

In the lower example, the downstroke has been slightly rotated and lightened to optically match the appearance of the upstroke.

When a curved stroke of generically circular radius extends from a vertical, straight one—as it might in the case of a lowercase a or f—it acquires a weirdly optical momentum that causes it to look like it's exceptionally extended, or like it's "flying away."

In the aforementioned characters (but in other instances, as well), this effect will generally make aligning the arc with the rest of the character below it somewhat difficult. To compensate, the arc must usually be pinched into a tighter radius, both at the point where it leaves the vertical and at its terminal. Rather than specific characters, the above examples show this optical illusion in a general, abstract way, so that it can be considered independent of any specific kind of instance. In each example, the uncorrected version appears to the left, and the corrected version to its right.

FORM PERCEPTION

**OPTICAL EFFECTS OF STROKE INTERACTION /
CONTINUED**

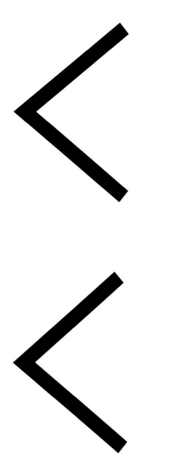

Diagonal strokes extending upward and downward from a single joint must be different lengths in order for their right-hand terminals to appear to align. In the upper example, the top diagonal appears to jut further to the right; additionally, it appears to be less acute than the bottom diagonal (more horizontal in angle).

In the example lower down on the page, these optical illusions have been corrected.

In general, you'll find that this same illusion comes into play between any two stroke configurations or forms that are situated one above the other. In both of the examples at the top of the page (the one that looks like a B, and the other, which looks like an R), the upper element appears not only to extend further to the right, past the lower element—but also appears larger (as well as heavier).

In both cases, the repeated examples toward the bottom of the page have been corrected to compensate for these illusions.

Horizontal strokes appear to change length when they join with other strokes. All of the horizontal stroke elements above are equivalent in length (the top-most one is the "master" for comparison), but all seem very different in length.

If a horizontal stroke is situated evenly, left to right, over a vertical stroke, it will appear longer to the left of the vertical than to the right (top). In the lower example, the left arm of the T-form has been shortened to appear the same length as the right arm.

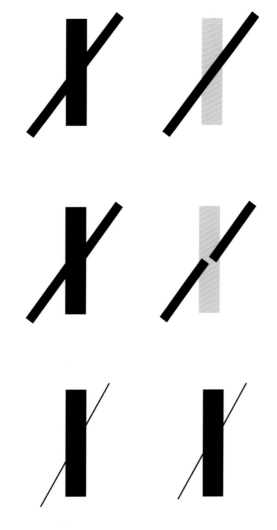

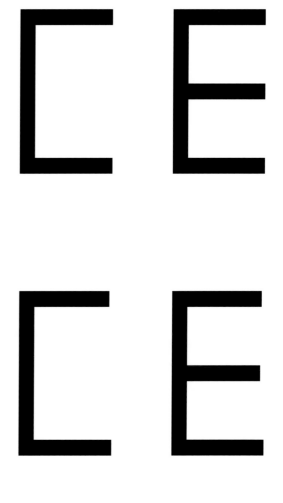

When three parallel, vertical strokes are evenly spaced (mathematically) in a horizontal sequence, the first two appear closer to each other than do the middle and third ones. This effect also occurs if the lines are angled. Again, the lower example in each pair has been optically corrected.

A diagonal stroke that crosses another (whether it, too, is diagonal or not) will appear broken, or discontinuous—as shown in the example at the top of the page. To correct for this illusion, the crossing stroke must be actually broken, and its right-hand side shifted slightly downward (middle example). This optical effect will be more exaggerated the greater the difference in weight between the two strokes (as shown in the bottommost example).

Horizontal strokes, or crossbars, that are of identical length as they extend from the upper and lower ends of a vertical (or, more specifically, along cap line and baseline) will appear to be different lengths: the cap line crossbar will appear longer, jutting out past the one at the baseline. If there also happens to be a central crossbar of identical length present, it will appear to stick out past the other two. In either case, the upper crossbar will need to be shortened, and a central crossbar will need to be shortened even more, if the crossbars are to appear to be the same length. As usual, the corrected versions of both examples are the ones lower on the page.

GEOMETRY: OVERALL HEIGHT AND WIDTH

Keeping in mind the optical variables discussed in the previous few pages, let's begin to look at how they come into play with regard to actual characters.

The first determinations a designer will have to make when constructing a new face are the general proportions of the characters as a set—how condensed or extended they'll be, relative to their height. That's the easy part. The difficulty arises in realizing that the characters within the set all must appear to be the same height and width. And so, the fundamental identity of each character's shape must first be addressed.

Every character is, in its essence, a rectangle (square), a circle, or a triangle. As we've seen, these shapes require a little adjustment in their relative sizes to make them appear optically equivalent—and that means the same adjustments must be made among characters whose overall shapes correspond to those generic, geometric forms.

Mathematically equivalent

Optically equivalent

Here, a little reminder that circular and triangular forms must be enlarged to appear equivalent in size to a square form.

HOA

The implications of such optical illusions are explicit in these fundamental forms—the rectilinear H, the circular O, and the triangular A. An A and O are always mathematically wider than an H; the upper and lower curves of an O must overshoot the cap line and baseline, respectively; and the apex of an A must typically overshoot the cap line.

HOA

HOA

Shown here are an H, O, and A set in different typefaces than in the main example above—a sans serif (top) and a serif (bottom)—simply for the sake of comparison.

The overshoot of the O above the cap line (in red) is similar in both faces.

Even the flat-topped apex of the sans serif A rises slightly above the cap line.

HOA

The H, O, and A shown on the opposite page are overlapped here to compare their relative widths, which are quite different. The more fundamentally geometric the letters in a typeface, the more exaggerated will be their width differences.

The three characters' relative widths are also diagrammed by the overlapped, horizontal bars immediately above the letters.

HOA

These three characters are set in a very condensed typeface—showing that as a font's overall width becomes more condensed, the relative difference in width among characters also decreases. The typeface in which these characters is set is so condensed that the O itself is more rectangular than it is curved—so, it is almost as condensed as the H.

To the right are the left-hand edges of the same O and H, greatly enlarged to show how small their width difference really is.

HOA

It's easy to note here that the serifs of the H extend past the outer contours of the O in this type style. Although the presence of serifs influences the apparent overall width of a character on which they appear, they're generally considered secondary structures with regard to determining basic width relationships. You'll notice that the H's stems are still well within the outer contours of the O.

Still, the stylistic aspects of many faces will often require some adjustment in thinking about these fundamental width relationships—especially in faces that aren't so generically geometric in their structure.

For instance—how does one think about width in a face such as this script, below?

PROPORTION

OPTICALLY CONSISTENT WIDTH

Visually matching the heights of different characters is relatively straightforward; the real concern is how similar in width they are or, rather, how close together their outer strokes appear—and, in concert, how similar are the relative sizes of their internal counters. In type design, consistent width isn't about physical distance from the left-most side of a character to right-most side, it's about density and interval: how a certain volume of space separates a certain amount of stroke information, left to right, in a way that appears the same in every character, after accounting for general geometric identity.

H

The capital H defines the "master" width for a face because its stems define a clear, absolute width that can be easily appreciated and used to evaluate the widths of other characters.

E F T

B P R

HAMO
BKES

Characters in faces of Roman proportion are of demonstrably different width—some are square in proportion, while others are of half-square proportion. The result is that their stroke/counter intervals are inconsistent. It looks great, but it's not useful for extended texts.

hamo

Characters in faces of modern proportion—in particular the lowercase—have varied empirical widths so that their heavier, dominant, vertical strokes all appear to be equidistant when set in text, making for even color and rhythm that enhance readability.

The forms above are primarily vertical in their structure, and are most similar in width to the H because they're basically orthogonal (despite the curves in the B, P, and R, which can be interpreted as rectangles of a sort). The E and F are typically more condensed than the

H because their open counters cause them to appear extended. The B, P, and R should be wider than the H—their curves should need to extend past the H's right-hand stem—but, because the H's two parallel stems are joined by a crossbar, it always seems more condensed,

and so the B, P, and R are usually a hair narrower in width.

The T is the odd man out in this set: It's physically wider than the H because its stem divides its crossbar into two apparently narrow arms that visually contract.

The basic width relationships between rectangular H, circular O, and triangular A are at play in this face, as expected. Again, this fundamental proportional idea is a starting point, and is useful for comparisons among similar form variants in all the characters. But, of course, all the other effects of stroke identity and interaction must be taken into account. Getting the dominant strokes in various characters to appear equidistant is a continual balancing act between every interdependent variable.

These variables begin to complicate matters when they involve diagonals and extreme stroke density, as happens in the characters below. The N, although it is formed with two strong stems that clearly define its width, must be drawn wider than the H because its diagonal stroke is so dynamic that it visually pulls the stems closer together. The K also is wider than the H, but not by much: its arm reaches the H's right-hand side and its leg extends further but, like the E or F, its open right-hand counter and diagonal "pulling" effect counteract its triangle-to-square relationships. The X is pure diagonal movement, pulling inward and pushing outward simultaneously—so its triangular qualities are in full effect, relative to the H's rectangular stability. The M is the widest of all capitals, simply because it contains the greatest number of strokes. These must be pushed apart to ensure similar stroke/counter alternation, as is found in the other characters.

A N K X M

O C S

Of the curved characters, other than the O, the C and S are the only ones that contain only curves in their structures. The C, like other characters with large apertures, is mathematically more condensed than is the O because it would appear too extended otherwise. The S is a study in conflicts. Its wave-form, ogee curve is so active that it pushes the character's upper and lower lobes outward, but its spine pulls its apparent width inward.

D G U

Like the B, the D and G present curves that are joined to stems, but their curves are full height. Because there's a rectilinear element in each (the stems), the D and G are typically more condensed than the O, but more extended than the H. The U, in which the bowl curve is joined to two verticals, is just slightly wider than the H. Its stems define a clear, similar width as do those of the H, but the bowl optically pulls them closer together, necessitating a slightly more extended width.

STABILITY

TOP-TO-BOTTOM BALANCE

It's important that all the letters in a face seem visually stable as they rest upon the baseline to minimize vertical activity and emphasize horizontal fluidity, facilitating the ease with which lines of text are read. Most alphabetic characters are bilaterally symmetrical (see page 66); but a good number are divided top to bottom, and these will potentially introduce up-and-down movement in a line of text that conflicts with the need for horizontally emphasized rhythm. To mitigate this problem, type designers, over time, have established that such characters should be divided in half at the midline between cap- and baselines: symmetry is visually restful.

That seems like an easy kind of consistency to accomplish. In fact, it's surprisingly difficult: First, because a mathematically centered stroke division will appear lower than optical center; and second, because of the variety of structures that form the upper and lower stories of the various letters. The challenge is further complicated by the fact that the upper stories of many such characters are closed, while the bottoms have counters that are open to the surrounding space. Even more frustrating is that the strokes involved are all different in identity and direction.

As with optically-consistent width, achieving the appearance of top-to-bottom balance means adjusting the locations of midline crossbars and the relative sizes of upper- and lower-story counters (as well as stroke weights) until a state of visual similarity is achieved.

The crossbar of the H at far left is mathematically centered on the character's height. The crossbar of the H at near left is optically centered. The difference in their height locations is shown by the two colored bars at right.

The crossbar in the A at far left is mathematically centered, but appears too high: This is because the lower counter, being open to the space below the character, is visually larger to begin with. Lowering the crossbar enlarges the upper counter (which is enclosed and, therefore, visually smaller) such that it becomes optically equivalent in size or volume to the lower counter.

In the K at far left, the joint is clearly above the midline. In the serif K (near left) the offset joint positions some stroke information below the midline, and some above, to achieve an overall visual centering (detail at right).

The lower crossbar of an uppercase F is typically at the character's actual midline. This causes it to appear lower than center, which helps keep the character from appearing top-heavy and unstable, as there's no baseline stroke information.

The crotch of the uppercase Y, on the other hand, is most certainly below the midline. Similar to the F, dropping the joint so low brings weight into the lower half of the letter so that it doesn't seem like it will topple over, given how much stroke information is up top.

BRS BRS

The empirical size of these letters' lower halves is larger than that of their upper halves, both in depth and width. The enlarged specimens, showing the letters split at their midline, confirm the top-to-bottom size disparity—as do their respective, isolated counters: the upper counter in each is clearly smaller than the lower. The red lines below mark the widths of each letter's lower half, compared to that of its upper half.

The return of the P's lobe to the joint at its stem is situated below the midline, adding weight to the bottom half that helps stablize it, much like the Y.

BRS P

D GG

In the uppercase D, top-to-bottom stability is typically achieved by orienting greater weight in its curve below the midline. Looking closely will also reveal that the upper part of the counter is narrower than the lower counter.

Achieving balance in the uppercase G usually depends on two strategies: First, the throat stem and/or crossbar (when present) is typically dropped below midline; in the case of the high-contrast serif form at right, the throat stem has been made significanrtly heavier in weight than the curved stroke.

The second strategy that is often implemented is the same as that for the uppercase D, in that the maximum weight in the G's bowl is concentrated below the midline.

STABILITY

LATERAL BALANCE / RIGHT-ANGLE FORMS

Characters also must appear stable from left to right. Once again, the strategy of choice over time has been to divide characters symmetrically along their vertical axis from cap line to baseline, so that the same amount of stroke information appears on either side. Achieving this lateral balance is relatively simple in the capital H—both of its stems are identical. The capital T, on the other hand, presents a bit of a problem to solve. Keeping it from appearing top-heavy happens almost automatically (remember that its crossbar must be physically lighter than its stem to appear the same weight; in most serif forms, its crossbar is of a markedly lighter weight). But we've seen that the optical relationship of a horizontal centered over a vertical means that one side must be wider than the other (see page 90); it also typically means that the longer dimension must be heavier.

Asymmetrical forms, like the capital E, F, and L require additional maneuvers. Our familiarity with these forms means we *expect* them to be fundamentally unbalanced and weighted on only one side. We understand that, unlike an H, they have no right-hand stroke to stablilize them. Even as we accept that condition, however, we still expect these forms to *feel* as though they're balanced, which may mean widening them more than is expected and, in the case of serif forms, adding extra weight to their right-hand sides by exaggerating the weight and activity of their serifs.

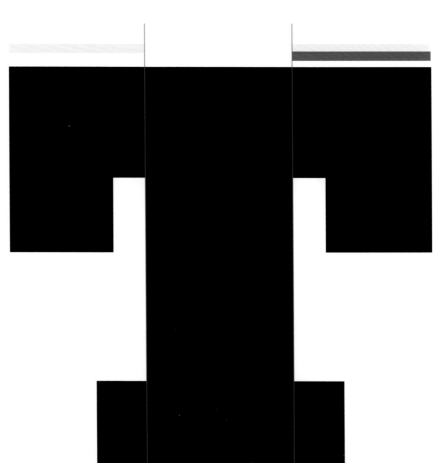

The arms of the sans serif T at far left are lighter in weight than its stem, which ensures that it won't appear top-heavy. The arms are different widths, as well, to offset the optical illusion that attends this structure (see page 90).

In the serif form at near left, not only is the right-hand arm wider than the left, but its serif is heavier in weight through the bracket; it also descends to a lower depth from the cap line.

The minute tolerances under discussion are shown here. The light gray bar denotes the measure of this slab-serif T's left-hand arm; the red bar denotes the measure of its right-hand bar. At this size, the difference in length is, perhaps, a millimeter or so at most.

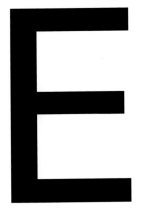

To think about (and, further, to see) an asymmterical character like the E as being balanced from left to right is a strange proposition—to be sure. It's clearly more heavily weighted on its left side, by virtue of a vertical stem that must be heavier than its crossbars. But, it's the contrast of the cross-bars' horizontal move-ment, their cantilevered quality, that creates this sense of balance: static solidity on the left, irreg-ularity and movement on the right.

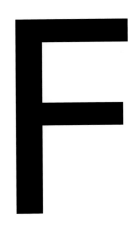

The uppercase F plays a similar game with the contrast of its stable stem and its extended crossbars as is experie-nced in the uppercase E. Its lower crossbar is noticeably shorter than its cap line crossbar (more so than in the E) and so introduces a point of comparison for the brain to ponder. It's probably a stretch to say this, but it's the added, unconscious intellectual involvement with the letter's right side that balances it out.

The design of the upper-case L is a different story altogether. When the width of its baseline stroke is the appropriate measure, the character's counterspace comes into a state of propor-tion that consists of two squares: again, a case of hidden visual math.

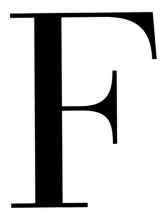

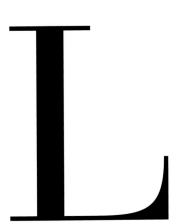

The presence of weighted finishing serifs (in a serif form, of course) adds to the balancing attributes already on hand in the structures of sans serif forms. In this high-contrast E, for instance, the delicate, hairline stroke weight of the crossbars creates an exaggerated contrast with the stem's bold

weight; the serifs bring added contrast to the form's right side; and each crossbar's length is clearly very different—adding to the degree of visual activity that the character's right-hand side offers in comparison to its static left-hand side.

The scale and weight of the finishing serifs are even more exaggerated in

the F and L, where there's less stroke information to carve out subtle geomet-ric spatial relationships. The baseline serif of the uppercase L is, perhaps, one of the most exagger-ated serif forms in the world of type design.

STABILITY

LATERAL BALANCE / CURVED FORMS

Generally symmetrical, circular forms—
the O in particular—seem relatively easy to
balance, just like the angular symmetrical
ones. An O, after all, is an ellipse whose
curves mirror each other, right?

Guess again. Even among faces designed
with uniform stroke weight and an upright,
rationalist axis, subtle adjustments must
be made in the curves to ensure the
appearance of uniformity: As should be
expected, the horizontally-moving (cap line
and baseline) curves will be lighter than
those traveling vertically, from top to bottom. Yet, even in upright-axis curves,
a very slight difference in curvature must
be enforced to make them actually appear
upright (the familiar expectation of an
oblique axis is so ingrained that mathematically symmetrical curves appear somehow
not quite right).

Laterally balancing the curved forms
becomes a more complex endeavor when
the axis is clearly oblique; the form will
appear to rotate to the left as its vertically-
oriented curve weights shift downward
on the left and upward on the right.

Forms that are primarily curves, but have
apertures and/or connect their curves to
vertical stems (the C, D, G, and U, the lowercase g, and numerals like the 2, 3, 5, and
6) impose the balancing considerations of
their angular counterparts on top of those
related to the curves. The S, notoriously, is
the bane of all type designers. Its rotational
symmetry and lack of a strong bounding
form make it a wily character to tame.

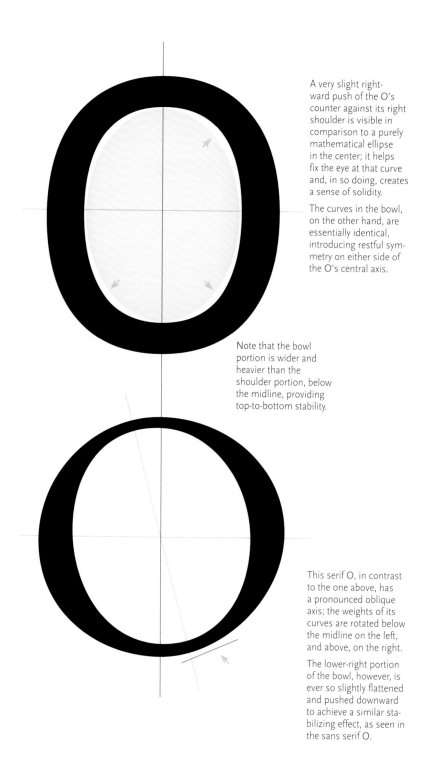

A very slight right-
ward push of the O's
counter against its right
shoulder is visible in
comparison to a purely
mathematical ellipse
in the center; it helps
fix the eye at that curve
and, in so doing, creates
a sense of solidity.

The curves in the bowl,
on the other hand, are
essentially identical,
introducing restful sym-
metry on either side of
the O's central axis.

Note that the bowl
portion is wider and
heavier than the
shoulder portion, below
the midline, providing
top-to-bottom stability.

This serif O, in contrast
to the one above, has
a pronounced oblique
axis; the weights of its
curves are rotated below
the midline on the left,
and above, on the right.

The lower-right portion
of the bowl, however, is
ever so slightly flattened
and pushed downward
to achieve a similar sta-
bilizing effect, as seen in
the sans serif O.

In the C and G of the
same face, as with the
O to the left (top), the
loss of symmetrical
weight on the right—
due to the breaks in the
curves (the apertures)—
is offset by a more pro-
nounced rightward lean
in their arcs and beaks.
The beaks in both
forms are empirically
heavier than the maxi-
mum stroke weight
in the bowls. In the G,
the presence of the
throat and crossbar
add information to fur-
ther balance the form.

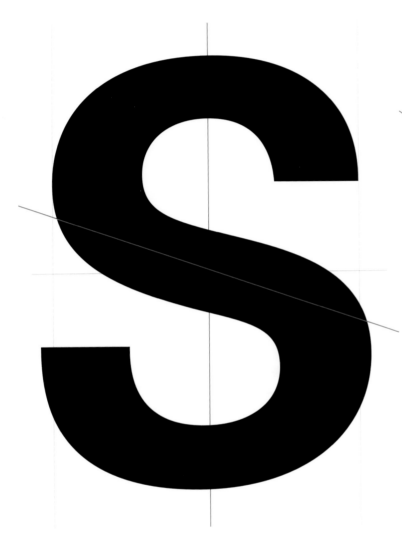

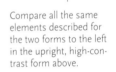

The serif S above has an oblique axis, which should cause the form to lean backward, to the left. To compensate, the arc at top right and the tail at bottom left are pushed outward, and the finishing terminals accentuate that adjustment with diagonal, outward shears. The spine itself cuts downward through the body at a steeper angle, optically pushing back against the oblique stress.

Compare all the same elements described for the two forms to the left in the upright, high-contrast form above.

As with the O, and most other symmetrical forms, the largest part of the form (and the heaviest stroke weight) is situated below the character's midline. But the real stabilizing element in the S is its spine, which carries the greatest stroke weight overall, and which reaches its maximum weight just above the lower right-hand bowl.

Because the spine is formed from a wave, or ogee curve—in which curves from the shoulder and from the bowl enter in a fluid motion and aren't as circular as the curves at top and bottom, the spine "reads" as a kind of diagonal that spans the character's body width and so pulls attention away from the "fly-away" curves at its terminals.

The activity of the terminals in this S are further made to seem stable through their flat finishes, and also through a subtle inward turn of the interior counter edges that redirect the eyes inward, rather than outward.

Analyze the numerals and the lowercase g in this group; look for specific details that correspond with those used to balance the other forms shown in this spread. In particular, take note of the number 2's more explicitly diagonal spine (weighted below midline) and its wide baseline stroke; the number 3's heavy terminals and leftward-thrusting central stroke; the contrast in movement between the 5's upper left stem and its bulbous bowl; the 6's rightward lean, as in the uppercase G; and the tight aperture at lower left in the lowercase g, which helps create the impression of a closed, symmetrical form below, as well as above, its baseline.

STABILITY

LATERAL BALANCE / DIAGONAL FORMS

As with the right-angle forms, diagonally-structured characters also should seem balanced across their vertical axes. Achieving this condition, not surprisingly, is less challenging for those characters which are bilaterally symmetrical: the capital A, M, V, X, W, and Y. The challenge remains, however, because the upstroke and downstroke diagonals of these characters are typically of different weights (even among those in monoline, or uniform-weight, fonts), and because the alternate directions of these strokes affect their apparent angles (refer to page 89).

Rotationally symmetrical characters, such as the N and Z, present additional considerations for achieving lateral balance, as do those forms that are asymmetrical from left to right: the uppercase K, for instance, as well as the lowercase y, and numerals like the 4 and 7.

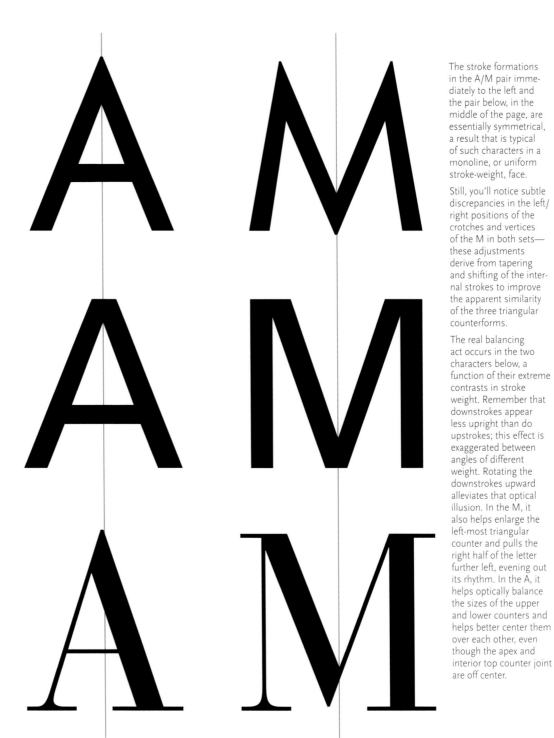

Extremely bold forms, such as this slab serif, tend to exaggerate the stroke balancing shifts off true vertical center.

The stroke formations in the A/M pair immediately to the left and the pair below, in the middle of the page, are essentially symmetrical, a result that is typical of such characters in a monoline, or uniform stroke-weight, face.

Still, you'll notice subtle discrepancies in the left/right positions of the crotches and vertices of the M in both sets—these adjustments derive from tapering and shifting of the internal strokes to improve the apparent similarity of the three triangular counterforms.

The real balancing act occurs in the two characters below, a function of their extreme contrasts in stroke weight. Remember that downstrokes appear less upright than do upstrokes; this effect is exaggerated between angles of different weight. Rotating the downstrokes upward alleviates that optical illusion. In the M, it also helps enlarge the left-most triangular counter and pulls the right half of the letter further left, evening out its rhythm. In the A, it helps optically balance the sizes of the upper and lower counters and helps better center them over each other, even though the apex and interior top counter joint are off center.

ZZZ

While the top crossbar of each Z is narrower than its respective baseline stroke, neither is centered: In both cases, it has been shifted slightly to the right so that it optically appears to center, rather than jutting out to the left.

NNN

In the sans serif N, the right-hand stem is heavier than the left; but its diagonal thickens as it moves upward into the top-left corner. In the serif N, the two joints are formed differently. In both cases, these adjustments derive from the need to make the triangular counters more similar in size.

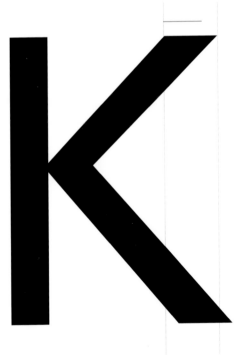

To balance the enormous, open counters and dramatic arm and leg diagonals with its static, stable stem, the arm and leg both flare as they extend rightward from the joint. The red line above the arm compares the thickness of the stem to that of the arm at its terminal.

Also note how the leg kicks out further to the right than does the arm.

In the serif K to the right, the leg is again heavier than the vertical stem; the arm, however, being an upstroke, is thin—and so weight is added in its finishing serif, both in its expansive brackets and in its extreme width. Compare the locations of its serif terminals, fillets, and overall position relative to the finishing terminal below it at the baseline.

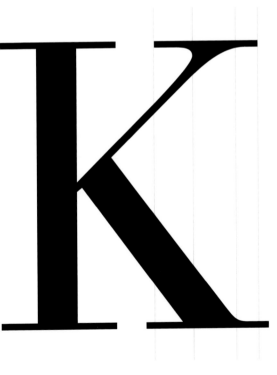

yy

In both of these lowercase y forms, each of a different style, you'll notice a slight deviation in the right-hand stroke as it moves downward past the baseline. By turning its angle slightly to the

right, the descender moves to a more stable, central position under the crotch.

44

The sans serif numeral 4 at left employs an extremely low crossbar that overshoots its stem, pulling the leftward thrust of the diagonal back to the right. Also note the

flat, or sheared, joint between the diagonal and crossbar. A similar strategy appears in the serif numeral (but with a sharp joint).

STRUCTURE

DIAGONAL ARCHITECTURE

Perhaps it seems counterintuitive to explore proportional relationships before examining structure itself—but proportional goals influence the structure of any given character, which must bend to achieve what proportion demands.

This flexibility in structure is most evident in the characters whose identities are defined by diagonals. The general body width of every font expresses an intrinsic "master" diagonal gesture, based on its aspect ratio (see pages 66–68), that is characteristic of that font. However, the capital N is the only character whose diagonal stroke will actually follow that angle— simply because the N's two stems define the body width and its diagonal connects their terminals.

In essence, diagonal strokes must be angled whatever way is necessary to build each character's structure such that it conforms to the optical width and stroke/ counter alternation that has been determined for the font. As the diagonals rotate from character to character, their perceived weights will change. And, as they join other strokes in different ways, their apparent lengths, weights, and angles will change.

The variables are so numerous and interdependent, it's easier to show the effect of a universal diagonal on character formation (at right, the top sequence), compared to the diagonals in a typically well-designed typeface (immediately below those). Each instance in a different character presents particular aspects for consideration.

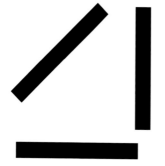

Along with the need to help position outer stroke material such that internal counters among characters are similar, one of the most influential aspects of the diagonals on structure is their apparent weight relationships to vertical and horizontal strokes as they rotate.

The other exceptionally influential aspect with regard to how diagonals are formed is the optical illusion that their angles are different, depending on whether they are downstrokes or upstrokes. Their apparent angles are also affected by their weights.

It's almost a silly exercise, but it makes an important point very clearly—so it's worth looking at: All of the forms in red, above, were drawn using diagonal strokes of the same angle and, further, all of the same weight. The incidental horizontal and vertical strokes also are mathematically equivalent in weight to that of the diagonal strokes.

At a quick glance, it's easy to see the results: Every character appears to be a different width and a different weight overall. Even though the diagonals are, indeed, identical throughout, they come to appear radically different in their angularity in some instances; compare the apparent angles of the K, for instance, with those of the N to its left and the W to its right.

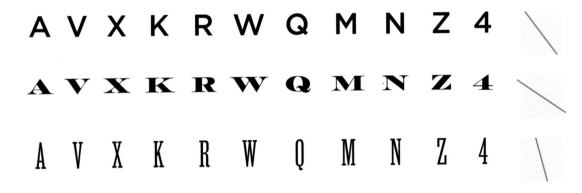

A V X K R W Q M N Z 4

A V X K R W Q M N Z 4

A V X K R W Q M N Z 4

Every typeface exhibits a general, "master" diagonal angle that derives from the aspect ratio of the face's body. It's most explicit in the uppercase N and X. The challenge in structuring the other diagonal-based characters is that their proportions require their diagonals to rotate away from the master angle in one direction or another. Much time is spent making adjustments to the opposing sides of the diagonal strokes, as well as to their joints, to help them seem more like the master angle as closely as possible in each character.

N K W X Z

N K W X Z

Additionally, all of the horizontal strokes appear too heavy, relative to the weights of the diagonals; and all of the vertical stems appear too light.

STRUCTURE

VISUAL DYNAMICS OF ANGULARITY

The angles of the various diagonals (in those forms that feature them) are what drive their other features: If the angle of a diagonal stroke is more horizontal than it is vertical, for instance, it will need to be lighter in weight than will the angle of a more vertically-oriented one—and so on.

But wait! A diagonal stroke has two contours—one to the left and one to the right (or an outer and an inner, or a top and a bottom—however you want to describe it). Because most diagonals join another stroke (or strokes), and these joint shapes all have different attributes, the two contours of a diagonal stroke are almost never parallel. (You saw that coming, right?)

In some instances, as in certain versions of the Q), the diagonal is free from joints at both terminals. In others—for instance, the R of many serif forms—the diagonal is revealed by curves (one at the leg's joint at the waist, the other trailing off the leg's finishing terminal). All these variables inform the actual angle of the diagonal within a given character.

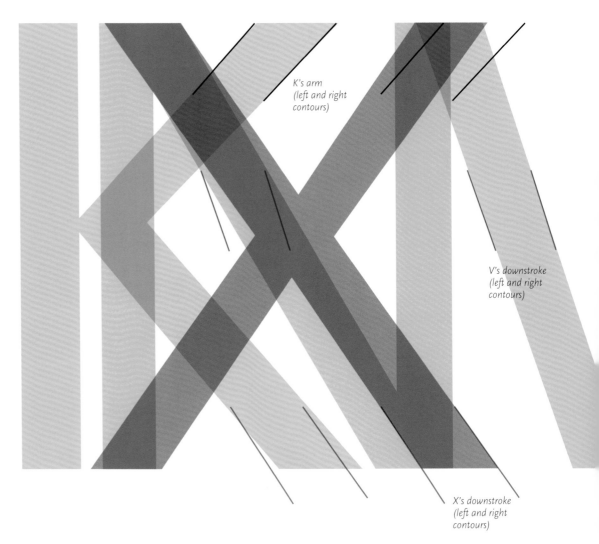

*K's arm
(left and right
contours)*

*V's downstroke
(left and right
contours)*

*X's downstroke
(left and right
contours)*

K N A V X M W

The greatly enlarged specimens of these characters—whose diagonals, at a text size, appear nominally similar—reveal the subtle compensations in angularity among stroke contours to achieve such optical consistency.

Overlays of characters with apparently similar stroke angles permit comparison of their respective general angles as well as the angles of these strokes' left and right contours.

Instances of specific left and right stroke contours are also provided, with each set color-coded for reference when it appears in different locations.

A's upstroke
(left and right
contours)

The leg of the uppercase R always presents an interesting challenge in terms of maintaining a similar diagonal angle, relative to other forms, because of its need to join to the character's upper lobe in the waist. Sometimes, in serif forms (as in the top example at left), acute flare on the leg's interior optically pushes the angle to appear more upright, and so "point" at the character's upper-left corner—mimicking, to some degree, the aspect ratio angle. In other forms (bottom left), the curves that append the nearly vertical leg cause its angle to appear less upright, and so follow the angle of another prevalent form, the capital A.

These two characters from a geometric sans serif both manage to achieve a similar logic in the angles of their respective diagonals: Each describes the aspect ratio angle of its particular character's width. The Q is virtually circular, making it more extended, while the R is slightly more vertical and condensed in its proportion. Although the actual angle of each character's diagonal element is appreciably different, they correspond to the same structural idea and so can be considered unified in that way.

STRUCTURE

CURVE LOGIC

Curves are heavily dependent on the body proportion. The uppercase O is typically a starting point for defining the curves; it's the widest curved form and, much like the N, suggests a kind of template for the quality of curves to be developed within other curved characters.

There are three primary considerations to address in establishing this "master" curve: First, and most important, is that its overall circularity (meaning, how truly circular is its radius, as opposed to how oval, or elliptical) should correspond to the proportion of the master width, based on its geometry (squarish, condensed, or extended); the O's master curve must translate into more complex forms such that it will appear similar in radius, even when split into semicircles or joined to stems or crossbars.

The second consideration is the fluidity of the curves—they should appear uninterrupted by bulges or flat spots.

Lastly, it's important to remember that a curved stroke embodies two, differing (but related) arcs simultaneously, on either side of the stroke's body. These should always flow away from each other as the stroke widens in its vertical direction and toward each other as it narrows toward its horizontal direction. The radius of an interior, or counter curve, is always smaller and of more rapid ductus, than is its corresponding curve on the exterior of the character, as defined by the stroke itself.

For comparison: A mathematically circular dot form.

Punching a purely elliptical counter through a dot or circle creates the odd appearance that the form is flat along its shoulders and bowls, and pointy at the cap line and baseline.

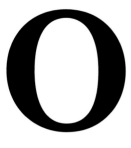

To counteract this optical illusion, the curve radii must be pushed outward in all four locations, as shown here.

The enlarged, transparent specimen (below) superimposes the original, uncorrected form in gray, and the corrected form (with its adjusted radii) in blueish gray.

This ovoid form—in which its curves transition into its side contours directly at 90°—demonstrates another optical illusion known as the "bone effect": the shape's vertical contours appear to bow inward, and the curved portions appear to bulge outward.

Any combination of extending the length of the transitions (slowing the ductus) by pushing the midpoint of the curve upward or pulling the juncture downward—as well as bowing the sides outward, even slightly—will remedy the bone effect, as shown in the corrected form, above.

Remember that curves must track each other as they transition from horizontal orientation to vertical. If the interior radius of a curve is identical to that of the exterior, the curve will become unacceptably heavy between the two radii (upper left). A tighter interior radius corrects this problem in the example to the right.

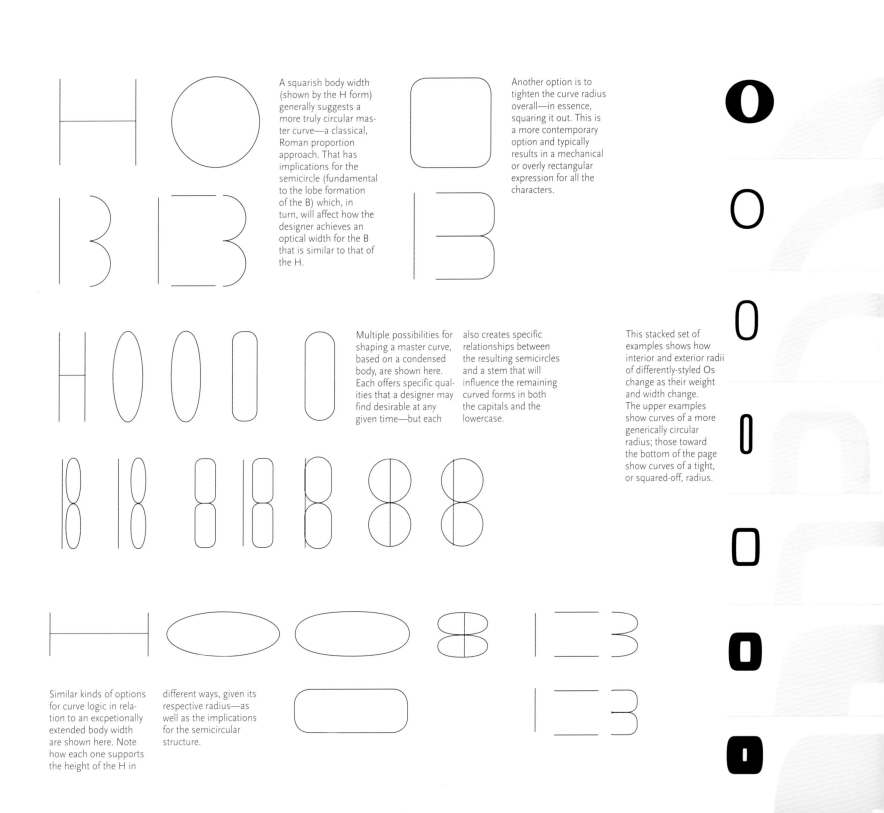

A squarish body width (shown by the H form) generally suggests a more truly circular master curve—a classical, Roman proportion approach. That has implications for the semicircle (fundamental to the lobe formation of the B) which, in turn, will affect how the designer achieves an optical width for the B that is similar to that of the H.

Another option is to tighten the curve radius overall—in essence, squaring it out. This is a more contemporary option and typically results in a mechanical or overly rectangular expression for all the characters.

Multiple possibilities for shaping a master curve, based on a condensed body, are shown here. Each offers specific qualities that a designer may find desirable at any given time—but each

also creates specific relationships between the resulting semicircles and a stem that will influence the remaining curved forms in both the capitals and the lowercase.

This stacked set of examples shows how interior and exterior radii of differently-styled Os change as their weight and width change. The upper examples show curves of a more generically circular radius; those toward the bottom of the page show curves of a tight, or squared-off, radius.

Similar kinds of options for curve logic in relation to an excpetionally extended body width are shown here. Note how each one supports the height of the H in

different ways, given its respective radius—as well as the implications for the semicircular structure.

STRUCTURE

TRANSLATING THE MASTER O CURVE AMONG OTHER UPPERCASE FORMS

The curves of the uppercase O are given precedence in the design process because, as noted, it embodies a primary geometric form (the circle); as such, it's one of the originating forms of the Western writing system (the capitals); it also represents one of the more basic vowel sounds in most languages, accorded a privileged status. In terms of form frequency, however, its expansive, full-height curvature is very rare among the various characters that contain curves. Most of the curves in the modern alphabet are found among the lowercase forms (compressed into a small area, and usually joined to other strokes). The uppercase C, D, and G carry the master O curve most explicitly, but all the other uppercase characters that incorporate it (B, P, R, S, and U) do so in the form of semicircles that often interact with other kinds of stroke.

Still, the general simplicity of these forms (as compared to those of the lowercase) offers an opportunity to compare how they each translate the master curve in different ways to maintain both similar radius and ductus, as well as overall consistency in body width and stroke/counter interval.

Shown here are a selection of the curve-based capitals in five faces whose master curve logic is radically different.

The master O curves are extremely circular, and the counter's curves are rotated, creating an oblique axis. The lobes of the B follow suit; the upper one overshoots the cap line to maintain the soft radius without pinching the lobe.

The master O curve in this italic is elliptical and slightly condensed; its weights are distributed somewhat evenly left to right, with slow ductus from thin to thick. The corresponding B's lobes show a similar elliptical quality and ductus.

In this condensed slab serif, the master O curve is relatively tight, but its ductus into the vertical portion is slowed by extending it further in each direction: down from the cap line and up from the baseline.

This bold slab serif emphasizes the mass of its stems, so the curves are of tight radius. On the exterior of the form, the curves are bowed outward to soften the shoulders and bowl; the interior radius is much tighter.

Similar to the bold slab above, this condensed face privileges the vertical. The sidebearing curves are essentially vertical stems. Unlike the condensed slab serif shown, the curves are relatively circular; in the B, they become more squared.

D G U

D G U

D G U

D G U

D G U

S

S

S

S

S

Among these three characters, the bowl curve in the U is the most different. It squares off slightly in the bowl so that it can join smoothly to the stems and maintain consistent stroke/counter interval.

A similar overshoot to the B occurs in the D and G. Note the spur on the G's throat—the mirror of the overshoot as it intersects the vertical stroke. The D's curve is more like that of the O; the U's curve, more like that of the B.

Among these characters, the U's curve is, once again, the most different—here, because it doesn't need to transition abruptly into an angled joint. Note how the G's upper curve drastically thins as it approaches its beak.

Of all the faces shown here, the curves among the characters are the most consistent in radius and ductus. This is because all are made to turn rapidly into verticals that define a more regular overall width.

The curves in these characters are a close second, in terms of consistency, after the bold slab above. Note the abrupt, angled joint between the G's bowl and its throat.

Each respective S in its stylistic group exhibits a wave-form curve that corresponds to the semicicular translation of the O's master curve; the S is, in essence, a pair of joined half circle forms, smoothed into a continuous curve. One can also consider the stabilizing quality of its spine in each case—always heavier in weight than even the heaviest points in the O's curves.

Interestingly, the S spines (when seen as diagonals, as described on page 101), each bear some relation to the master N diagonal of their respective typefaces. As that diagonal rotates from more acute, or upright, to more horizontal, so too does the spine in the corresponding S-form.

The one exception to this observation can be found in the bold slab serif. While the N's diagonal describes the aspect-ratio axis, the S's curve is forced into a more horizontal orientation so that the character will maintain its exterior verticality and overall width, while ensuring its interior counters are shaped and sized similar to those in the capital B.

**INTRICACIES OF CURVE FORMATION
WITHIN THE LOWERCASE**

Although the majority of the curves in a full character set are found in the lowercase, it's also true that the curves in these characters are all modified from that of the master curve by virtue of their interaction with other strokes—vertical stems and horizontal crossbars—and, further, by the individual structural conditions imposed by dense stroke information (the a and e), ascenders and descenders (the b, d, f, g, q, and p), and occasionally condensed widths (the f, r, and t).

Compounding those issues in most serif forms (and, often, those of a humanist, sans serif style), is the presence of an oblique weight axis. As with the architecture of diagonals (see pages 102–107) and that of the uppercase curves presented prior, the curved components of the lowercase must be allowed to flex organically in order to achieve not only an overall similarity in radius and ductus, relative to the master O curves, but also meet their respective characters' structural requirements and maintain apparent width, proportion, density, and rhythmic consistency with each other, and with the uppercase.

Some fundamental, optical aspects to consider in the lowercase curves are illustrated in detail on this page, using characters of a humanist sans serif with a slightly oblique axis; on the opposite page are examples of the lowercase from each of the five faces used to illustrate curvature in the uppercase on the previous page spread.

oe as
pntrf
g

The overarching logic that describes the curve variation in this—and most other—lowercase character sets is that of a "pinching" of the master O curve. It happens in varying degrees from character to character: some are more clearly circular all around, supporting the basic curve, while others force the curve to join vertical stems. This pinching is most evident in the branched forms (n, m, r) and in the link and bowl of the g. The f here shows a more expansive, o-like curve that extends its ascender far to the right, but this condition is atypical of the character—most often, its shoulder radius is quite severe.

ag

In a sans serif of upright axis and more geometric consistency, the curves of the lowercase a and g very much mimic each other, in all locations, from arm to bowls to lobes to descender.

oaegpfqstnru

oaegpfqstnru

oaegpfqstnru

oaegpfqstnru

oaegpfqstnru

LIGHT AND DARK

PROPORTION AND STRUCTURE TO RHYTHM, DENSITY, AND COLOR

Within a given typeface, body proportion and intervals between stroke and counter, left to right, establish its characteristic rhythm—it may be loose, open, and expansive, or tight, compressed, and concise. These variables also establish a color, or textural gray value, that is similarly characteristic: A single font may be relatively light or dark compared to another (see pages 58, 75, and 80).

Each face also exhibits a fundamental weight—the relation of its strokes' thickness (or thicknesses) to its height. Stroke weight, like all other variables in type design, must fluctuate from character to character to maintain consistent density among all in the set, accommodating for each one's particular structure.

Further, each varied face within a family (Roman and italic, medium and bold, condensed and extended) must share structural and rhythmic attributes, even as their color and proportion change. With regard to text families, the goal is to ensure that the visual continuity of rhythm in a line of text remains undisturbed as specific elements within that text are emphasized through style changes—styling them as italic in a line of Roman text, for instance, or calling them out with a bold weight within a book- or medium-weight line of text. This brings us to the last of the fundamental optical issues of type design, that of light and dark.

Each of these typefaces exhibits a characteristic color and rhythm—established, as we have seen, by its unique totality of width, shaping, contrast, and stroke/counter interval.

Lorex ipsuf dalor kuisnegit ullamc

Lorex ipsuf dalor kuisnegit ullamcorper t

Lorex ipsuf dalor kuisnegit ullamcorpe

Lorex ipsuf dalor kuis*negit u*

Lorex ipsuf dalor **kuisne**

Lorex ipsuf dalor kuisnegit ul

The specimens above show the interaction (and integration) of stylistic variants within a family.

The top specimen shows how the Roman and italic forms support each other in color and rhythm, despite their posture and width differences.

The specimen in the middle, above, presents words (in dummy text) that are differentiated by weight—yet still maintaining the appearance of overall stroke/counter interval and rhythm as styles change from extra light to extremely bold.

The bottom example presents similar consistency in weight, but the words change in width—from super-condensed at the far left of the line to extended at the far right.

orper triqua pellentesque ad magnificat ⅼⅼⅼⅼⅼⅼⅼⅼⅼⅼⅼⅼⅼⅼⅼⅼⅼⅼⅼ

qua pellentesque ad magnificat ////////////////////////

triqua pellentesque ad magnificat ⅼⅼⅼⅼⅼⅼⅼⅼⅼⅼⅼⅼⅼⅼⅼⅼⅼⅼⅼ

lamcorper triqua pellentesque *ad magnificat*

git **ullamcorper triqua pellentesqu**

amcorper triqua pellentesque ad

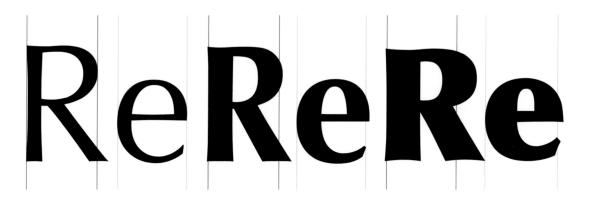

In all the specimens above, some interaction between the weight of the characters in each style variant and the width in each must be at play—how else could each line of mixed styles be continuous in its rhythm and color?

The specimens of uppercase R and lowercase e, at left, hint at the answer: there must be some correspondence between the width of a character and its weight.

LIGHT AND DARK

**THE INTERRELATIONSHIP OF
WEIGHT AND WIDTH**

At its most basic, the width of a character and its weight respond to each other in a reciprocal, inverse relationship. The more extended a character is, relative to another, the heavier its strokes must be, so that it appears to be the same weight as a more condensed counterpart (because its larger counters will appear to lighten it); conversely, the more condensed a character, the lighter its strokes. This fundamental logic becomes more complicated when resolving stroke-weight consistency between curved and angular forms, forms with contrast among strokes, and forms of relatively different amounts of internal stroke information—but it remains a consistent logic, nonetheless.

It follows, therefore, that the widths of bold-weight characters must be mathematically greater in measure than the widths of regular-weight and light-weight counterparts in the same family; and again, conversely, that the stroke weights within extended characters must be mathematically heavier, overall, than those of their regular-width and condensed-width counterparts. This visual reciprocity is easiest to see (and the most revelatory) in an upper-case, sans serif E—which, not surprisingly, perhaps, was the first exercise with which I was tortured in my college Letterforms class (and why the E shown in the Preface is so sentimentally important to me).

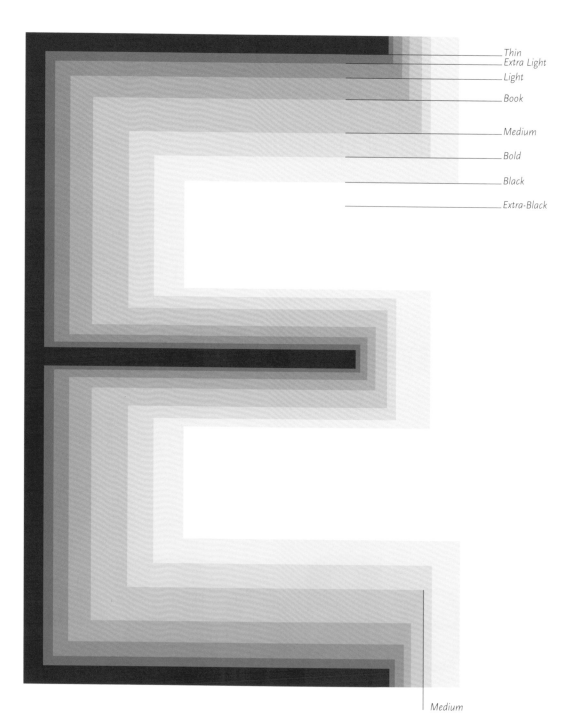

Thin
Extra Light
Light
Book
Medium
Bold
Black
Extra-Black

Medium

E E **E**

These three stylistic variants in the same font change in weight—from light, at the far left; to medium, in the middle; to bold. The light E's strokes open its counters dramatically, so it must be purposely condensed to remain visually the same width as the middle E. Conversely, the bold character's strokes compress the form's counters, causing it to visually contract—and so must be purposely extended in width.

E E E

These three characters are of the same weight, but their widths are different: condensed at the far left, regular width in the middle, and extended on the right. Here, the opposite is true: The condensed form causes its counters to contract, making it appear bold—so its strokes must all be purposely lightened in weight; because the extended E's strokes expand the form's counters, the character would become visually lighter—and so, its strokes must be made heavier to compensate.

E E E E E E

To maintain continuous color in relation to its Roman counterpart, the oblique set of forms at far right—which are typically condensed—are slightly bolder in weight.

exm*exm*

LIGHT AND DARK

STROKE GROWTH, WIDTH, AND DENSITY

When the strokes of characters expand from lighter to bolder weight, they do so in a particularly organic way: growing outward from the basic, archetypal skeleton of their given character—almost as if their heaviness bleeds outward from their hairline, linear architecture, or appends muscle mass to a bone.

This outward expansion, however, is tempered by the necessity of maintaining overall width dimensions (not just within a particular weight variant, but also between weights, to ensure consistent rhythm across a line of text in which instances of heavier and lighter variants might appear in sequence). For that reason (as you'll see in the capitals shown here), most of the aforementioned bleed is concentrated inward: The counters become steadily smaller and more compressed as the character becomes heavier, while the outer widths generally remain more consistent in their dimensions.

As a result, the structural adjustments in each character that compensate for their weight change can be quite dramatic; curve radii and ducta become sharper and diagonal strokes, especially, must rotate considerably to retain their structural and stylistic qualities.

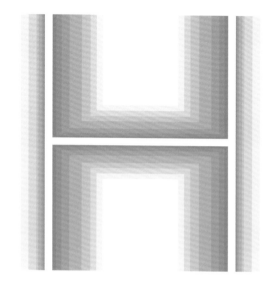

The greatest expansion in stroke weight within these characters takes place internally: The strokes bleed inward, compressing the counters as their weights increase. This is because these three forms are among the most extended in their typeface—meaning they can't grow laterally too much before sacrificing width- and stroke/counter interval continuity between the lightest and boldest weights in the family.

The already compressed structure of the B forces the counters to become extremely small as its strokes expand in weight from light to black. As a result, characters like the B that incorporate a great deal of stroke information in their structures—such as the R, the M, and the lowercase a, e, and g—must be given careful consideration when developing weight families.

Forms that feature diagonals as their primary structure undergo the most radical changes as their weight increases—but not very consistently with regard to the locations of such changes. In the uppercase Y, the change in the angles of its arms is quite pronounced, while its centrally-located vertical stem area accepts the weight expansion without really affecting the character width at all.

In the K, the most pronounced changes occur in the arm: as its weight increases, its angle rotates upward to keep the stroke expansion from widening the character. The same is generally true for the leg, which can be seen to rotate inward, to the left—but not quite to the same degree as in the arm.

HAMBURGEFONTSIV
hamburgefontsiv

HAMBURGEFONTSIV
hamburgefontsiv

HAMBURGEFONTSIV
hamburgefontsiv

HAMBURGEFONTSIV
hamburgefontsiv

These specimens, stylistic variants within the same sans serif family—light and heavy forms of regular width first, then light and heavy forms of condensed width, following—demonstrate the impact of weight and width variation on overall spacing. As the counters in each style expand, so too does their normal, or comfortable, spacing. As their internal counters become compressed, the opposite occurs.

LIGHT AND DARK

**WEIGHT CORRESPONDENCE BETWEEN
UPPERCASE AND LOWERCASE**

Weight and width compensations among individual characters, as well as between lighter and bolder, condensed and extended, variants in a family notwithstanding, the lowercase characters in a set must appear to be the same weight as their uppercase counterparts. In general, the rule of thumb is that the strokes of the lowercase in any given face tend to be a hair lighter than those of the uppercase, in every respect. It's simply a matter of the lowercase stroke information being concentrated within a smaller area: Just as the strokes of a condensed capital must be lighter in weight than those of a corresponding regular-width character to maintain a similar density of stroke/counter ratio.

In an overall light-weight face, the difference in stroke-weight measure between upper- and lowercase characters is minimal; the heavier a face becomes, the more exaggerated the difference in weight between uppercase and lowercase characters. Extremely bold faces often necessitate unusual adjustments in lowercase proportion and structure: Because their width dimension can't increase too much without sacrificing line rhythm, sometimes the x-height of the lowercase is marginally enlarged so that the volumes of their internal counters, relative to their stroke density, can remain in similar ratio as found in the lighter-weight family variants. Other options, including radical thinning of internal strokes, as compared to those that define a character's exterior, as well as tapering and exaggerated notching between stroke joints, may also come into play.

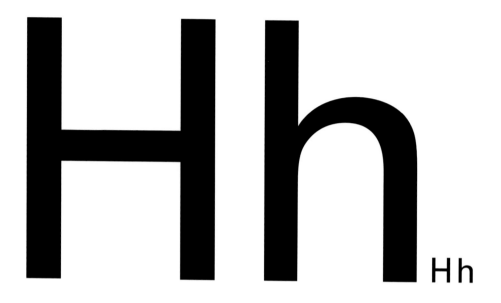

Even though the ascender of the lowercase h is free from the stroke density of its x-height tall, branched component, it still must remain similar in weight to those components.

At a small size, the capital and lowercase form appear more similar in weight. The greatly enlarged specimen, below, shows the relatively minimal difference in stem weight between the two forms.

hok

Just as with the upper-case forms, differences among the weights of strokes of rectilinear, circular, and triangular or diagonal identity are found in the lowercase.

The darker colored-block here is the relative weight of the vertical stems; the middle-value color represents the weight of the diagonals in the k; and the widest, light-valued block shows the relative thickness of the o's curved strokes.

H h   O o   A a

H h   O o   A a

As the overall stroke weight increases from lighter to bolder among weight variants in a family, the resulting compression of counters necessitates that contrasts in stroke weight—especially at the characters' joints—becomes more pronounced. In these examples, the red bar represents the maximum stroke thickness in each character of a given weight; the gray bar represents corollary minimum stroke thickness.

XXXXXXXX

When the weight range within a family becomes extreme—especially toward the extra bold end of the spectrum—it sometimes becomes necessary to increase the x-height of the bolder weights' lowercase in order to accommodate the dense stroke information among its characters, while still maintaining a similar stroke/counter ratio at the same time.

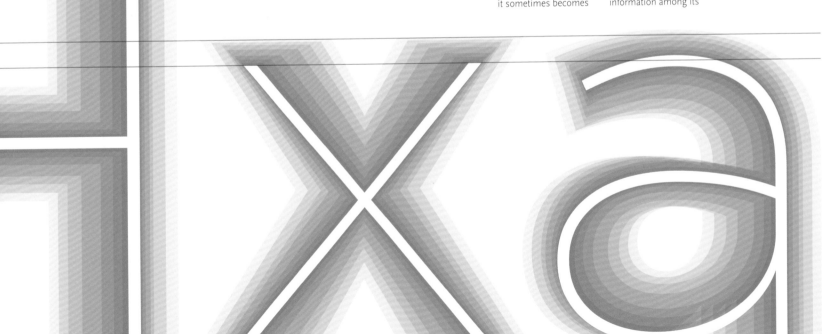

LIGHT AND DARK

**COMPENSATING FOR WEIGHT GAIN
AT THE JOINTS**

Locations where strokes come together intrinsically carry more weight than do the individual strokes themselves—no real mystery there. The challenge is to alleviate such excess weight without sacrificing the prevailing stroke architecture and weight, or the stylistic elements of the face (as it has been defined) in each instance.

To do so, type designers employ a variety of strategies. Most often, strokes are subtly tapered as they approach the joint in question. In other instances, the counter enclosed by the joining strokes is imperceptibly (or perceptibly, if it's a stylistic idea) extended into the joint area—what is called a "notch" or "ink-trap." Occasionally, the challenge is best met by altering the structure of a joint more dramatically by shifting its parts, altering the angles or radii of the strokes entering it, or radically thinning them. These kinds of adjustments must be supported by similar formal elements in other structural locations among characters in the rest of the set.

 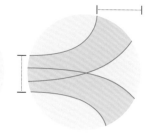

One option for alleviating excess joint weight is to force the counter around or under the joint to intrude into the joint area—either subtly (top), or as a bold notch or ink trap (bottom).

A common strategy, especially for joints between diagonals, is to taper the strokes as they approach the joint so that, when they do cross into each other, the combined weight is similar to that of the heavier ends of the strokes.

In this G, the throat stem is shortened so that the bowl's curve returns upward to meet it in a fluid joint; the illusion of continuity it creates alleviates the perception of weight gain in this location.

The curves of the B's upper and lower lobes converge into a single, lighter-weight horizontal crossbar at its waist—after first thinning out as they enter the return from top and bottom.

Characters with orthogonal joints—those between vertical and horizontal strokes—rarely require any weight adjustments because the natural weight relationship between thinner crossbars and heavier stems obviates it.

Rather than introducing a notch or ink trap, another strategy is to slightly offset the meeting place of converging strokes so that the joint just isn't as heavy.

X
Instead of simply breaking the upstoke of this X and offsetting it across the downstroke (see page 91), both diagonals are actually broken and the counters from all four directions push into them slightly.

In the lowercase a, below, joint areas are simply thinned using a common logic: the arc is the heaviest of the three horizontally-oriented curves; the middle stroke is lighter; and the return, at bottom, is the lightest.

k r

a k r

a k r n

Unless the stroke of a branch originates from a stem at a lighter weight than that which it will achieve once it extends into the branch's curve, the joint will appear uncomfortably thick and heavy, as it does in this example. Below, at left, is the typical structure for this kind of branching form. Further below is an exaggerated shift in weight from branch origin outward that is typical of exceptionally bold forms.

Q Q Q

In the monoline Q above, the tail crosses the bowl. As it does so, it is pinched ever so slightly to lighten the area where it crosses—seen more clearly in the enlarged detail.

In this Q, the tail emanates from the lower portion of the bowl and extends horizontally along the baseline. Its origin point is treated like a branch, beginning at a lighter weight before thickening as it extends to the right.

In extremely bold forms, such as this slab serif a, the only option is to radically exaggerate the thinning logic described for the lighter, monoline a shown above it. Even though these internal strokes are exceptionally different in weight from the rest of the letter, being flexible this way with their weights allows this form's exterior weight to correspond more closely to that of its counterparts in the typeface.

k b

Above are a variety of joint structures that are possible within a K-form that may help minimize weight gain at its joint.

The return of the lobe to the stem in this heavy slab-serif b demonstrates the possibility of a super-exaggerated notch. This idea follows similar logic employed in the lowercase a shown to the left.

The link between the eye of the lowercase g and its bowl (or loop) is often a location where weight increases undesirably. In modern g forms, like that to the left, above, the strategy is usually to thin and deepen the

descender, while the bowl strikes, or rides along, the baseline. In many older-style and serif-form versions, the eye is raised above the baseline, with the link cresting along the baseline instead.

COMDKHV
PSZVUYQ
efjpdbql
yarnithg
AXIS NOT 90°
CURVES LIGHT
POINTY
POINTY

With a firm grasp of character structures and the optical aspects that inform their creation, the next step is to actually go about designing. But where does one begin, and what process should one follow to get from an initial idea to a sound, stylistically cohesive end result?

Whether the plan is for a complete text or display face, or a finite set of letters as a brand wordmark, the first thing is to get comfortable with making letters by hand. Eventual digital production aside, most type designers work manually. Hand-drawing simultaneously builds manual control and visual sensitivity to form while working to achieve the desired goals previously described. Deciding on a particular style follows; then a process of defining its characteristics; and, ultimately, adjusting them, character by character, until all within the set appear visually related.

Evolution

**STRATEGIES AND
PROCESSES TO HELP
GUIDE THE BUDDING
TYPE DESIGNER**

LEARNING TO WRITE (AGAIN)

Everyone learns to make the letters of the alphabet in grade school. As a result, day-to-day writing is so second nature that properly forming archetypal, alphanumeric characters proves surprisingly difficult for many designers. The challenge is often exaggerated for many younger designers because they don't often do much physical writing—mostly typing. The spontaneous, gestural lyricism of writing is, nonetheless, fundamental to the liveliness of designed fonts, and yet one must still be able to control character formation with purpose.

Drawing fuses neural pathways between input (seeing) and output (making)—through practice, analysis and intuition become one, effectively allowing the maker to physically feel what is seen and to see what is felt, on the fly, as it is happening in real time. In the jump from refined drawn or painted forms to clicking around a screen adjusting Bézier points in software, this well-developed synesthetic facility eventually allows a designer to better understand the moves he or she is making on screen, despite the disconnection between mouse and creation space.

A student's early attempt at drawing formally constructed archetypes shows how unusually difficult this seemingly simple task may often be.

The student's lack of confidence in confronting standard structure and proportion—as well as the discomfort with manually using a tool to draw—comes through in different ways: awkward shaping; inconsistent character height, width, and spacing; flatness or egginess in the circular forms; and inconsistent stroke weight.

Although these issues were eventually overcome, and the student was able to compose a page of characters in one shot or, "at a stroke," it's easy to see here the initial need to sculpt each form by redrawing and correcting strokes with an eraser to help discover them.

DESIGNER UNKNOWN / USA
PURCHASE COLLEGE SUNY
Timothy Samara, instructor

TOOLS

The physical act of drawing characters also invokes the individual characteristics of the tool being used; very often, it's the quality of each medium's special marks that drives the stylistic quality of a font—qualities that are likely to be overlooked if one is simply building characters with line segments in a software environment. In addition to simply becoming competent with character formation, it's important to experiment with a variety of tools to interrogate their potential for stylistic influence—simply by becoming aware of them through use.

It's helpful to have two different erasers on hand: a white, hard, graphic eraser (top) for major corrections; and a soft, kneaded eraser (bottom) for more delicate corrections.

For brush or pen drawing, any black calligraphy ink will do. Bottles of ink sometimes come with droppers in their caps—which can also be used as a drawing tool.

A selection of pencils with different weights, or densities, of graphite, is useful for different purposes. Darker densities (3B to 9B) are best for stroke writing (discussed on the page spread following) because they help exaggerate stroke density a

nd modulation when desired. Lighter densities (H, 2H) are good for marking guide lines. Pencils may be sheathed in wood (A) or, alternatively, unsheathed (B) as solid graphite sticks.

Charcoal is a great alternative to graphite, especially for looser or more gestural drawing. It comes in three forms: as a sheathed pencil (C); in vine form (D), which is very light in density; and as compressed sticks (E), which is dark.

Designers will want a variety of brushes for different purposes: Flat brushes (F) are ideal for basic stroke drawing; it's best to have a range of widths—¼", ½", and 1". Rounded brushes, like those used for watercolor (G) can be used for stroke formation when one wants to modulate the stroke by changing

pressure, as well as for filling stroke areas that have been first drawn with pencil. Chinese or Japanese brushes (H) were made for calligraphy.

A calligraphy pen (I) is ideal for sharper, more refined drawing, as well as for stroke wriitng. Different tips, or nibs, may be used for different kinds of stroke shaping.

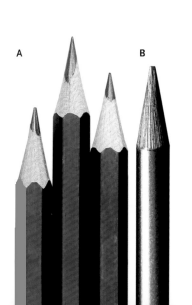

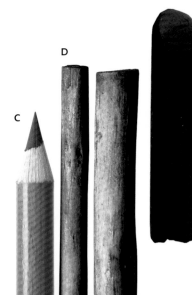

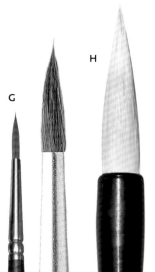

EXERCISING EYE & HAND

STROKE WRITING / PENCIL

As a first step in developing the rigorous eye/hand coordination needed to draw and refine type forms, no exercise is more effective than stroke writing. This method enforces strict goals to be achieved: beginning with making individual strokes exhibit a specific weight and dark/light modulation, and further, maintaining the stroke quality while ensuring consistent proportional relationships throughout a sequence of characters.

This writing should be done with a dark, 3B-density (or darker) graphite pencil (which makes weight control more difficult). Each character is drawn "at a stroke"— in one motion, without erasing—and the designer then analyzes the result, correcting discrepancies in subsequent, newly formed characters. In this way, one comes to objectively appreciate successes and overcome the influence of failures until the hand intuitively gravitates toward "rightness" in the forms.

Desired Goals

Vertical strokes must be unequivocably vertical (perpendicular to baseline).

Diagonal strokes must appear to be of equivalent angle—whether "downstrokes" (dominant) or "upstrokes" (subordinate).

Curves must be circular—not elliptical or "egg-like"—without bulges or flatness.

All strokes must appear to be the same height, regardless of their respective shapes or directional movement.

A consistent overall weight must be achieved in the straight strokes (whether orthogonal or diagonal) and specifically modulated: heavy at the attack or entry, lightening into the stroke body, and heavying up again at the finish, or terminus— with smooth, unbroken transitions.

The overall weight of the curved strokes (and their internal weight modulation) must match that of the straight strokes—but in reverse (heavy in the body and light at the entry and terminus).

Independent strokes must be evenly spaced and of optically similar overall proportion. Once letters are formed, every letter must maintain consistent proportion (clearly full or half square, if drawing forms of Roman proportion, or clearly optically even in width, if modern in proportion).

Letters in sequence must maintain consistent cap-height, spacing interval, and baseline—without rising or falling across the line, left to right.

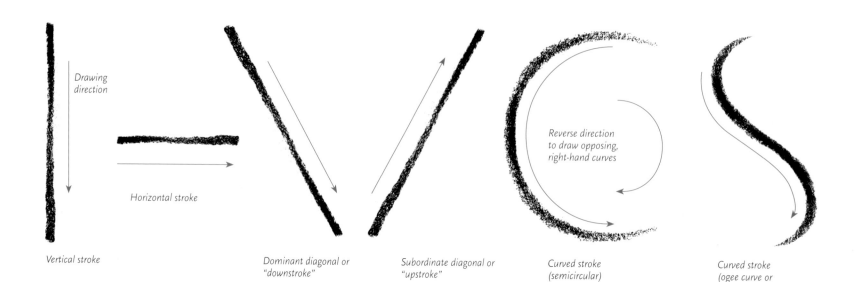

Drawing direction

Horizontal stroke

Reverse direction to draw opposing, right-hand curves

Vertical stroke

Dominant diagonal or "downstroke"

Subordinate diagonal or "upstroke"

Curved stroke (semicircular)

Curved stroke (ogee curve or "wave-form")

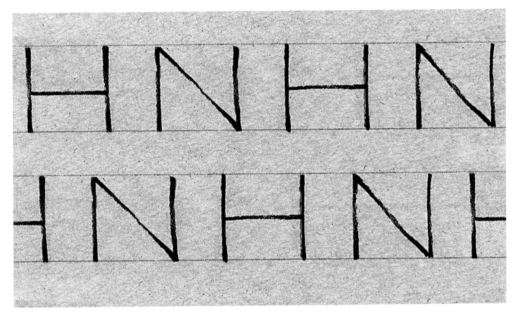

Many letterform instructors have their students begin with independent, single strokes, but it's less abstract, and more immediately relevant, to start with two basic capitals—the H and N.

From left to right, draw an alternating sequence of these two letters at full-square porportion; the spaces between the letters should be half their width. Beginners will want to do so on drawn guides for cap line and baseline (it's okay); after a while, however, continue without guides to more rigorously train the eye and hand.

Continue row after row down the page. From there, introduce additional angle-based forms—E, F, K, T, X, A, and so on—being careful to maintain their respective full or half square widths, as well as consistency in all other variables. Alternate among the various characters in random order.

Next, get comfortable drawing the curves, beginning with the C (the semicircle) then the O (conjoining opposing semicircles), and finally, the S (two half-size semicircles joined in a fluid, continuous gesture, forming a wave)—before moving on to the combination structures, like the R, B, and P and the G, D, U, and Q.

Keep mixing up the order of the letters to avoid repetitions and patterns from line to line, which can confuse the eye and direct the hand to repeat errors.

This exercise begins with Roman square proportion; it's good to start this way because evaluating width and spacing is initially easier, due to the strict geometry of the forms. After you've become accomplished at consistently rendering letters of Roman proportion, however, transition into drawing sequences of letters in modern, or optically even, proportion.

At this stage, introduce lowercase letters (which don't exist in Roman square cap alphabets), following the same methods and looking to achieve the same kinds of regularity among all their variables—and in comparison with those of the uppercase.

EXERCISING EYE & HAND

STROKE WRITING / BRUSH OR PEN

Writing with pencil establishes basic structural control; writing with brush or flat-nibbed pen builds on that skill and introduces the variables of weight and contrast to be mastered. Thus begins the process of understanding the organic interaction of light and dark, and the relationship between stroke contouring and counter shapes.

The primary concerns at this stage are the angle of the brush or pen—which can be explored for its effect on the relative weights of thins and thicks—and the consistency of the wrist's position, which must remain constant despite changes in stroke shape and direction.

Any black calligraphic ink works well; use a flat brush or pen nib width that feels appropriate for the size at which you'll work and the overall weight you'd like to explore. Begin writing with a constant pressure; as you become more accomplished, investigate changing the pressure you apply—and when—to add yet another dimension to the quality of the strokes.

25°

A tool angle of 20°–25° from horizontal yields a historically subtle weight contrast between vertical and horizontal strokes.

0°

Holding the tool at 0°, oriented at pure horizontal, creates extreme weight contrast between thicks and thins.

65°

Angles greater than 45° will reverse the historical weight relationship between strokes—verticals will be light and horizontals, heavy.

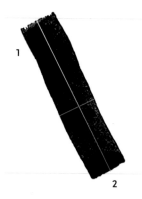

The straight strokes—whether vertical, horizontal, or diagonal (downward or upward)—are made in a single motion from cap line to baseline. Given the width of the tool and its angle, the stroke terminals will exhibit a triangular shape and so must typically overshoot the cap line and baseline.

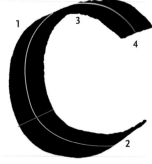

Full-circle forms are made using two semicircular strokes—left side first, followed by right side. For letters like the C, the second stroke stops short to create the form's beak.

In a historically-based approach, not only is the tool held at a consistent angle, but the wrist is also kept stiff, without rotating, as the hand moves through the stroke, regardless of its direction; hand, wrist, and forearm act as one from the elbow forward. Together, these two strategies ensure that the tool deposits stroke weight in the conventional places even as the stroke changes shape or direction.

Similar to pencil writing, the spine of the S is drawn as an uninterrupted wave (really, a fluid joining of two semicircles, as previously shown). Terminals to the left and right of the wave's central axis can be added with shorter, truncated opposing curves as in the C above.

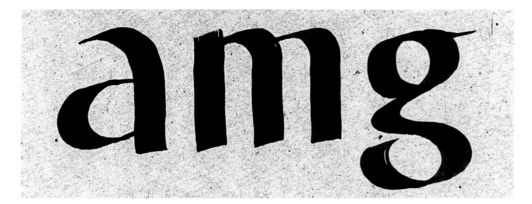

Experiment with different tools—this character was written with a soft, wide-nibbed calligraphic marker. Along with changing pressure, tool angle and wrist rotation will also create different effects on stroke terminals, joints, and contrast. Understanding how they do so reveals possibilities for refined formal concepts later on.

As with pencil writing, begin simply, with basic angle forms (H and N) before adding more complex ones, then curves, and then proceeding to the lowercase.

Maintaining consistency among the usual variables in a particular study set is critical for developing patience and control: consistent height, width, weight, contrast, spacing. But don't let that stop you from defining different variables—a more condensed

or extended body width, less or more thick/thin contrast—for exploration in a different set. Once you decide what those qualities will be, however, stick with them throughout.

TOWARD A NEW DESIGN

VISUAL INTEREST AND INSPIRATION

There's no better reason for wanting to design a new typeface other than "I want to design a new typeface"—the question, really, is what that typeface is going to look like: Serif, sans, slab, or script? Should it be for text or display? Bulbous and fluid or rigidly geometric, or a little bit of both? What makes you tingle creatively?

The inspiration for a new face can come from anywhere. Absent the directive of a design brief for a real-world project, the first place one can look is within studies produced during stroke-writing practice; maybe there's a particular combination of shaping, weight, and tool-mark details that catches your attention because it stands out from others.

Another source for inspiration might be something seen in the neighborhood or coming and going from work: a few characters seen on a grocery store sign (how would the rest of that alphabet evolve?) or the numbers of a building's street signage. Alternatively, it might be a question of visually translating a feeling—"I want to make letters that are powerful, or slinky, or elegant, or dangerous, or sexy."

Not so surprisingly, many type designers are fascinated by the history of the craft: A huge number of newly-developed typefaces are based on historical precedents. Many designers, deeply enamored of a particular historical period or innovator, choose to reinterpret such sources in their own way, focusing on specific aspects that interest them.

It's not really about "doing it better than Grandjean did," or simple hero worship—the goal is to reveal some quality hiding in the source. Sometimes, this impulse is guided by a desire to refresh a font of some pedigree that, because of its historical context, deviates from currently-desirable norms—a 15th-century serif with a tiny x-height that could become more useful if its lowercase were enlarged, for example.

In looking for an idea to pursue, one might uncover a rarity: an obsolete, custom drawn logotype; a specimen cast only in lead and never digitized; or one that appeared as a headline in an old catalog, but was never seen again. As cultural aesthetics change over time, typefaces of one style or another inevitably go out of fashion. Reviving a disfavored style, or one that enjoyed only limited use, can be especially fulfilling, and the results may resonate with contemporary audiences.

Up-and-coming type designer Tré Seals is interested in typographic expressions that surface during protest marches and political demonstrations. The banners in this photograph, taken in 1948 during a march in support of the iconic Argentine first lady and activist Eva Perón, provided inspiration for several fonts in his catalog—one of which is featured in the last chapter, on page 216.

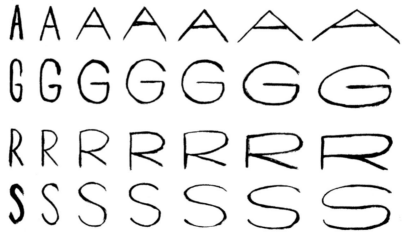

Nothing beats methodical exploration as a way of identifying interests. Beginning with a rote investigation of basic characteristics, such as character width (as is shown here), can help corral overwhelming possibilities into more finite categories for consideration. In working this way, one discovers very quickly what one really likes (and doesn't).

DESIGNER UNKNOWN / USA
PURCHASE COLLEGE SUNY
Timothy Samara, instructor

The Garamond face—a specimen of the original's capital and lowercase A is shown at left—is famously popular for revival. At last count, there were more than 100 cuts produced in the intervening 400-odd years since Claude Garamond first drew it. Four such reinterpretations are shown below the original; all four exhibit a modern convention—a significantly enlarged x-height—but each presents a unique take on its source.

For some reason, when I doodle (which is often), the lowercase f captures my attention. Drawing different variations of the form of a letter that one happens to like a lot is both good practice and a way of mapping intuitively appealing traits that could ultimately lead to a new font. At left is a random selection of such doodles.

Combing through old advertisements, one is certain to find a variety of custom logotypes with interesting traits that could easily inspire a complete character set.

Outdoor signs, building numbers, even a single digit from an old catalog like the one seen here, can provide enough source material for developing a complete character set. Although such sources might lead to a revival, their basic traits need not necessarily become the basis for a historical period piece. A contemporary designer can translate such a source's features as he or she likes, easily creating a new font that is engaging to contemporary audiences.

Never overlook a happy accident! A slip of the hand while stroke-writing produced a curved crossbar that this student designer found intriguing. A process of pencil sketching and then hand-painting led to the refined set of characters at right.

MATTHEW ROMANSKI / USA
PURCHASE COLLEGE SUNY
Timothy Samara, instructor

WISHFUL THINKING

Yet another approach to defining an idea for creating a new face is allowing oneself to simply wonder: "What if?"

Despite the availability of roughly 200,000 fonts, there are a lot of gaps in the offering. Try to find a super-condensed sans serif with extreme stroke-weight contrast, for instance; there are, perhaps, five such faces of any quality. "What if I made something like that?" Identifying a set of characteristics that don't already exist in combination presents the delightful possibility of making something that no one has seen yet.

Such inquiry into the unknown can be driven by purely visual interest, or ideas that are more conceptual, or even narrative, in nature: "What would the offspring of a particular serif and sans serif face look like?" or "How would a typeface that captures the essence of George Orwell's dystopian novel, *1984*, appear?"

AaGgRr
HhPpWw
SsMm

The designer of this face determined that he'd like to develop a slab serif of medium, relatively uniform weight—but with notched and wedge-shaped serifs, instead of the usual abrupt or curved-bracket sort that is far more common.

ANDREW SCHEIDERICH / USA
PURCHASE COLLEGE SUNY
Timothy Samara, instructor

In 1988, German graphic designer Otl Aicher developed a four-part super-family called Rotis, based on the idea of hybridizing Univers, a neo-grotesque sans serif, and Times Roman, a transitional serif. One of the four families is an actual hybrid—a semi-serif, shown here.

AaGgRrHh
PpXxSsMm

RaeGmHh

Here, a selected set of extra-condensed, sans serif characters with extreme contrast in the stroke weights—which, incidentally, I designed in my *Letterforms* class while I was in college.

CONFRONTING A CHALLENGE

A last (or perhaps, first?) possibility for determining the paramaters of developing a new typeface is that of resolving some acknowledged problem or difficulty in how some class or style of face is constructed.

One will find, for instance, that certain characters in faces with extreme characteristics—say, those that are super bold and exceptionally condensed or extended—are often, frustratingly, out of step with their character counterparts because of conflicts between their required stroke formation and the aesthetic requirements imposed by the font's overarching visual language.

Still other challenges that may offer opportunities involve how font styles are affected by the medium in which they appear; as well as fundamental difficulties that attend a font's basic structural framework—for instance, achieving improved evenness of color in a monospaced typeface.

Dimensional
Planetarium
Metaprotein
Interstitial
Neutralizer
Playfulness
Magnetized
Governance
Mechanical

Streamlined
Coffeehouse
Nonresident
Schoolroom
Influential
Carbonator
Qualitative
Sketchbook
Omniscient

Semiconductor
Triangulation
Magnetosphere
Precipitation
Electrostatic

Repeatability
Investigation
Perpendicular
Marketability
Architectonic

In developing Operator, a new font offering, font house Hoefler & Co. decided to tackle a couple of challenges posed by typewriter type, a form that—while instantly recognizable and popularly appealing (despite the fact that typewriters haven't been in use for a few decades)—isn't all that flexible.

First up: Creating a broad range of weights for the style, which is notorious for having only one.

Second: Introducing an equally robust italic version (actual typewriter italics tend to be somewhat anemic) in all the weights available in upright form.

Last: Addressing the form's mechanical heritage, its fixed-width construction. Or, rather, throwing it out: Operator is designed with natural, optically consistent widths and spacing.

Still, a determination was made that a true monospaced version might be desirable after all, so a companion family was created. It still exhibits some of the frustrating characteristics of fixed-width forms but, ultimately, these were mitigated through clever character shaping and subtle weight variations, resulting in a remarkably even color in text.

FREEHAND PENCIL SKETCHING

It's possible, of course, to begin developing a new font by working directly from roughed-out characters made with a brush, pen, or other tools, but constructing (or reconstructing) them more methodically with pencil and eraser provides far greater control—whether working investigatively and testing as one goes or attempting to distill a rough idea into one that is more specific in its characteristics.

Drawing is a very personal skill, and all of us are comfortable doing so in our own way. Two different approaches are recommended here, but feel free to draw in the way that works best for you. However you do it, the most important aspect to address in visualizing the forms is to be able to understand the relationship between positive solidity and negative counter shaping.

One way of drawing letters is to grow the mass of a character's strokes outward from its archetypal skeleton. Start with delicate lines to rough out the character's basic shaping and proportions, and then continually add more stroke mass.

Use a white graphic eraser or pink eraser to delete darker marks; use a kneaded eraser to smooth edges or remove lighter marks without disturbing the darker ones.

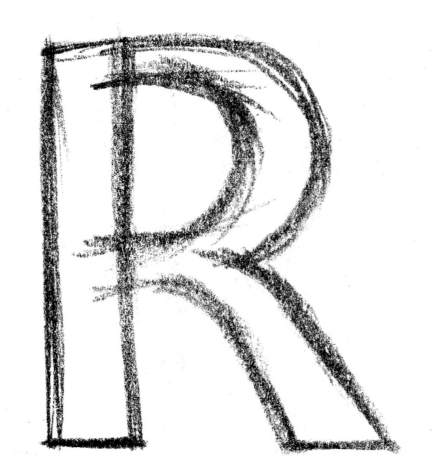

Most people focus on contours when they draw; it's easier to plan and see the overall shape this way than it is by following the beefed-up skeleton method described on the opposite page.

Using an eraser to edit drawn contours will help sharpen and clarify them. Again, use a hard eraser for more aggressive, corrective work and a kneaded eraser to fine-tune, as needed.

What will be lacking from the contour approach is being able to see the positive/ negative relationship between stroke and counter—until after the contour has already been drawn.

Spend some time darkening in the stroke areas defined by the contours as you go. You can always correct later, but being able to tell how dark or light the strokes really are, earlier on, is more informative. In any event, cross-hatching or diagonal shading both work well to generate an adequately solid stroke form. Be sure to cover

contour lines at joints or other locations inside the stroke areas themselves (they can inaccurately influence the appreciation of movement). If necessary, shade or crosshatch again, but darker, and in an alternate direction.

CONSTRUCTION METHODS

MAKING A STROKE LIBRARY

Another means of discovering a new typeface concept's DNA is to construct characters using a selection of premade marks, in different combinations. Generating an inventory of different stroke shapes, weights, and tool-mark details that can be mixed together in a variety of combinations offers an opportunity to compare the visual effects of such combinations to help determine which might be the most interesting—without the pressure of trying to achieve a specific result from the outset.

The more marks with different attributes, the better. Along with making individual, isolated strokes, also consider including continuous, rhythmic elements. These can be useful for extracting connective material to help with serifs and joints, as well as for suggesting overall rhythm—especially if a script form is the goal.

Elements created as a library can be combined physically—by scanning or photocopying them and then splicing them together manually—or purely digitally, by bringing scans of the elements into an image-manipulation software program.

CONSTRUCTION METHODS

REFINED PAINTING

Now, however, we're gonna kick it old school. Yes (of course), it's possible to proceed from a refined pencil sketch—or even a rough brush drawing—directly into digital construction. But coming to know even more specifically what one's intentions are by translating preliminanry studies into an exceptionally clarified state can only ease the process. That translation means committing to pure positive/negative visualization in the form of painting the letters on boards.

The process outlined here is intended to make one's visual intentions clear and understandable—not to simply produce clean forms for the sake of cleanliness. Painting refined forms on boards helps identify decision points for resolution ("Are this stroke's contours parallel from cap line to baseline or not?") and, so, provides more accurate (and physically stable) masters to scan for later digital work.

Tools and Materials

2- or 3-ply hot-press (smooth) illustration board

A set-square (triangle): Translucent plastic, with one edge measuring at least 10" (4.5 cm)

Studio knife and (steel) ruler

Pencils: HB and 3B weight

White drafting or artist's tape

Plaka (tempera paint): One bottle each of black and white

Ruling pen

Two no. 6 round brushes

Two containers for water

Two small plates or palettes for mixing

1

Use tracings of pre-drawn letter sketches to define a uniform size for the boards that will accommodate all of the letters to be painted at a height of 4" to 5" (8 to 10 cm). Be sure to account for wide letters, like the M and W, and provide enough depth for the ascending and descending characters.

Plaka is a casein-based tempera that dries to a velvety matte finish and won't reconstitute when it gets wet—which makes it ideal for correcting. Mix in enough water to achieve a consistency like that of heavy cream while remaining opaque.

It's important to keep the two colors separate, hence the two brushes, the two water containers, and the two small mixing palettes suggested above. This obsession with separateness is solely about not compromising the ability to appreciate pure positive against pure negative—which will

become an issue if either the black or white becomes tainted. Further, Plaka takes a little while to completely dry. A hairdryer can help speed up that process; or, you can enjoy a little rest between each round of painting.

At the same time, the boards should be narrow enough in width that the letters painted on them can be reviewed and evaluated side by side as close to each other as possible, but still with comfortable space between.

2

Before cutting the boards from a larger sheet, prime the working side with white Plaka: Use a wide brush with extremely soft bristles (one with bristles made from rabbit hair is ideal). Mix the white Plaka with enough water to achieve a consistency like skim milk (thinner than the consistency you'll use for corrections later).

Cover the board from edge to edge in one direction with generous, even strokes, working quickly to lay a thin film of the Plaka cross the surface in one direction, and—while it's still wet—do so again in the opposing direction. The board will warp slightly from the moisture in the Plaka (that's okay).

When the working side is dry, flip the board over and repeat the process on the back; doing so will undo the warp and, once dry, the board will return to being flat.

Priming the board with white Plaka creates a ground of the same color that will be used for corrections so that any color difference between the board and the Plaka itself won't be distracting.

3

After the board is dry, measure out one master letter board at the size you have established. Use a set-square (tri-angle) to establish true perpendicularity in the measurements.

Cut out the master letter board with a studio knife or utility knife. Then, use the master board as a template to trace out the dimensions of the other boards. Use a sharp, H-weight pencil for greater accuracy.

Mark the cap line, mean line, baseline, and descent lines along the master board's left-hand edge; use the triangle to extend them very lightly, with the pencil, left to right, across the board. Position a new board to the right of the master and match the positions of the cap line, mean line, baseline and descent line. Repeat this method until all the boards have identical guides drawn across them. Use the triangle and a ruler to ensure all the guides are parallel.

CONSTRUCTION METHODS

REFINED PAINTING [CONTINUED]

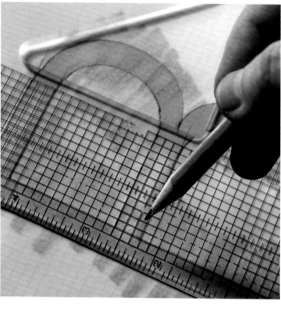

6

After the contours of the straight strokes are drawn, use the appropriate brush to fill in the blank areas of the straight strokes. You can always correct mistakes with white Plaka later, but be as careful as you can to minimize the need to do so.

4

If you haven't already, carefully trace the sketch of each letter onto tracing paper with the H-weight pencil.

Turn each tracing over and, with a 3B-weight pencil, scribble on the reverse side to cover all the areas described by the traced form on the front side.

For each letter, choose a board marked with guide lines. Turn the tracing of a letter back over (right-side-up) and position it to rest on the baseline. Use the triangle to ensure that its stems are truly vertical to the baseline.

(For characters without vertical stems, you'll have to eyeball it.)

Use small pieces of white tape to gently adhere the tracing to the board. Using the H-weight pencil once again, retrace the contours of the letter; this will transfer the darker, 3B graphite from the back of the tracing sheet onto the board itself. Use the triangle when tracing vertical and horizontal contours.

5

Time to paint! Mix black Plaka (using the brush, palette, and water designated for black). The consistency of the Plaka should now be viscous, more like heavy cream in consistency.

Fill the brush and drag it across the tines of the ruling pen to deposit the paint between them. Tighten or loosen the adjustor nut to open them such that the pen will draw a line roughly 1 point in weight.

Draw the contours of the letter's straight strokes with the ruling pen, held against the edge of the triangle. When you get to corners, cross them (as shown above). You'll remove the extra line lengths by covering them with white Plaka, which will help you achieve sharp corners.

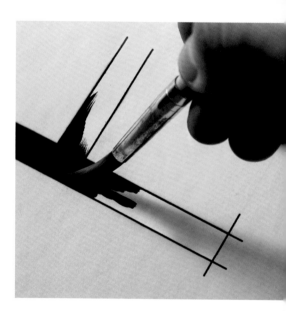

A no. 6 round brush works best for this paint-ing process.

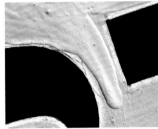

If the Plaka gets too thick and lumpy, use a fine-grit sandpaper to sand it down.

8

Then, using the white Plaka, begin the task of correcting weights, widths, and curve shapes as needed (us-ing the brush, palette, and water designated for white Plaka). This process will take some time (especially for the curved forms).

Work back and forth between white and black to continually edit the forms, comparing them to each other in groups as you go.

7

Once the straight strokes are filled in, paint any curved strokes freehand, carefully following the transferred contours on the board.

It's okay to rotate the board when painting curves—or, for that matter, when filling in the straight strokes—there's no rule that the board must remain oriented toward you in any particular way.

Take your time and be as precise as you can, but keep your hand moving fluidly. If you make a mistake, remember that you'll be able to correct it later with white Plaka.

While one character's strokes are drying on its board, go on to another; repeat steps 5 through 7 for each board until all the letters are painted in black.

Completed boards for two different styles of capital R.

PREPPING FOR DIGITAL WORK

All font-design software allows for working directly—jumping intuitively, so to speak, into defining stroke, character width, weight, and shaping parameters—using a program's drawing tools, without reference. On the other hand, they all also allow for importing scans to serve as a basis for construction, and it's a good idea to proceed this way.

It doesn't really matter whether scanned characters are relatively rough or highly refined (although it's easier to start working effectively if the scanned models are, in fact, very tightly developed). What's important is how the scanning is accomplished so that they're as useful as possible once one starts working with them.

First, scan each character at full size, at a resolution of at least 300 DPI—or higher. The scans should be grayscale to capture the maximum amount of information.

Next, open the scans in an image manipulation program and alter the levels to achieve a high-contrast version of the image (this will also sharpen its contours).

Last, readjust each image's levels so that white areas remain absolutely white—but so that black areas lighten to a 20% gray value. Doing so will allow you to see Bézier points and their line segments on top of the scanned reference images more easily.

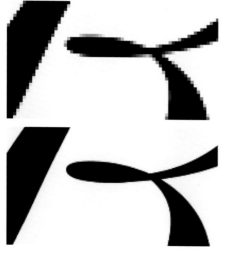

The information in a low-resolution scan of only 72 DPI (top) will not likely be sufficient to accurately trace subtle forms with vector drawing tools; note the detail that is present in a 400 DPI scan of the same form (bottom).

Once all the characters are scanned, enlarge the canvas or artboard. Position a cap line and baseline (mean line, if needed) and arrange all the individual characters' images along the baseline guide.

Scale any characters that are slightly off in size, taking into account overshoots for curves or diagonals.

Along with general adjustments to ensure the images are a consistent size, also address their verticality: Position vertical guides along a given character's outer and inner stem contours for reference; rotate and/or skew the images until their vertical stems are perpendicular to the baseline and parallel to the vertical guides (if that's desirable for the design concept).

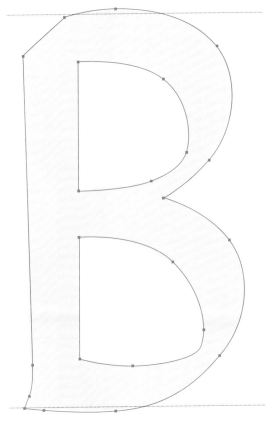

When tracing the scanned reference, use as few Bézier points as possible, but position them where the greatest control will be needed. Curves usually require control at locations where they change in radius or direction, especially near joints.

Avoid the urge to autotrace the character images (whether you're working in a general drawing application or one specifically designed for font work). Auto-tracing will introduce too many Bézier points along the scanned image's contours to be useful; too many points can also potentially confuse the software and corrupt the file.

Every step along the way presents options for clarifying one's intention for the characters' attributes. One can easily alter the direction a design will take by making a decision about how it is traced, as seen here in the vector outlines based on the same scanned character.

PROCESS STRATEGIES

BEGINNING WITH THE CAPITAL H

No matter how one is going about it—sketching and then scanning or refining through painting beforehand—the crux of designing a font is about making basic decisions about attributes for a limited selection of characters, and then carrying them out among the remaining ones.

For newbies, the best place to start with this decision making is with the rectilinear forms, because they are the simplest and will provide the clearest, most concrete of defining characteristics. Of these, the capital H is the most informative: One can clearly see its height to width relationship, its stroke weights, and basic terminal- and joint-shaping without confusion. As new kinds of characters are added, the designer will be forced to compare their logic with that already defined—implying a continual revisiting and retrofitting of newly discovered characteristics to forms previously developed.

The process outlined here can be followed through a process of drawing, painting, tracing, cutting and pasting, or by purely digital means, as a designer's skill and interest warrants.

Master measurements

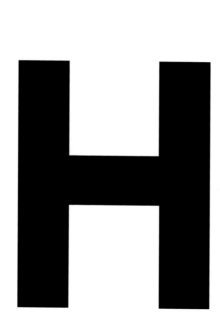

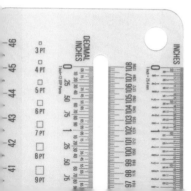

The measurement in question will need a finely detailed ruler with increments as small as 1/64" (0.4 mm).

Decide on a general style.

Construct the H at a cap height of 4–5" (8–10 cm), establishing its width, weight, contrast, and any characteristic features, including modulation, terminal and joint shaping, serifs, and so on. The steps shown here begin with an H of bold, relatively uniform stroke weight.

Measure the character's overall width and those of its stems and crossbar.

Yes: Measure them.

Build the remaining right-angle forms using the master measurements to start: Knowing that all the characters' widths and stroke weights are the same, it will be easier to first appreciate their resulting visual differences—and will provide a sense of how much these measures may need to change in each.

Working at a cap height of 4" (8 cm), stroke weights may vary from 1/32"–3/64" (1–2 mm) thicker or thinner; character widths, by as much as 1/8" (6 mm), or slightly more, narrower or wider.

H E F T L

As first constructed on the opposite page

H E F T L

The same forms, corrected

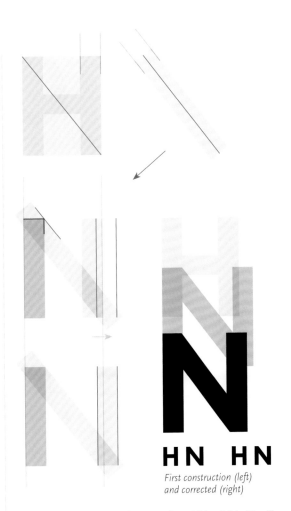

E F

T L

N

HN HN

*First construction (left)
and corrected (right)*

Among sans serif forms—in which the A may be made with a flat or pointed apex—the A's angle may be defined generally in the two ways shown above.

Among serif forms, the A's angle is often defined as falling from a point at the center of the N's body, along cap line, to the N's right stem at baseline.

**K M X Y Z
V M W**

Note variants of M structure

Compare the widths and weights of the right-angle forms, as derived from the master measurements, and correct for discrepancies.

Consider joints for shaping and opportunities for stylistic qualities. The joints in this character set are neutral in their shaping.

Use the aspect ratio of the H to rough out the master diagonal for the N at the same measured weight as the H's vertical stems.

Instead of forcing the diagonal to meet the width of the H, orient it over a copy of the H stems as shown. It will overshoot the right stem; reposition it to meet the left corner of the right stem at the baseline.

The width of this N will be too extended—more than is needed to optically match the width of the H. Further, the joints will likely be heavy, even if for a light-weight face. Thin the stems and/or notch or taper the diagonal to ease the weight in the corner joints.

The angle of a diagonal varies (see pages 104–107) but, basically, there are two kinds: the one defined by the N (the aspect ratio) and another, more acute, angle that characterizes the A. All the other diagonal forms' angles fall between these two extremes, which can be used to help construct them. First, therefore, develop the A.

There are three simple ways to help determine the A's angles from the N; these relationships are fairly consistent among type styles (top).

After the A is formed, construct the remaining diagonal characters, basing their angles, widths and stroke weights on the information provided by the A or the N as seems most appropriate.

BEGINNING WITH THE CAPITAL H [CONTINUED]

HO HO

*First construction (left)
and corrected (right)*

Next: the curved forms. Explore the radii of different ellipses, focusing on the upper-left quadrant of the body, to identify the desired curve logic for the font. Duplicate the radius into the remaining quadrants to form a rough O; use the master width and stroke measures of the H to initially organize and weight the quadrant curves.

The roughly constructed O will be light and condensed compared to the H. Adjust the stroke weights and width of the O to optically match those of the H. Compare the counters to ensure similarity in overall volume relative to the stroke density.

Use the corresponding quadrant curves of the refined O to form the shoulders and bowls of the C, D, G, and U.

Delete portions of the right-hand side to create apertures for the C and G; copy the H's stem and position it on top of the curves of the D, G, and U to determine the locations of these letters' respective vertical elements.

Add the G's crossbar. Test its height position, relative to the height of the stem and the depth of the beak above it, as well as its horizontal dimension. Consider whether it should be spurred or not.

Test tail options on the O to build the Q.

Translate the curve logic of the C, D, G, and U into the hook of the J; consider the Q's tail shaping with regard to the J's tail length and shape, as well.

Cutting and splicing   *Tracing and splicing*   *Digital scaling*

**EFHIJLT
AKMNVWXY
BPRCDGOS**

**SKOMLTY
ABFUXIKJO
ZINJQPSV**

**LOREM IPS
HAMBURGE
FONTSIV**

Use the right-hand shoulder and bowl of the O to discover the lobe and waist formation of the B. You can do this by tracing each (or cutting a copy apart) and then overlapping them so they're spliced together; as an alternative, scan the O and, in imaging or drawing software, scale it vertically, compressing it to about half its height.

Each method has its pros and cons; you'll need to tweak the curves and their weights either way so that the curve is smooth (if spliced) and so that the upper lobe is slightly smaller than the lower one.

The B's lower lobe makes a good reference for the P (which will need to be condensed slightly); the P then gives rise to the R by

acquiring a leg—the angle of which can be determined from the diagonal of the N or the A as a rough beginning. Consider the transition of the R's leg from the waist, as well as the shaping of its finishing terminal, for stylistic possibilities.

Build the S by inverting the upper B lobe and connecting it to the lower lobe with a thick spine. Compare the diagonality of the curve to primary diagonals, like those of the N or X—the curve should appear, flow through the spine, and come to resolution around that diagonal such that the axis of the curve feels similar to the literal diagonal.

Test the overall uniformity of the characters by ordering them in a variety of random sequences and reproducing them at different sizes to see where individual forms stand out compared to the others; continue to correct the characters in the set as needed.

PROCESS STRATEGIES

BEGINNING WITH THE CAPITAL R

For designers who are more accomplished or, at least, more comfortable with the complexities of form, beginning with the capital R allows one to establish all of a font's characteristics at once: body proportion, curve and diagonal shaping, transitions between straight strokes and curves, and several kinds of joint.

It's a lot to consider all at once—especially for beginners—but, on the other hand, taking into account all of these variables in one character from the outset means less back-tracking from discoveries made later during the process. The roadmap that the capital R delineates is far more comprehensive, even if it requires more complicated evaluation in the initial development stage.

At right are a series of questions posed by each major element of the capital R to the designer. The answer the designer gives to each question provides a clue as to how that roadmap will be revealed.

Sans serif or serif—and what kind? Bracketed or unbracketed? Horizontal joint, or sloped and modulated?

How does the cross-stroke transition into the shoulder? What's the radius of the shoulder's curve? How rapid is the ductus into and out of the curve?

Does the crosstroke extend in a truly horizonal direction? Is it the same weight as the vertical? How far does it extend (and so, what kind of width is it establishing for the entire form?

Is the stem of uniform weight or modulated?

Are the two cross strokes the same weight or different? Are they thins, as compared to the stems, as thicks?

Does the bowl of the upper lobe mirror the shoulder, or is it shaped differently? When does the bowl turn into the middle cross stroke?

How is this joint formed— from a horizontal, a curve and a horizontal, or from two curves? Does it meet the stem or is it detached? If it's detached, how far is it from the stem?

Does the leg extend abruptly from the upper lobe or transition smoothly from it? Is the leg a true diagonal or is it a curve? How far does the leg extend past the lobe above it?

Is the baseline terminal the same as, or different than, the cap line terminal of the stem above?

Are the contours of the leg parallel? Does the leg itself flare or modulate? Is its baseline terminal flush to the baseline or is it sheared? Does the leg turn outward and trail off or does it turn and end abruptly?

There are so many variables that comprise an uppercase R that it would be impossible here to map the results of every decision that could be made about them.

Instead, the process outlined here will focus on the specific characteristics of five highly differentiated styles, and how they're translated across the various uppercase forms.

That discussion focuses on major structural categories, rather than a step-by-step process (as outlined in the previous section), but the same process logic may still be applied.

This medium, sans serif R is constructed of mostly neutral geometry. Its strokes are of uniform weight, the curvature of the upper lobe is more or less circular, and the leg is a nearly isometric diagonal that points from lower right corner to upper-left corner. The curves of the lobe are distanced from the vertical stem by truly horizontal cross strokes that extend relatively far from the stem before the curves begin.

In this sans serif R, which is slightly condensed in its width, the stem and leg are noticeably modulated. This modulation follows in the curve of the upper lobe, especially as it moves leftward to join the stem. The upper contour of the shoulder overshoots the cap line and then dips slightly before rising again into its joint with the stem, in the upper-left corner of the form. The upper counter is semicircular, but the bottom one is purely triangular, the result of the leg being a straight diagonal. Unlike the sans serif specimen above, the lobe and leg join each other at a location that is quite close to the stem, without significant cross-stroke formation.

Even more condensed than the form above, this serif R also shows a waist joint that occurs close to the stem. This form is shaded, having pronounced contrast between thins and thicks. Its serifs are relatively extended, and segue into the stem with brackets of a relatively sharp radius and ductus. The transition from the upper-left corner into the shoulder, however, is a little more fluid, with a slower ductus. The leg is constructed of a curve—or, rather, the diagonal quality of the leg is only appreciable for a short distance before it curves into the waist and upward from the baseline. The leg is finished with a small ball-like serif.

This slab-serif R is unusual for its rectilinear formation, which extends to the shaping of its curves—all of a tightly squared-off radius and rapid ductus. Overall, the character is slightly bolder than a medium or regular weight. Its strokes are generally uniform in weight, although the horizontals are slightly lighter. The angle of the leg is more upright; as with the specimen above, its angularity is somewhat absorbed by curves in the transition into the waist, and outward, along the baseline, where the stroke finishes abruptly in a flat terminal that is cut at 90° to the direction of the stroke.

This R is exceptionally condensed. As a result, its counters appear vertically elongated, and are only twice as wide (or less) as the width of the stem. The character is also sans serif and of uniform weight; the far-right joint between lobe and leg is deeply cut to alleviate weight gain. The leg in this R is a purely vertical stem that transitions in a rapid curve from the waist, mirroring the radius of the shoulder and bowl.

PROCESS STRATEGIES

BEGINNING WITH THE CAPITAL R [CONTINUED]

R H E F T L I
R H E F T L I
R H E F T L I
R H E F T L I
R H E F T L I

R B P D U J
R B P D U J
R B P D U J
R B P D U J
R B P D U J

The capital R defines attributes for different archetypal structural groups, and any one of them can be the first area of focus for development—but beginning with the right-angle forms is easier, especially for beginners.

Even though the R is asymmetrical left to right, its right-hand side offers enough information to derive the width of the capital H. Once that width has been established, one can proceed to the remaining right-angle forms as outlined on pages 146 and 147.

Note how the character widths, stroke weights, modulation, and joint shaping are each reflected among the right-angle characters that accompany the respective R styles.

While the R's upper lobe provides information for shaping similar forms in this group, these forms also benefit from seeing how the right-angle forms develop in terms of their widths. The overall width of these forms is driven by how far the R's horizontal cross-strokes (or, lack thereof) separate the lobe from the stem.

Notice how the relative circularity or squareness of the R's shoulder and waist curves is translated among its accompanying forms in each case. In particular, compare the overshoots of the modulated sans serif (second from top) and the upper-left joints between shoulder and stem.

The shaping of the J's tail is also a detail that responds very specifically to the R's curvature in each case, most noticeably in that of the condensed serif set (middle row).

R **O Q C G S**

R **O Q C G S**

R O Q C G S

R **O Q C G S**

R O Q C G S

R **N A V W X Y K M Z**

R **N A V W X Y K M Z**

R N A V W X Y K M Z

R **N A V W X Y K M Z**

R N A V W X Y K M Z

The curved forms among the characters in each style reflect the radius, ductus, axis, and shading of the R in each case.

In the modulated serif style (second row from top), the lift of the R's shoulder, creating the overshoot above the cap line, is reflected in a slightly oblique axis in the other forms.

The curved, uniform-weight sans serif forms in the top row are nearly true circles; in the

condensed serif set (middle row), they are ovoid—their R's upper lobe is also generally circular, but its condensed width requires similar condensing throughout, which compresses the O, Q, and other curved forms.

Note the deep beaks of the C, G, and S in the super condensed set in the bottom row.

Last, but not least, the diagonal structures. The leg of the R in each style is radically different in its formation. In the sans serif at top, the leg is very nearly the same angle as that of the N's master diagonal; the other angle forms also show diagonals that are more closely related in angle. In most of the other sets, the angles are not so similar to that of their respective R's leg: in the three bottom-most rows, the leg of

the R is sufficiently stylized that it doesn't provide much information for defining the diagonals in the other forms. For that purpose, the N must be developed first, based on the width of the H, in order to determine how the diagonals will be best expressed throughout.

PROCESS STRATEGIES

BUILDING THE LOWERCASE FROM ESTABLISHED CAPITALS

In those limited, formal courses devoted to typeface design, the capitals are always the starting point in the process of designing a font (because their construction, as complicated as it may be, is yet simpler than that of the lowercase).

Once the uppercase character set is designed, the next step is to develop the lowercase characters that will accompany them. The most important relationships to be established between the lowercase forms and their uppercase parents is discussed in detail in Chapter 2: Legacies.

What follows here is a methodology aimed at simplifying the very complicated process of designing lowercase forms once an uppercase character set has already been developed.

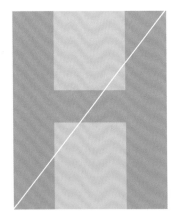

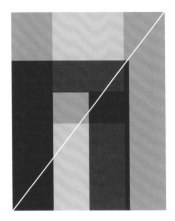

Before proceeding, test the implications of the developing x-height on the a and e, the two most challenging characters because of stroke density.

Map the aspect ratio of the H from the already-designed capitals to establish an approximate proportion for the lowercase.

Rather than an x, draw a rectilinear n-form whose stroke weights match those of the H. It is easier to understand the lowercase width by using this simplified form.

Compare the n-form to the H; its strokes will appear heavy and its counter more vertical because there's more stroke information in a smaller space. Adjust the n-form accordingly.

Place the H and the adjusted n-form side by side: the counter above defines the prospective ascent and descent measures.

Duplicate the geometric n-form. Close its baseline counter and split it in half with horizontal strokes to approximate the density of the a and e that will eventually develop.

Adjust the closed form's stroke weights and, if necessary, enlarge its height to help alleviate excess density. Doing so will affect the ascent and descent measures.

Remove the extra strokes from the closed n-form and compare it to both the H and the original, rectilinear n-form.

Check the resulting ascent/descent measures to see if they will accommodate future forms like the f and g.

Don't design the a and e yet—some more information is needed.

Draw an x to optically match the n's height, width, and weight. Take into account the potential need to offset the x's upstrokes on either side of the downstroke.

At this point, cut a stem from the H to create the lowercase l; duplicate the l and cut it to the x-height to create the i, minus its tittle. The tittle will be added in a later step.

Shrink the capital O to match the optical height of x and thicken its strokes to match. Replace the n's flat top with a similar, tighter curve that flows from its right-hand stem back to its left-hand stem. The curve of this rough branch will need to be pinched slightly because it's turning from a vertical and, technically,

coming to a finish just as it strikes the left-hand stem, instead of benefiting from the full width of the o's outer curves.

Repeat the n and overlap its strokes to build the m.

Cut the n's branch to reveal the rough r.

Adjust the counters and the branch weights among these three forms as needed to compensate for the differing amounts of stroke info in each character.

PROCESS STRATEGIES

BUILDING THE LOWERCASE FROM
ESTABLISHED CAPITALS [CONTINUED]

ıp np
pbdq

Direct reversals from the p

pbdq

Corrected characters

Place the i-stem over the left-hand curve of the o and extend it downward to the established descent line to roughly form the p, the basis for the lobed forms (p, b, q, d). Finesse the transition from lobe into stem, using the n's branch for reference.

Flip and reverse the p to rough out the b, d, and q.

The reversals will reveal subtle discrepancies in branch-joint weight and counter stability among the lobed forms—keep the heavier branch at the mean line and expand the inner counters downward to lighten the branches at the baseline.

To make a rough f, extend the r's stem and shift the branch upward to the cap height; delete the flat terminal and thicken the branch to match the curves in the o.

Add a crossbar of the appropriate weight, positioned to hang from the mean line.

Now, with the discovery of so much curve and joint logic, take care of a few simple issues:

Examine options for shaping and height position of the i's tittle; differentiate the lowercase l from the uppercase I; duplicate the i and rotate the upper shoulder of the f to roughly define the descending hook of the lowercase j.

To form the t, invert the f and raise the crossbar to hang from the meanline; shape the ascender as desired.

For a modern g, trace the f's shoulder and upper stem. Invert and composite with the q. Copy the o's lower bowl and overlay as shown; drop the loop to the descent line; then adjust the curves.

For an oldstyle g, see the steps outlined on the page opposite.

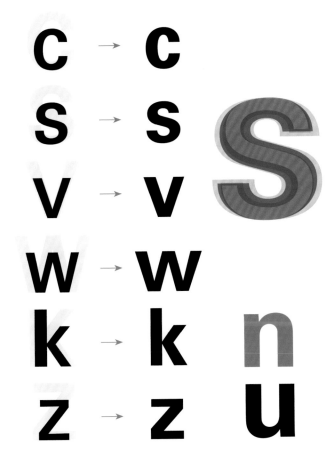

Reduce the capitals C, S, V, W, and Z to the established x-height.

For the k, reduce only the arm and leg of the capital as a unit. Adjust the weights and widths of these forms and integrate any relevant characteristics, such as joint notches, tapering, and spurs or serifs.

When thickening these characters' weights, keep in mind how strokes grow from center outward, horizontally (refer to page 118).

Invert the n to form the u.

Many contemporary sans serif fonts incorporate an old-style lowercase g (along with other serif attributes). This kind of g starts with the o, stacked and reproportioned to create desired upper/lower counter balance and to fit the descent depth. A lowercase s, slightly rotated, provides great potential for designing a conventional link—but it might be useful to look at joints in the uppercase R, A, and K, as well as link options in a variety of faces.

Trace or digitally composite elements of the g, s, and n to roughly construct the a; smooth and join the parts, as needed.

Duplicate the o and splice in a crossbar to form the e. Compare the shoulders, bowls, and counters of these to each other, and to those of the g and n.

As with the uppercase, test the characters by ordering them in a variety of random sequences and words.

BEGINNING WITH THE LOWERCASE

Anyone who has ever read anything will immediately realize that the bulk of all typographic text is disproportionally represented by lowercase forms. It stands to reason, therefore, that it would make sense to begin designing a typeface intended for extensive reading by developing the lowercase character set first.

Yes! That *is* a good idea—but it's one best approached once one is already competent in the basics (meaning, structuring capitals first and evolving the lowercase after)—mostly because the number of variables involved is multiplied (more kinds of shapes, and greater irregularity among them).

Still, if one is feeling up to the challenge, beginning with the lowercase characters is an excellent way to suss out the functionality of a font design, and many of the parts of the lowercase letters are somewhat similar, so components of forms designed earlier on in the process can basically be flipped, left-to-right or top-to-bottom, to generate rough forms of other characters. All along the way, of course, it will be necessary to compare the results of such mechanical construction methods and adjust them, as needed, to ensure the various forms' visual stability and stylistic integrity.

Define the height/width ratio and curvature of the o, as well as the desired degree of contrast. Decide on general style, too: serif or sans serif.

Explore the relationship between verticals and the curvature to define the branch and lobe forms, using h and p as controls.

The upper terminal of the p defines the prospective x-height and, therefore, also the prospective ascent and descent measures.

Working from the h, develop the branch forms n, m, and r, following the steps described on page 155. Use the p to develop the other lobed forms b, d, and q, following the steps on page 156.

Once these characters are resolved with respect to their relative widths, weights, contrast, and shaping, follow the steps on pages 156 and 157:

use the r to develop the f, j, l, and i; use the f to develop the t; and then the f, q, and o to work out the g (if of the sans serif variety, as described on page 156, or see page 157 to develop a serif, or oldstyle, g).

Invert the n to form the u.

a e x

g s n

q c s kvw

p 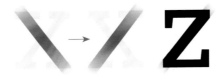 z

From this stage forward, use parts from the characters already defined to create the a and e.

Refer to the methods described on page 157 to help guide these characters' development.

The s may be drawn freehand or, alternatively, first constructed mechanically by splicing together the shoulder of the q and bowl of the p within the established x-height (the arc of the a can also be helpful) before smoothing out disconnections.

Draw the x: its height derives from the baseline of the h and the flat terminal of the p.

Use its proportion, stroke weights, and optical compensation strategies to help establish the arm and leg of the k, and the v, w, and y.

Invert the x downstroke to generate the z upstroke, which may require some adjustment in angle and weight to optically match.

Map the aspect ratio of the n from the lower-left edge of its left stem, extending the diagonal upward to the right and through its branch corner to meet the cap line defined by the h ascender. Separate the left stem from the h; duplicate it and orient the two stems to correspond to the aspect ratio diagonal. Split the form top to bottom with a crossbar to form a capital H.

Then, proceed to develop the uppercase as described on pages 146–149.

PROCESS STRATEGIES

**ON TO THE NUMERALS AND
ANALPHABETIC SYMBOLS**

Numerals (or numbers) follow the same structural, proportional, and stroke-weight logic as letters and should exhibit all the formal logic that is established for the alphabetic characters in an evolving font.

However, there are two distinct structural possibilities for the design of numerals: those that are based on the body of the lowercase and, like those characters, include ascenders and descenders—what are called *Oldstyle* or *text figures*—and those that are more closely derivative of the capitals in proportion, called *lining figures.* Oldstyle, or text figures, set seamlessly within lowercase text; lining figures are designed for mathematical applications in which figures need to appear vertically aligned for value comparison or tabulation. Most contemporary typefaces include both kinds of numeral.

Analphabetic symbols (more popularly referred to as *glyphs*) include symbols like the ampersand, the "at" sign, percent sign, punctuation—the exclamation point, question mark, quotes, comma, period, brackets, and so on—and accent marks, or diacritical symbols. All of these should appear to be visually related to the proportions and shaping details established by the letters in a character set.

0123456789

0123456789

Two examples of Oldstyle, or text, figures are compared here to show the stylistic relationship between the numerals and characters of the corresponding lowercase. Note the variation in the ascender and descender forms in the 3 and 5

0123456789

0123456789

0123456789

All three sets of lining figures, above, correspond to the uppercase forms in their respective styles—but all are clearly more condensed in width and, sometimes, are drawn slightly shorter than the height established by the cap line (as is true for the set of numerals in the example in the middle). The strategy here is to help more clearly differentiate the numerals from the capitals, as these often appear together in acronyms, notations, and in tables of numerical data.

Il1
Il1

Differentiating the uppercase I from the lowercase l presents a challenge that is compounded by the similarity of the number 1.

5S
38

These two sets of characters are easily confused at a glance, especially when set in small sizes. The presence of angles in the numbers helps.

Ø ⊙
O O

The zero can be distinguished from the capital O in a number of ways. Sometimes, it's given a slash; alternatively, a small dot is positioned in the middle of its counter. An oldstyle zero is typically distinguished from a lowercase o by being drawn with a uniform stroke weight.

& % ? ! @ " ( ) { } ü î ñ ç é

& % ? ! @ " ( ) { } ü î ñ ç é

& % ? ! @ " ( ) { } ü î ñ ç é

& % ? ! @ " ( ) { } ü î ñ ç é

& % ? ! @ " ( ) { } ü î ñ ç é

& % ? ! @ " ( ) { } ü î ñ ç é

Again, the general approach to developing analphabetic symbols, or glyphs, is the same as it is for any other characters: they should reflect the width, stroke/counter alternation, overall weight, contrast, curvature, and angularity present in the letters.

Above is a comparison of selected glyphs and letters in their respective typeface styles.

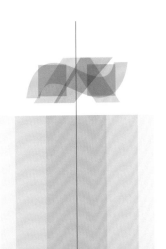

Diacritical marks, or accents, also follow the visual attributes established by the letters in their particular font.

Dot-like marks typically reflect the shaping and relative proportion of the lowercase i's tittle; angle forms, like the circumflex, translate the angles and joint shaping of the diagonal forms; curved elements, like

the tilde and cedilla, correspond in curvature and gestural rhythm to the larger curves, and details like tails in the J and Q, or the finishing stroke of the R's leg. Diacritical marks are generally simply centered over their letters.

One of the most fascinating aspects of letter-form design is how robustly flexible it is—the basic shapes of characters may be revised and reformed in almost infinite ways, creating new styles from within a strict, and seemingly limited, number of variables. This freedom can be attributed to the iconically distinct recognizability of the various letters' forms. If an A looks enough like an A, for example, it will read as such, and it takes a lot of manipulation to render an A unrecognizable.

Taking liberties to transcend mere function and impart meaning, or narrative, is fundamental to developing display faces, titling, and, most especially, brand marks, where conveying ideas beyond the explicit is critical.

Designers who understand historical precedent are, oddly, in a better position to liberate their investigations from historical models and so innovate new forms with great integrity, formal sophistication, and resonance.

Reinvention

ENVISIONING STRUCTURE AND STYLE IN NEW WAYS FOR NARRATIVE AND CONCEPTUAL EXPRESSION

RIFFING ON FUNDAMENTALS

EXPLORING INTRINSIC GEOMETRY

A specific, geometric configuration of strokes is what makes a letter identifiable for what it is—but that geometry also offers wide latitude for new versions of what it *could* be. Within a single-letter archetype, each stroke's shape, angle, weight, joint formation, and detailing expresses one possibility of many; even slight alterations to any one of these characteristics can create a dramatically new form.

Investigating the geometric relationships of structure and stroke formation in a particular form archetype depends on identifying the kind of structure intrinsic to that archetype: Is its structure defined by angles (and what type?) or curves? Where do its structural components join? And, what can happen when these limited variables are pushed to their extremes?

This extensive study of an uppercase K first explores the possibilities inherent in only the variables associated with the joint between the stem, arm, and leg.

In this study, all variables remain consistent, except for the relative lengths of the strokes—in the top row, arm and leg lengthen, shorten, or disappear altogether.

In the middle row, the stem grows from baseline to cap line, and then recedes upward.

In the bottom row, the designer examines the effects of obscuring strokes from around the area of the joint outward.

The study below investigates the possibilities afforded by digital distortion, creating the illusion of planar perspective in the form and, sometimes, as a result, altering its posture, from reverse oblique to italic.

The K studies on these pages were graciously provided by Jerry Kuyper.

Testing the basic variables of weight and extension, in combination, results in a comprehensive look at how much variation is possible in the most fundamental aspects of the structure.

The column of regular-weight forms (far left) compares the effect of different terminal shapes in the arm and leg; the second column (near left) shows the exaggeration of those effects when the form is significantly bolder.

This study examines the effect of changing weight distribution among the stem, arm, and leg.

Contrasts between contours reveal additional interesting possibilities.

Here, the designer investigates the contours of the form as outline and inline strokes, and the effect of weight changes to the structure of the joint.

The deep understanding of a particular letter's geometric structure allows a designer to see possibilities for creating rich, inventive letter signs, as in this logo for a stationery company called Kids Art Cards.
TIMOTHY SAMARA / USA

In this group of related studies, the designer tests a variety of serif formations.

EXAGGERATING NORMS

Most variation in the look of different typefaces results from the slight emphasis of particular aspects: one is a little more extended, or its serifs are sharper, and so on. Radically accentuating such basic formal qualities will immediately result in new, wildly expressive forms. Extremes of width, weight, and contrast in stroke weight may be just the beginning. Other possibilities might include altering the top-to-bottom proportional relationship in characters so they are top-heavy or bottom-heavy; skewing an italic form's angle axis far past the customary 12–15° off vertical; or super rotating the interior counters of curved forms to create excessive tension between their outer and inner elliptical contours. Stroke terminals also are elements that can be super stylized, as are joint shapes.

Extra. Bold. Ultra. Fine.

These hyperbolic characters exaggerate the contrast of stroke weights and the size of their dot-like forms—balancing serifs, tittles, and punctuation. In addition, the flare of curves within strokes overtakes what are typically straight strokes, as seen in the baseline of the capital E and B, and in the diagonals of the lowercase x. The energy of this face is further compounded by its setting on a rising baseline.

MADELINE DENEYS / AUSTRALIA
OLD SCHOOL NEW SCHOOL
Victoria Grow, instructor

Aa Bb Cc Ee Hh Kk Mm Pp Rr Ss Tt

In these condensed sans serif characters, a pronounced contrast in stroke weights accentuates the extreme rotation of the curved forms' axis off center. The x-height of the lowercase is unusually large; and the lower stories are clearly larger than the upper ones.

ERIKA FULTON / USA
PURCHASE COLLEGE SUNY
Timothy Samara, instructor

R Q N G K B

A relatively restrained character set with minimal contrast in weight gains added interest through an exaggeration of circularity, established by the Q. Note the extension of the R's and B's shoulders as they return to, and cross past, their stems; further, the diagonals of the R's leg and the N's dominant stroke, as well as the leg of the K, are drawn as curves; the upper-left joint in the N reveals a curvaceous terminal. The face is further characterized by the exaggerated size of the upper stories and counters, evident in the R, N, and K, and in the low rise of the G's throat.

MAXIMILLIAN POLLIO / USA
PURCHASE COLLEGE SUNY
Timothy Samara, instructor

REINTERPRETING ARCHETYPES

Of course, just because a particular character is archetypally configured from particular shapes doesn't mean it must always be made so. It's important to recognize that a character's form is not ncessarily wrapped up in the presence of curve, diagonal, or stem—what is truly important is that the stroke information made available in its design corresponds to readers' expectations of what its parts do, in relation to each other, to elicit recognition of the form as one character or another. A rectangle, triangle, or irregular blob can replace a curved stroke, for example, so long as it can be interpreted as fulfilling the structural function of the stroke that has been replaced.

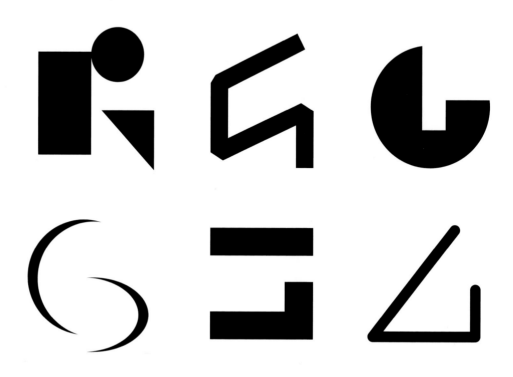

This character set reimagines all of the lowercase forms as structures composed of disconnected, parallel lines whose terminals are softly rounded.

PAONE DESIGN ASSOCIATES / USA

Wolos Capital

In looking at this logo for a financial services firm, one is reminded how little information is really necessary to recognize a letter—in this case, a capital W.

The success of this mark lies in its designer's recognition of a simple truth: that any two dots describe a line between them.

MOVING BRANDS / UK

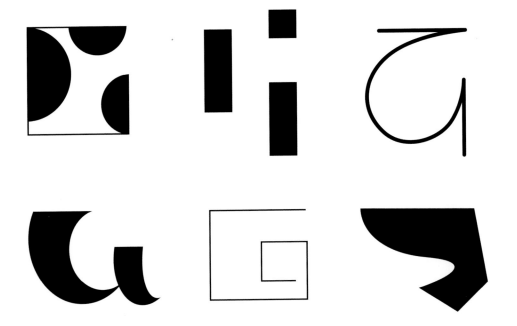

This array of variations on the form of a capital G suggests how far the characteristics of a form's archetype might be pushed. Although this study was developed without a brief in mind or for any particular project, it demonstrates how liberating such thinking can be, and how useful: Consider each of these a letter-based logo, for instance. Among the limited number of iterations shown here, one could envision brand marks for a variety of clients.

This logo for a Swedish construction firm builds an S from angled planes—a complete reversal of the character's archetype, which is fundamentally about a single curve.

ATIPO FOUNDRY / SPAIN

The many alternate characters created as part of this font illustrate, in practical terms, how varied the archetype of even a single letterform can be reinvented.

TYPOTHÈQUE / NETHERLANDS

RIFFING ON FUNDAMENTALS

IMPOSING A VISUAL IDEA

It's a short leap from exaggerating a structural norm, or reinterpreting how an archetype can be changed and remain recognizable, to feeling free enough to introduce a purely formal gesture, or conceit, into the visualization of letterforms. Such imposed conditions might be structural in their basis—for instance, altering the characters' conventional distribution of stroke weight—or it might be more surface-related—interrupting the characters' basic shapes with a pattern. Given that conventional drawing media impart specific mark shapes and textures, allowing evidence of such media can even be considered a visual conceit if they demonstrably affect the shaping of characters and aren't simply textural embellishments.

Contrary to convention, the weight in these forms is located around their joints, creating an interesting tension between geometric and organic qualities.

DESIGNER UNKNOWN / USA
PURCHASE COLLEGE SUNY
Timothy Samara, instructor

A pattern of lines, in the negative, interrupts the continuity of the characters' stroke formation in this experimental face. Further, the characters themselves have had a specific weight logic imposed on them: the left-hand side of the characters is constructed of a lightweight stroke or strokes, while their right-hand side is made of heavy ones. The reversed line pattern creates the impression of secondary, positive line patterns, as well.

DESIGNER UNKNOWN / USA
PURCHASE COLLEGE SUNY
Timothy Samara, instructor

ACEHIRT

The character set shown here was derived from a project about water scarcity; the visual idea was to reduce the amount of stroke information—especially at the joints—to convey the idea of drying out. The remaining heavier elements, smoothly modulating into nothingness, seem to be getting absorbed into cracks in the surface.

DESIGNER UNKNOWN / USA
PURCHASE COLLEGE SUNY
Timothy Samara, instructor

EAOR
efakgrx

Two visual ideas were imposed on the characters of this set: First, the forms are primarily rectangular and skewed to appear in perspective; second, their internal counters have been skewed in the opposite direction.

In this character set, regularity of proportion and shaping take a backseat to two imposed visual traits. First, the overall language is one that emulates crystalline planes, creating facets within each of the letters.

Second, the forms are made using a pen or marker, and that tool's casually varied line weight is retained to impart a softer, more organic counterpoint to the geometry of the facet-like construction.

RIFFING ON FUNDAMENTALS

EXTREME MASH-UPS

In the previous chapter, the idea of hybridizing characteristics from different style classes was discussed as an option for inventing a new typeface. The assumption in that context was that the intention in doing so would be to seamlessly integrate those characteristics and still frame the desired design outcome in terms of a conventional, unified text style.

Why stop there?

By all means, see what happens if one carries that thinking a little further—or much further!

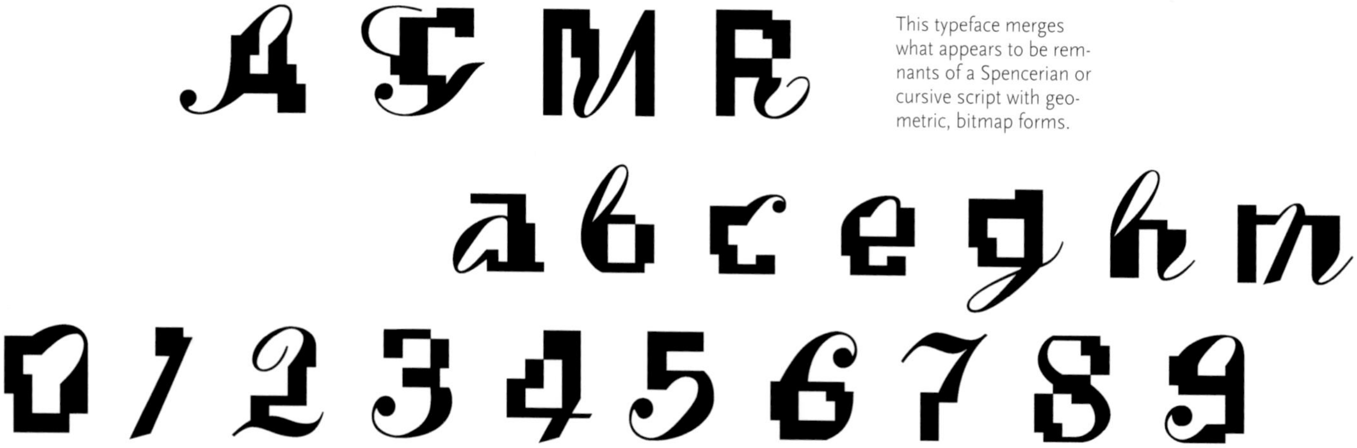

ADEFGHN

befh

0123456

This typeface merges what appears to be remnants of a Spencerian or cursive script with geometric, bitmap forms.

NTUZ

mrtuvxyz

789

This hybrid of transitional serif forms with those of a rounded, geometric sans serif, was designed by P. Scott Makela—a designer aligned with the Post-Structural movement of the 1980s and 90s. It makes no bones about the disconnect between its stylistic components, allowing their boundaries to crash into each other and, sometimes, their formal elements to cross those boundaries.

ADEFHIKNO

RSTUWY

adefhiknorst

uwy

0123456789

At first glance, this bold, extended, rectilinear sans serif seems quite normal—especially compared to the other specimens shown on this page spread. Closer inspection reveals a simple, but effective, hybrid solution that integrates hard-edged, linear strokes with irregular, textured brushstrokes.

DESIGNER UNKNOWN / USA
PURCHASE COLLEGE SUNY
Timothy Samara, instructor

GETTING SPONTANEOUS

It's hard to let go. Designers often forget that typography's origins lie in calligraphy (okay technically, that's not true, but the point here is more important than that). The point is that type is about writing; writing is gestural and spontaneous, and a type designer can embrace that visceral truth as a starting point, even if the outcome is a tightly regimented translation of written form that isn't even a script. Greek and Roman writing, if one recalls, were originally hacked, primitvely, into the surfaces of stones—and are inarguably beautiful as a result.

So, one might just accept the visual power that gestural writing offers, warts and all, in the quest for a new kind of form. That might mean keeping the textural evidence of the tool as part of the design, or eliminating it altogther in favor of a refined form that yet retains the spontaneous quirks of its source.

A script alphabet with a rough, calligraphic approach that embraces the texture of a dry brush, finds elegance in the form of curled, swash-like terminals and a delicate sway in a number of the stems.

Working spontaneously to generate rough forms as part of an investigation may point the way toward an overtly calligraphic approach in the end—but it just as well may not. The rough study at far left, made using a piece of inked cardboard, could simply suggest unusual structures and details to incorporate into a more refined or constructed face, as shown in this character.

DESIGNER UNKNOWN / USA
PURCHASE COLLEGE SUNY
Timothy Samara, instructor

Taking a slightly different tack, the forms in this character set aim for a suggestion of control as a counterpoint to their extremely aggressive gesture by enforcing a contrived, triangular structure on the curves.

AGMRS

abeghm

AGMQRS

adefgkm

Both of these script forms retain clear evidence of their calligraphic origins, despite having their contours cleaned up and their proportions regularized.

The script at top follows a chancery model that displays an occasional inline—a detail just as revealing of its pen-drawn origin as are its sharp, flat terminals. The script immediately above is less refined with regard to width and weight consistency, allowing the irregularities of its drawing to live as they were made.

NEW TOOLS, NEW OPTIONS

RETOOLING THE OLDSCHOOL

Familiarity with using studio tools to accomplish specific tasks can blind one to their potential if used in unexpected ways. For instance, the form language most typical of a wetly inked brush is one of sloping, wiggling, curvaceous, interconnected, river-y blobs—but see what happens if the brush is slapped onto the working surface: a new kind of mark! Investigating how varied the possible uses of a tool may be can yield critically important knowledge.

Tools typically used for one purpose can also be appropriated for other purposes, like drawing. An eyedropper, for example, exists to deposit drops of liquid; if it's dragged across a surface while being squeezed, it makes lines, not drops—and these can be changed by altering the duration and force of compression on the dropper's bulb.

Printing methods, including cutting reliefs from potatoes (and inking them), as well as using stencils to alter how one is affecting a drawing surface underneath, both offer beautiful alternatives to directly gestural mark making.

The character studies to the right were made with an eyedropper to help the designer understand the variety of marks it could make among different forms.

After extensive investigation, the designer selected those attributes that provided the greatest formal consistency and translated them into the character set below. She chose to keep some explicit evidence of the dropper's inking irregularities while refining other elements in the set.

DESIGNER UNKNOWN / USA
PURCHASE COLLEGE SUNY
Timothy Samara, instructor

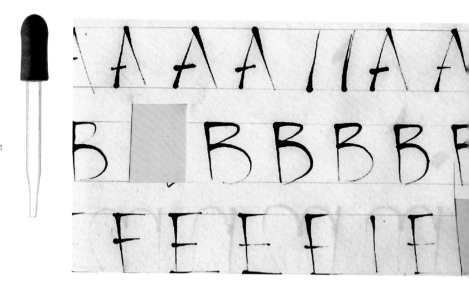

Dramatic new effects can be achieved with an exceedingly familiar tool by simple means:

The N at far left was drawn by cinching two brushes together with a rubber band. The E to the immediate left was made by covering a toothpick with paint and rolling one end of it.

DESIGNERS UNKNOWN / USA
PURCHASE COLLEGE SUNY
Timothy Samara, instructor

The characters in the set below were created by inking a block of wood—pulled from the furniture of a letterpress.

DESIGNER UNKNOWN / USA
PURCHASE COLLEGE SUNY
Timothy Samara, instructor

Paper offers wonderful potential as a drawing medium—from a conventional approach (ripped strips) as seen in the large A below; to more inventive ones, as with the set R E A to the left, made by gluing a white sheet to a black sheet and then peeling off the top layer. In the image at the bottom of the page, stencils and spray paint were used to investigate texture.

DESIGNERS UNKNOWN / USA
PURCHASE COLLEGE SUNY
Timothy Samara, instructor

GRAPHICAL ALTERATIONS

Instead of drawing forms from scratch, manipulating existing ones offers yet another avenue for discovering unexpected typographic ideas. The emphasis here is on the word "unexpected": rather than aim for a predetermined effect, test a multitude of alterations without a goal in mind to remain open to a greater array of options.

Choose a single capital or lowercase letter with which to work. The letter selected may be of any style, but keep in mind that its particular formal qualities will be affected by graphical explorations in different ways than might another. In that regard, it might be helpful to test alterations on two or more differently styled specimens. Arrange several instances of the letter(s), at a height of roughly 2–3" (5 to 6 cm), on a single page and print a relatively large number of copies.

Perform a different manipulation on each instance of the letter(s), making sure the result of each is clear and dramatic. Manipulations may be accomplished digitally but, again, overfamiliarity with software can sometimes limit one's thinking—get out of your comfort zone and explore manual techniques that you're less likely to be able to control.

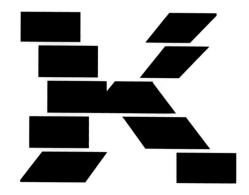

Any basic strategy—for example, slicing—can be explored in a number of ways each yielding a different effect. The K above was sliced horizontally with a studio knife and its parts shifted laterally. Had it been sliced vertically, or at an angle, the effect on its structure would have been different.

The K to the left was traced onto a thin, spongy surface, cut out, and then sliced in multiple directions. Scanning it and increasing its contrast simplified the results into a solid, purely positive/negative image.

The K at lower left was simply ripped and then photocopied in successive generations to pull out a gritty texture along its ripped edges.

Letter studies on these pages
KEVIN HARRIS / USA
SCHOOL OF VISUAL ARTS
Timothy Samara, instructor

The manipulations shown here comprise a number of hand-generated solutions that range from cutting and reordering parts, to pasting printed graphic elements together, to crumpling, to redrawing with a marker and ruler. With a little time and imagination, hundreds, if not thousands, of unique strategies may be invented and tested individually or combined. An abridged list of possibilities is provided as a jumping-off point at lower right.

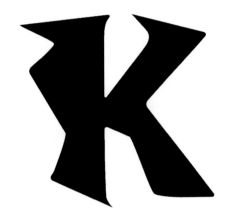

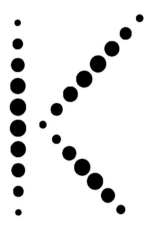

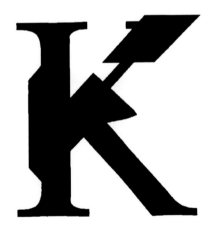

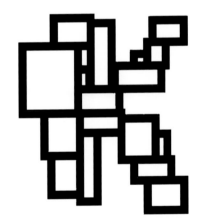

Sample Strategies

Scribbling / Rough tracing / Outlining / Contour drawing / Erasing / Shredding / Smearing / Folding / Tearing / Disintegrating / Scratching / Scoring / Rubbing / Roughening / Slicing and dicing / Shifting parts / Soaking / Puncturing / Perforating / Burning / Spattering / Photocopy degeneration / Remaking with foreign elements /

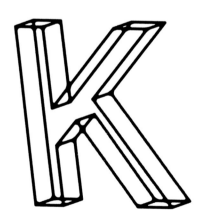

MODULAR CONSTRUCTION

On the other hand, pursuing entirely digital investigations is certainly an option— and there's no more fundamentally digital formal structure than that of the pixel or, considered more expansively, working with a repeated module to build letterforms.

It goes without saying that drawing and image-making software are ideal for this kind of approach because of their facility for automated repetition—copying and pasting, rotating, inverting position, and so on. The process can be extremely rapid and generate a huge number of variations to compare in a short time.

One chief consideration when using a modular approach is the "resolution" of the grid—how many units high, how many deep. The fewer units there are, the more challenging it will be to differentiate similar forms, like an O and a D, especially because curves may not be available. Still, working with a square, pixel-like module isn't the only option. The module itself may be any shape, and one need not necessarily restrict oneself to only one module shape. For that matter, the modular elements need not be arranged on a grid structure at all.

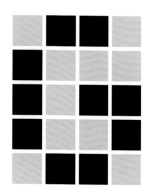
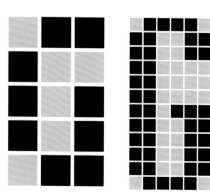

A square grid of two different resolutions— one coarse, or made of fewer modules (far left) and one that is much finer (near left) show the effects of this fundamental characteristic on the possible complexity and detail of the letter made with each.

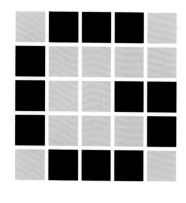
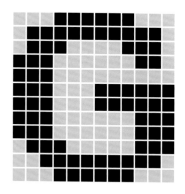

Further altering the field of modules by reducing the number of units left to right—in essence, enforcing a condensed character width—greatly exaggerates the difference in overall presentation that the letter will achieve.

Modules need not necessarily be square or follow the notion of a pixel. Here, two faces each use a module of differing shape and complexity, although both order the modules on an orthogonal grid.

Another variation to explore is the use of more than one kind of module shape. In the typeface to the right, two basic forms—a square and a trapezoid, or a sheared rectangle—were recombined, sometimes being allowed to overlap to create the appearance of other shapes.

In the extended typeface below, a rounded line segment, a dot, and a diagonal detail element merged in a somewhat binary, or digital, formation.

Modularity can also be conceived as a kind of dimensional construct, as in this typeface. The characters' strokes are selected instances of the parts of a wireframe figure (above); each level's horizontal axis was also made available to help introduce strict horizontal strokes into the forms.

DIGITAL MANIPULATION

Software tools themselves offer an abundant source for altering letter shapes to find new kinds of form. Most designers tend to be comfortable using such functions as distortion or warping, or filter operations, on pictorial material, but they are often reluctant to examine the effects of these techniques on type. Less experienced designers (in particular, students) and those who lean toward dogmatic thinking tend to be overly concerned with what they perceive as type forms' sacred quality. Get over it—and get your digital freak on.

Whether one chooses to construct a few basic character shapes with which to work or simply set a few from an existing font, the vector-based tools of an illustration program provide the most direct means of interacting with type forms in a digital environment— given that these forms are vector shapes that consist of points, the line segments that join them, and their interior fill colors.

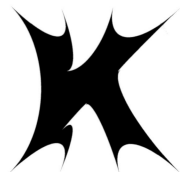

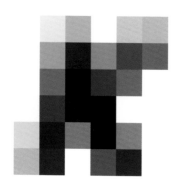

Bitmap-based imaging software encourages photographic, or continuous tone, experimentation which, based on the pixel as its medium, can range from softening of contours to creating pattern forms, and from overlaying transparent splices of shapes in that blend positive and negative in unexpected ways to creating distortion and textured surfaces.

Selecting points or segments around a type form and moving them, or transforming selected parts using the editing transformations (such as scaling, warping, and shearing) are several of many options such software allows. Another is to apply filters to the selected outline forms.

As ready-made effects that are commonly recognizable (and, sometimes, somewhat cheap or cartoonish), the filters require testing how altering their respective parameters might yield less expected results (for instance, increasing or decreasing the number of generators in a wave-texture filter, or the amplitude and direction to be applied). A single filter can transform the same target in hundreds of ways—and there are hundreds of filters.

PHOTOGRAPHIC STRATEGIES

The interplay of light and dimensional form that photography entails offers unique possibilities for altering letter structure. The medium of photography is now, essentially, a digital one. Trying to find an actual film camera is difficult and usually expensive; developing and printing photographic images from film negatives, even more so (as well as being time consuming, and requiring specialized expertise).

In recent years, however, digital cameras and their software (even inexpensive ones, or those integrated into smartphones—have been developed to include functions that mimic some of the effects that were possible with conventional film cameras: long exposures to allow blur as the camera is moved while the shutter is open; multiple-exposing two images in one frame; allowing light to leak into the camera; flash effects; and so on.

It's important to keep in mind that image scanners and photocopiers, as well as cameras, are photographic technologies. These can be used to generate chance effects by moving a letter image across the imaging bed while being scanned; holding a print of a letter away from the bed, or at an angle, or inserting some kind of refractive material as interference, can also affect the scanned image in interesting ways. Last, but not least, of course, the photographic filter operations in imaging software are ripe with potential.

Photographing the play of light across volumes in space and then masking them into existing forms is a simple strategy for involving photography.

The characters above were created this way, using an image of a metal, roll-down security gate as a source image.

Another strategy, and somewhat more complicated, is to isolate components from photographed scenes, and then composite them; equally interesting is the tactic of projecting letters across objects or environments to deform them, and then photographing them—or lighting cut-out letters to cast shadows and doing the same. The images captured can then be processed to change their densities and contrast as one likes.

One of the most readily available strategies— and one that is exceptionally fun—is moving subjects on the bed of a scanner or photocopier as the input head moves from one end to the other. Moving the subject slowly will produce more continous warping effects (as shown at left), while abruptly repositioning the subject will typically introduce a choppy, staggered, and fractured result in the image.

KEVIN HARRIS / USA
SCHOOL OF VISUAL ARTS
Timothy Samara, instructor

Because the photographic medium is now inherently digital, imaging software is an easy go-to for generating visual effects that riff on those one could only create with a camera in the past. Blurring, for example, is more easily accomplished by using the tools of such a program than it is by shaking a camera during a long exposure.

The added benefit is that, like filters in vector-based drawing software, photographic effects filters also may be controlled as to how they affect subject matter through options for changing their parameters. All three of the B specimens here, for example, are instances of different kinds of blur control.

High-contrast photographic film that exposed only the highlights and shadows in an image, while leaving the midtones out, used to be the only way to achieve a detailed, high-contrast image of the kind above.

Fortunately, changing the value and density levels of an image using software will accomplish the same effect—and more varied ones— within seconds.

The characters shown here began life as rough forms cut from tissue paper that was then crumpled; the designer tested different lighting situations and, in combination with rubbing charcoal onto some of the surfaces, succeeded

in generating photographs that revealed the crumpling in exceptional detail. The images were altered digitally and, eventually, different parts were composited together.

RHIANN IRVINE / USA
PURCHASE COLLEGE SUNY
Timothy Samara, instructor

TELLING STORIES

FEELINGS MADE VISUAL

Both pictorially and nonpictorially derived strategies may be used to powerful effect in the formation of letters. The intrinsic form language of a typeface, established by its stroke-and-counter alternation, weight, width, and details, automatically carries nonpictorial narrative. Interpretations of elegance, romance, or sensuousness attend typeface styles that are lighter and more linear, express fluidity in the modulation of weight in their curves. Light, extended typefaces seem graceful, open, and calm, while bold ones read as aggressive, authoritative, or loud.

Beyond such basic formal qualities, though, a designer might also incorporate abstract or illustrative elements that evoke a variety of emotional experiences or states of mind. The specific tool used to make the forms will itself add its own language of effects—in concert with, or even independent of, the designer's choices of proportion and formal detail. The diagonal, linear pattern of a brush over a textured surface may lend a sense of connectivity, as well as environment, to a bold, authoritative face.

This bold, italic slab serif leans engagingly to the right; its thick, rounded strokes feel soft and cuddly, but perky.

The font at right combines script elements—which impart an unstudied, honest quality—with an exceptionally large lowercase whose proportions seem almost childlike.

The light, extended sans serif below is relatively stately, but it also exudes a sense of calm—because of its wide dimensions—and directness, which results from its light-weight, open counters, and crisp terminals.

These fonts, on the other hand, come across as sinister or dangerous.

The top specimen conveys these qualities through its torn, seemingly violated contours and the unreliable distribution of weights; some of its counters are also eye-like.

The specimen in the middle also exhibits disturbingly irregular contours, as well as strange growths from its strokes, suggesting tendrils, or perhaps pins,

holding them in place so they don't escape.

The specimen at the bottom is formed of bold verticals that descend from shallow crossbars and terminate in pointy shapes, suggesting an iron gate. It also makes reference to gothic or blackletter types from the Middle Ages, which are commonly associated with films of the horror genre.

A G M R

A G M R

These two typefaces feel fragile; the exceedingly light sans serif (top) seems brittle, as though it's about to come apart, while the textured sans serif (bottom) could be interpreted to be formed from glass or ice.

A G M R

A G M R S

A G M R

The grouping of fonts above feel dynamic in different ways: through energetic, diagonal splicing that causes the forms to vibrate, almost electrically (top); through extreme extension and sleek, monotone strokes that expand with great velocity across the page (middle); or through extreme boldness (always a contributor to a sense of power) and an exaggerated backslant, which causes the forms to feel as though they've suddenly, and unexpectedly, lurched—the feeling is enhanced by the intrusion of sharp, angular counters (bottom).

A G M R

A G M R

A G M R S

In these typefaces, unsual stroke shaping and graphical details might be interpreted as exotic, mystical, or alien, depending on the context in which they might be encountered.

A G M R

A G M R

A D G M R

In this grouping, all of the faces convey a quality of artificiality or contrivance, mostly because they appear to be purposely constructed of disparate elements—the elements don't seem likely to have come together naturally. The middle example has the quality of a machine or toy; the one at bottom shows evidence of having been hewn from a surface.

EVOKING TIME AND CONTEXT

Whether it's in fulfillment of a project's design brief and communication goals, or just for the pure fun of it, investigating typographic forms from other eras, cultures, or locales can be a solid basis on which to develop a new font. First, consider that the formal aspects of many existing, older typefaces are characteristic of the time and place they were created, as well as of specific technological conditions.

For a given project that requires it—say, designing a titling treatment for a poster about a Baroque architecture exhibit— a designer may be more apt to follow the relevant historical model more closely, producing a kind of "period piece." On the other hand, reinterpreting the form language of a historcial face in a less refer- ential way, by simplifying or abstracting it, can lead the way to creating an appropriate allusion to the historical subject that is, nonetheless, fresh and contemporary.

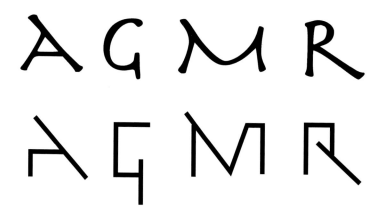

The font immediately to the left is a translation, or reinvention, of an ancient Greek form. It has been somewhat stylized and made more regular in its rhythm than is true of its historical precedent. Below it, however, is a geometric reinterpretation that carries this historical baggage, but casts it in a more contemporary voice.

Similar to the examples at the top of the page, these two typefaces are based on blackletter forms. The one to the left is a systematic, highly reduced interpretation. The one above is more referential of its source, although its stems have been thickened to an extreme and its details also have been simpli- fied. Further, the lower- case has been enlarged to a more contemporary proportion; and the sty- listic logic between the uppercase and lowercase has been brought into a greater state of unity or correspondence.

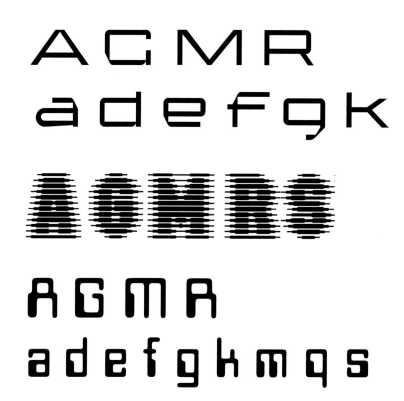

Both of the fonts above are likely to remind one of the 1950s, for different reasons. The top specimen is an industrial script that refers to automobile styling from that era.

The specimen immediately above is constructed of graphical forms that refer to the same period's most prevalent artistic genres—Biomporphism and Abstract Expressionism.

All three of the specimens above exhibit qualities that convey notions about technology and, perhaps, of science or the future.

In differing contexts, they might come across as historical or even campy, like a B-grade science fiction movie, or as rather forward looking.

These three specimens speak to the Victorian age in England and the U.S., the period roughly from 1880 to the early 1910s. The top specimen captures the geometric organicism of English Art Nouveau; the specimen in the middle is similar to many wood-type slab serifs that gained popularity in England and the U.S. during that period; the specimen at the bottom combines details from period-relevant architectural styles, like the Arts & Crafts or Mission style, as well as wrought ironwork that was characteristic of architecture in Chicago and New York at that time.

VERNACULAR MESSAGES

The tool or method used to visualize a new type form may itself derive from some commonly understood source, typographic or otherwise—a vernacular experience. Designers might draw inspiration from all manner of day-to-day, "undesigned" visual sources: the dot-matrix printing of sales receipts and customer information on airline tickets; a supermarket's painted promotional signs; street graffiti; forms used by scientists to diagram or model a particular kind of data; and so on.

Of all well-liked vernacular references, typewriter type is probably the most beloved. It occupies a strange territory in cultural consiousness, somewhere between nostalgia and old-school mechanical chic; a kind of office-punk realm that is both prosaic and weirdly symbolic.

A G M R S

a d e f g k m q

! ? & @ $: ; " "

The quick brown fox jumps over the lazy dog.

Many branches of science have their own, particular graphical gestures for visualizing aspects of the natural world. This typeface draws upon methods used to represent molecular and atomic structures, like benzene rings and peptides. Much like chemistry itself, it assmebles a palette of elements— solid strokes and inline strokes, strokes with flags for terminals and those with dots—and organizes them in a near-modular structure to form the characters.

DANIELLE WEINBERGER / USA
PURCHASE COLLEGE SUNY
Timothy Samara, instructor

H N T J U C Y
F A L E O G S
e a n g f i h t c
0 1 2 3 4 5 6 7

Next to (or, perhaps, ahead of) typewriter type in the lexicon of designers' typographic indulgences are graffiti forms that first surfaced in the late 1970s in urban America—reviled as vandalism and then, later, accorded a place of prestige in the art world.

Graffiti walks a line between display face and script form. Like other major classes of letter style, it too occurs in a variety of subclassifications that encompass calligraphic styles, block lettering, inlines, outlines, and shadow styles, as well as decorated and illustrative ones.

As a script, it's the most contemporary kind in a long continuum of such faces—and likely the edgiest of them all.

Day-to-day, commonly lived experience is the backbone of vernacular expression. People from all walks of life, working in the home or in an office, are always making things; if they're not artists or designers by education or profession, those things come into being from a place of honesty and authenticity, never mind a little naïvete.

The realm of home crafts and housekeeping, especially that which occupies a fond place in collective memory, is a wellspring of charming visual languages. This typeface evokes one such trope: hand-embroidered samplers of a bygone time.

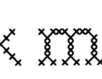

TELLING STORIES

CONCEPTUAL NARRATIVES

Yet another option for narrative story-telling through the design of a font lies in incorporating pictorial, as well as abstract, formal gestures that capture more complex associations. A face that is intricately constructed of industrially-evocative details, for instance, may refer to iron architecture; irregular contours and weight changes may suggest a rough-hewn material, like stone; sharp, partially edited outlines may suggest the unknown in a difficult experience. The more stylized the form, the more specific or concrete its message is likely to be.

This approach is exceptionally well-suited for developing a bespoke house face as part of a branding system, but especially for the development of a client's identifying wordmark. The details of a complete typeface will give specific character to the communications produced as part of such a system; used to visualize a single word or short phrase—like a logotype or a book title—the letters' form language will un-pack its multiple potential meanings and emphasize a particular understanding.

Even a single word with an apparently unequiv-ocal meaning, such as the one above, can be unpacked, shaded, and otherwise transformed into a conceptual allusion to some specific aspect of its meaning.

The second example hints at dimensionality and enclosures of space. In the middle, hairline strokes articulate mini-malist apertures within

The example at top uses volumetric forms that speak to architecture's play of mass and light.

the geometry of a square, a hypermodern aesthetic.

In the fourth example from the top, small blocks suggest bricks and the modularity of construction.

The example at the very bottom, which includes characters that are missing strokes and others that are blunt cut, express the mono-lithic and primitive heritage of building or, perhaps, suggest the architectural style known as Brutalism.

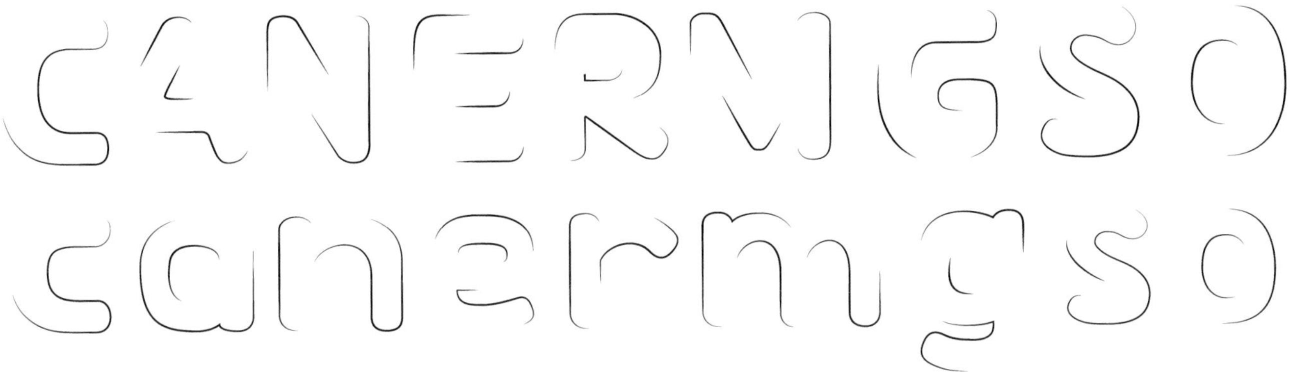

CANERMGSO

canermgso

This character set was designed to represent Cancer Management Centers, its disappearing strokes meant to suggest the disappearance of tumors and a progression to remission.

DONALD BRADY / USA
PURCHASE COLLEGE SUNY
Timothy Samara, instructor

In this typeface, developed for BioBank, a life sciences, company, the designer established a group of robust capitals whose shaping mixes sharp, technological angles and sloping, organic forms, alternating in their relationships from character to character.

The massive stroke area of each capital form encloses (and appears to protect) dot-like, cellular details and circuit-like linear counters.

DESIGNER UNKNOWN / USA
PURCHASE COLLEGE SUNY
Timothy Samara, instructor

ABCDEF
GHIJKLN

THGOSEIRFNL

enghridoftls

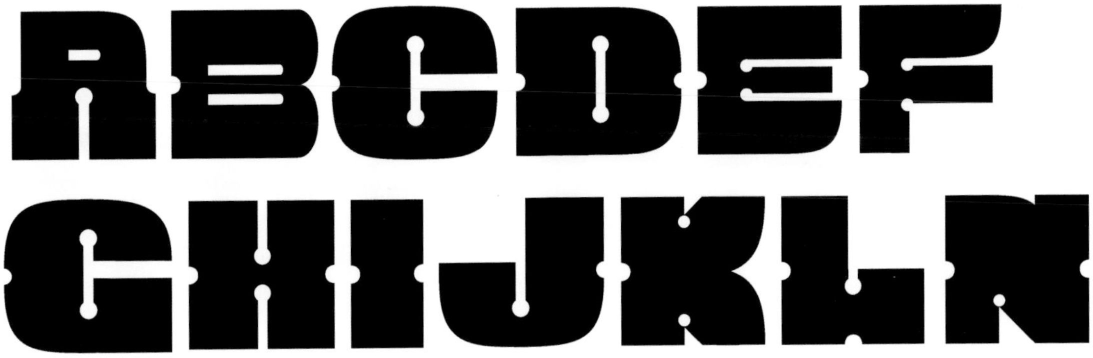

A house face for the High Line, an urban park reclaimed from an elevated train track, references the iron couplings and luminous sheen of the tracks; a horizontal inline detail visually connects the uppercase letters all at the same level, creating a space that suggests a path through a dense city environment.

PHILLIP WONG / USA
PURCHASE COLLEGE SUNY
Timothy Samara, instructor

OBJECTS AS INSPIRATION—OR FORM ITSELF

At the most image-like and extremely narrative end of display-font design options are those whose stroke structures are derived from pictorial forms. A designer may choose to pursue this idea in a very literal way (assembling characters' strokes with actual images of objects, whether naturalistic or stylized); alternatively, he or she may prefer a less direct visualization, opting instead to identify recognizable formal qualities of the objects under consideration and then translate them more abstractly.

Although it's important to keep an eye on the legibility of exaggerated experiments, it's equally important to remember that the alphanumeric characters are remarkably resilient when it comes to manipulation—designers often have a lot more leeway for experimentation than they may initially suppose. Ultimately, it's this robustness of the Western alphabet's structure that allows for reinterpreting its forms, and so continually evolving it in new ways.

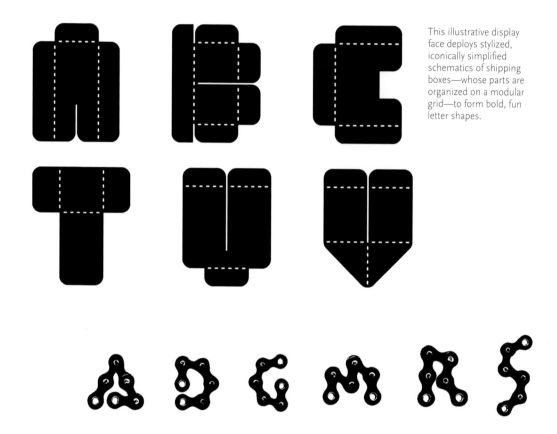

This illustrative display face deploys stylized, iconically simplified schematics of shipping boxes—whose parts are organized on a modular grid—to form bold, fun letter shapes.

The inspiration for this character set, developed in relation to a poster promoting a rock-climbing organization, was—well, rocks. A combination of irregularly rounded forms and sharper, jagged ones interact in different ways from character to character.

Much of the designer's attention concentrated on finding consistencies in the contrasts that occurred in each instance, despite the fact that sharper and rounder forms would confront each other in different locations. Further, the irregular weights of each character were adjusted so that relatively similar weight values

and weight changes would appear in every character. The result is a somewhat seamless overall weight, shaping and proportion logic that carries throughout.

ANDREW SCHEIDERICH / USA
PURCHASE COLLEGE SUNY
Timothy Samara, instructor

Similar to the font inspired by stones on the opposite page, these letters play with the tension between organic irregularity and systematic relationships. Note the similarity in proportion and ovoid shaping between the eye of the lowercase e, the lower story of the lowercase a, and the upper lobe of the capital R.

Further, each letter incorporates three line weights and a more massive element to establish uniformity from erratically organic material.

JESSICA DEANGELIS / USA
PURCHASE COLLEGE SUNY
Timothy Samara, instructor

Photographs of bicycle-chain segments were processed into high-contrast outlines to construct the characters of this font. Using images of the actual object imparts a casual, comfortable naturalism to the characters, while maintaining a slightly industrial edge. As a system of lines made from joined dots, the typeface is technically a modular construction. An interesting tension arises as a result of the individual character shapes being limited by the physical mechanics of the chains themselves: a modular concept, disturbed by an imposed irregularity.

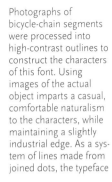

Even the most prosaic of office materials can find their way into the formation of typographic shapes that elevate the lowly object—even while they bring the highbrow notion of type design back down to Earth.

Since 1990, the number of available typefaces has increased more than tenfold—from perhaps 30,000 to nearly 500,000, based on some current estimates. Add to that an uncountable number of letter signs, wordmarks, and titling treatments, and the magnitude of typographic exploration approaches the astronomical in scope. Assembled here are examples of typeface design and lettering recently produced for all kinds of application. Whether created for extensive reading in an editorial context or for a single product name on packaging, each exploits knowledge of the discipline's history and respects its precedents. This is so even when the goal is to fight them and reinvent accepted forms to create a newly conceptual experience.

The State of the Art

**A SHOWCASE
OF CONTEMPORARY
DIRECTIONS IN
LETTERFORM DESIGN**

COMA DISPLAY FACE
BARNBROOK / UK

This bold, geometrically constructed inline face wryly comments on popular culture with elements that evoke electronic networks and toys, pill cases, and sporting apparel.

TREMOLO FAMILY
TYPOTHÈQUE / NETHERLANDS

An extensive range of calligraphic semi-serifs incorporates solid-stroke, inline, shadowed, and two-tone variants—along with idiosyncratic details (note the tittles!)—to offer numerous expressive, yet craftsmanly, options for the typographer.

COMA / IS / THE / TORPOR / THAT / WE / LIVE / IN / EVERY / DAY / OF / OUR / LIVES

Calligraphers

Influx Artiste

Brainwasher

Middle Earth

Snoop Doggy

Megalomania

Revolution 46

Rock & Rolla!

BEVERAGE BRANDING
MUCCA DESIGN / USA

This wordmark for a brand of energy drink brewed from guayusa (an Amazonian tree leaf) employs inline detailing to suggest its regional heritage in a contemporary, sans serif presentation.

CANELA FAMILY
COMMERCIAL TYPE / UK

This warm, quietly confident serif began life as an interpretation of Caslon, but shed its explicit serifs in favor of gently flared terminals that recall the classical texture of stone-carved Roman types.

REAL ESTATE BRANDING
SOMEONE / UK

A handsome and sober, yet elegant, monogram for a refurbished and repurposed multiuse property (Devonshire Quarter) concisely merges the two letters of its initials.

QUARTO FAMILY
HOEFLER & CO. / USA

This robust serif draws from 16th-century Dutch display faces created by Hendrik Van den Keere. Its arresting design results from controlled contrasts: strong verticals and lavish curvature; steadfast rhythm and sudden, sharp turns; heavy thicks and razor-bright serifs.

Großstadt
WARSAW
Adjacency
Lavorazione
TYTUŁÓW
Psychologist

EQUITABLY
Promulgated
CAMPANARIO
Uomgængeligt
GRECQUES
Repülőtérrel
NOMINATION
Idiosyncrasies

Civilization Netherlands
Lichtenstein Architecture
Photography International
Meadowgrass Michelangelo
Knightsbridge Composition

WRIGHT
ADAMA

ART AUCTION HOUSE BRANDING
THIRST / USA (TOP)

A high-contrast, all-capital, italic form with intriguing ligatures and missing strokes conveys credibility and a sense of risk taking.

BEAUTY & LIFESTYLE BRANDING ANAGRAMA / MEXICO (BOTTOM)

Extreme contrast, pronounced joint details, exaggerated proportions, and a unifying diagonal lend chic energy to this exquisitely classical serif wordmark.

MR. K SCRIPT FACE
JULIASYS STUDIO / GERMANY

Julia Sysmäläinen, the designer of this fluid, energetic script, exploits OpenType's capacity for extensive alternate glyphs to generate a specimen that is at once tightly refined and yet very humanly spontaneous in its presentation.

IDEAL SANS FAMILY
HOEFLER & CO. / USA

Instead of rigid austerity, this humanist sans serif family exudes warmth and organicism by flouting geometry in favor of classical, hand-drawn details and proportions.

Outstanding Capital Stock

Globex Associated Broker

Settlement to the Market

Opening Rotation Order

Assigned Short Position

Fundamental Research

Exchange Supervision

Conversion Premium

Depository Transfer Cheque

Open End Investment Trust

Mutual Capital Certificate

Electronic Trading System

Quoting in Inverse Terms

Cross Exchange Trading

Daily Settlement Price

Automated Exchange

TELECOM BRANDING
MOVING BRANDS / UK

A friendly, dimensional, script-form logo gives rise to an equally friendly, bespoke, sans serif family by lending its signature curves—especially in un-conventional locations.

ABGMRQKS
adefgklmptx
0123456789

ABGMRQKS
adefgklmptx
0123456789

ABGMRQKS
adefgklmptx
0123456789

ABGMRQKS
adefgklmptx
0123456789

JASAN FAMILY
STORM TYPE FOUNDRY / CZECH REPUBLIC

This contemporary sans serif also approaches its design from a calligraphic, less-machined standpoint. Subtle modulation and variation in joint details contribute to a sense of honesty and accessibility in the family's extensive weight and width variants.

gnr

chефбг

Zz£&@

Nærøyfjord

WATERFALL VIEWPOINT 5 MIN.

Yggdrasil

Stalheimskleiva E16 ↗

pižmo tůně

Декадентный

HOTEL BRANDING
MUCCA DESIGN / USA

The house type style of a boutique hotel—rooted in the square-shouldered, industrial sans serifs of the early 20th century—draws upon the ad hoc mixing of multiple widths and weights by job printers during that era to render a visual language for the brand that is both casual and rigorously mechanical.

REAL ESTATE BRANDING
THIRST / USA

An algorithmic generator is used to continually reconstruct the logotype of a high-end commercial developer.

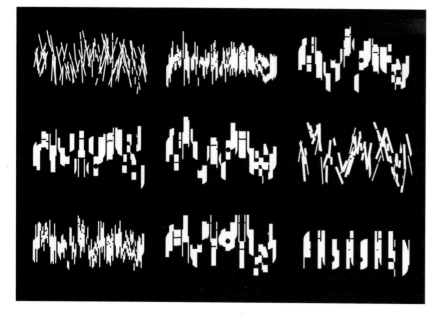

FRANCIS FAMILY
TYPOTHÈQUE / NETHERLANDS

Although the members of this high-contrast, sans serif family may be used effectively in a more conventional way for extensive text applications, the critical innovation here is its gradient options, which allow for rhythmic compression and expansion of text on the fly.

Light
Light Italic
Regular
Regular Italic
Medium
Medium Italic
Bold
Bold Italic
Heavy
Heavy Italic

FRANCIS INSIDE
FRANCIS OUTSIDE
FRANCIS RIGHT
FRANCIS LEFT

REMARKABLE TEXT PATTERNS ARE POSSIBLE BECAUSE EACH GRADIENT STYLE CONTAINS 2,690 GLYPHS THAT ARE SELECTED AUTOMATICALLY USING OPENTYPE'S CONTEXTUAL ALTERNATES FEATURE. THESE GRADIENT PATTERNS CAN BE APPLIED TO INDIVIDUAL WORDS, OR TO WHOLE LINES OF TEXT.

TO INFORM IS TO EDUCATE TO INVESTI— GATE IS TO INNOVATE TO DENY IS TO DENIGRATE AND TO FORBID IS TO FEAR

ICOH FONT
SEALSTUDIO / USA

This experimental display face by up-and-coming type designer Tré Seals riffs on drawing templates once used by architects.

Its unforgivingly mechanical quality is offset by a number of alternates that include condensed, extended, stenciled, and filled-counter options.

LIFESTYLE BRANDING
CHERMAYEFF & GEISMAR & HAVIV / USA

This letter-sign logo for a fashion company called Beehouse reconstructs the company name's initial in the hexagonal form of a beehive's honeycomb.

REAL ESTATE BRANDING
CHERMAYEFF & GEISMAR & HAVIV / USA

Another letter-sign logo, this time for a luxury, urban high-rise building—The Parkhouse—reveals its signature initial from an interrupted configuration of concentric circles.

MORTAL WHITELINE FAMILY
STORM TYPE FOUNDRY / CZECH REPUBLIC

The relentless geometry of this family's proportions and structure comes alive in its angularly cut terminals—truly visible only in its bolder weights, or in the light weight when set at large sizes—and in an in-line version that is almost electronically luminous.

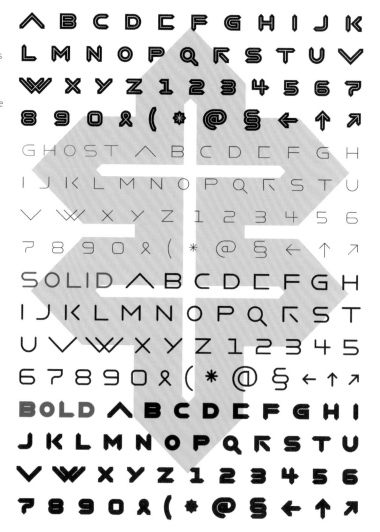

ARCHITECTURE FIRM BRANDING
PARALLAX / AUSTRALIA

A clever deconstruction of architectural details yields a brandmark that is exacting in its iconography, yet playful and creative.

EDITORIAL HEADLINE TREATMENT FAITH / CANADA

Letterforms constructed from sartorial details—buttons, seams, collar yokes, and so on—provide a fun take on the craft of tailoring in the headline treatment for a fashion magazine article.

VIVHO DISPLAY FACE
ESTUDIO PONCE CONTRERAS / SPAIN

The designer of this topically-informed typeface brings a note of optimism to what is usually a morose matter through bold, almost child-like forms that mix anxious sharpness and effusive circularity, lightning-like danger and romantic iconography.

INVESTMENT FIRM BRANDING SOMEONE / UK

This type-driven identity conveys the notions of interconnectivity and building (of wealth) through a bespoke, inline sans serif that integrates a modular construction approach.

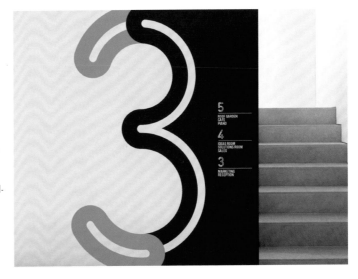

STENCIL MIX DISPLAY FACE ESTUDIO PONCE CONTRERAS & UN MUNDO FELIZ / SPAIN

Very simply, here is a display font that provides an array of letter styles, each available as an alternate for every character or glyph. All are unified by virtue of their drawing as stencil forms.

CULTURAL FESTIVAL BRANDING THONIK / NETHERLANDS

The identity program for the most recent iteration of a longstanding Dutch cultural festival trades on a stencil font that, in addition to its inherent characteristics, features a tremendous selection of character ligatures.

"RENIEGO DE LOS HUMANOS: SOLICITO UN PASA-PORTE DE PÁJARO"

DALA FLODA FAMILY
COMMERCIAL TYPE / UK

If there's any font offering of the stencil variety that has captured the imagination of designers in the past five years, it's this one—unexpectedly, and elegantly, based on Rationalist serifs of the 18th century.

VESTVÅGØY

Letterstaafje

ANTIQUITY

Lithography

BREUKELEN

Gleichmäßigen

PHILOSOPHY

Northumberland

EUCLID STENCIL DISPLAY FACE SWISS TYPEFACES / SWITZERLAND

This stencil variant distinguishes itself with stroke breaks that are independent of the letters' joints.

ABGMRSQ

gleefully mechanical

0123456789!

REAL ESTATE BRANDING
ANAGRAMA / MEXICO

A high-contrast, stencil approach ligates characters in this sharply austere, elegant wordmark. Note the graphical inclusion that substitutes the E's middle crossbar—and the visual completion of the R by the E's detached serifs.

EDITORIAL TITLING TREATMENT FAITH / CANADA

The extreme contrast—and unusual weight distribution—in these numerals elicits a sense of historical continuity and forward-looking futurism.

FASHION & LIFESTYLE BRANDING
MOVING BRANDS / UK

This monogram for a company called Material World is a concise, well-crafted hybrid of the initials of the client's name.

REAL ESTATE BRANDING
THIRST / USA

The logo and flexibly pro-
portionable modular alphabet designed to promote
a high-end rental property
draw from the building's
architecture and 1930s
typographic experiments
from Italy.

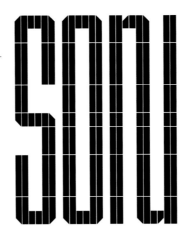

**FINANCIAL SERVICES
BRANDING**
MOVING BRANDS / UK

The dynamic interaction
of two cubic forms re-
imagines the inital S of the
client's name and suggests
a percent sign.

**ENTERTAINMENT
BRANDING**
CHERMAYEFF & GEISMAR
& HAVIV / USA

This letter-sign logo for
Screen Gems integrates
the forms of an S and G
with an iconic representation of a film reel.

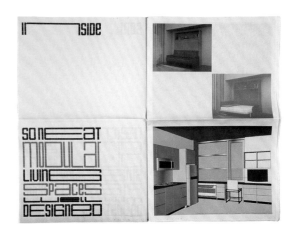

CULTURAL ENTITY BRANDING
PAONE DESIGN ASSOCIATES / USA

This letter-sign for the Greater Philadelphia Cultural Alliance (a nonprofit organization) merges the entity's initials in a single form, supported by a graphical language suggesting its community influence.

STEEL TRADING BRANDING
CHERMAYEFF & GEISMAR & HAVIV / USA

A custom, squared-off sans serif wordmark accompanies an abstracted letter-sign, both evoking an robust, industrial quality.

BEAUTY & LIFESTYLE BRANDING BARNBROOK / UK

The brandmark for Japanese fashion house Shiseido's men's fragrance reorients the Z character of the product name to form its terminal character, the N. Together with the type style's classical, Roman construction, the result is an elegant, but robustly masculine, style.

KRSNA DISPLAY FACE
SWISS TYPEFACES / SWITZERLAND

A bizarre set of character alternates—some combining linear, modular structures and others that incorporate pointy, diagonal strokes—come together with a set of more conventional set of geometric, sans serif capitals to create a font with unusual possibilities.

ART EXHIBITION BRANDING FAITH / CANADA

This wordmark incorporates alternating widths, high-contrast stroke weights, and idiosyncratic details to capture the Surrealism of an art exhibition's subject.

THEIR MONUMENTS STOOD—MASSIVE AND RESPLENDENT—OVER 11 DAYS

Cities of common ownership, private property & the sharing economy

DIE NORD-SÜDLICH AUSGERICHTETEN LÄNGSSTRASSEN ERHIELTEN NAMEN

Lățimea maximă (nord-sud) 178 km, este între între Cap Blanc și punctul

PICTOPIA DISPLAY FONT
UN MUNDO FELIZ / SPAIN

Created to support a series of sociopolitical icons, this irregularly contoured, condensed sans serif

provides an edgy feel for text and headlines without compromising the icons' massive, aggressive visual qualities.

VEIÐAR ALVEG VIÐ STRÖNDINA ERU MJÖG MIKILVÆGAR FYRIR

Przy rozmiarze klatki 9 × 11 cm oznacza to w przybliżeniu

Afterwards master distillers confirmed specific gravity

OVERTLY ALLUDED TO THE MODERNIST IDEOLOGY IN LATE 2001

Célébré comme l'un des peintres figuratifs américains du

DRUK FAMILY
COMMERCIAL TYPE / UK

Too extensive to show here, the Druk family of dramatic sans serifs comprises a system of some ten weights, each available in a variety of widths and intended applications—condensed and wide styles for text; super condensed and super extended styles for display; and everything in between. The family's overall stylistic qualities are derived from Dutch printers' grotesques from the first part of the 20th century and, so, carry with them the imprint of that stylistic era—updated for a contemporary sensibility.

MÅDER
Skrifað
Holding

The grand ceilings of the library echoed aghast

DEZENAS DE EVENTOS CULTURAIS DURANTE O VERÃO

TOWARDS THE ROLLING SOUNDSCAPE APPROACHING

Desemneazã o individualitate conştientã de sine

A B C D E F
G H I J K L
M N Ñ O P Q
LOVE SUMMER
PICTOPIA_68
TYPE
LA POLICE S'AFFICHE
AUX BEAUX ARTS
R S T U V W
X Y Z 1 2 3
4 5 6 7 8 9

UMF*

Morandi Serif

MORANDI SERIF LIGHT
abcdefghijklmnopqrstuvwxyz
ABCDEFGHIJKLMNOPQRSTUVWXYZ
12345678910

MORANDI SERIF REGULAR
abcdefghijklmnopqrstuvwxyz
ABCDEFGHIJKLMNOPQRSTUVWXYZ
12345678910

MORANDI SERIF HEAVY
abcdefghijklmnopqrstuvwxyz
ABCDEFGHIJKLMNOPQRSTUVWXYZ
12345678910

MORANDI SERIF BLACK
abcdefghijklmnopqrstuvwxyz
ABCDEFGHIJKLMNOPQRSTUVWXYZ
12345678910

Morandi Grotesque

MORANDI GROTESQUE LIGHT
abcdefghijklmnopqrstuvwxyz
ABCDEFGHIJKLMNOPQRSTUVWXYZ
12345678910

MORANDI GROTESQUE REGULAR
abcdefghijklmnopqrstuvwxyz
ABCDEFGHIJKLMNOPQRSTUVWXYZ
12345678910

MORANDI GROTESQUE HEAVY
abcdefghijklmnopqrstuvwxyz
ABCDEFGHIJKLMNOPQRSTUVWXYZ
12345678910

MORANDI GROTESQUE BLACK
abcdefghijklmnopqrstuvwxyz
ABCDEFGHIJKLMNOPQRSTUVWXYZ
12345678910

ABGMRS
adefgoptx
**ABGMRS
adefgoptx**
ABGMRS
adefgkoptx
*ABGMRS
adefgkoptx*

RESTAURANT BRANDING
MUCCA DESIGN / USA

These type families were developed to publicly characterise an Italian trattoria in New York City, responding to its casually elegant Italian country décor.

The challenge was to retain the authenticity unique to informal dining experiences in Italy without establishing a contrived quality for the brand.

The serif and sans serif families both deploy idiosyncratic details in their characters' contours—and subtly purposeful inconsistencies in character weight and proportion—to deliver a recognizable brand character that still feels charming and personal.

SANGBLEU FAMILIES
SWISS TYPEFACES / SWITZERLAND

For some time, the Sangbleu family has been expanding to provide new possibilities in color and expression. All of the members of the family exhibit noticeable stylistic elements that, while slightly divergent, all carry a kind of delicate romanticism—from the Empire version (top), a high-contrast, Rationalist serif; to the Sunrise version, its semiserif counterpart (second from top); to the original BP versions released a few years ago, consisting mainly of exceptionally light, calligraphic forms (third and fourth from top) with eccentric details.

ART BIENNIAL BRANDING
THONIK / NETHERLANDS

A custom sans serif with structurally-dependent add-on strokes conveys the industrial character of a contemporary art festival's cultural context and its various venues.

EQUIPMENT MANUFAC-TURER BRANDING
CHERMAYEFF & GEISMAR & HAVIV / USA

This clever letter-sign logo encapsulates the product offering of the client, Magirus, who produces ladders for use in the construction industry.

s[edition]

DIGITAL ART GALLERY BRANDING BARNBROOK / UK

Punctuation (the brackets) effects a sophisticated play on words in this logo for an online gallery of art works that, technically, don't exist.

WINE PRODUCER BRANDING PARALLAX / AUSTRALIA

This monogram for Ministry of Clouds, a premium vintner, is based on cloud classification symbols and the crystal structure of ice.

Art Mediation/Art Education
Kunstbemiddeling/Kunsteducatie
Guided tours, kids & youth workshops, family events and more
Rondleidingen, kinderen- en jongerenworkshops, familie-evenementen en meer

June 2 – September 30, 2012 · Genk, Limburg, Belgium
The European Biennial of Contemporary Art · De Europese Biënnale voor Hedendaagse Kunst
La Biennale Européenne d'Art Contemporain · Die Europäische Biennale für Zeitgenössische Kunst

NEWSLETTER MASTHEAD
PAONE DESIGN ASSOCIATES / USA

Abstracted characters live side by side with letter-like elements from musical notation to create a unified character set in this titling treatment for a music organization's periodical publication.

PROTOTYPE DISPLAY FACE
BARNBROOK / UK

A hybrid font offering whose specimen text, below, pretty much captures its intent.

PROTOTYPE IS A UNIVERSAL ALPHABET WITH A VERY CONTEMPORARY IDENTITY CRISIS. IS IT OLD OR NEW? UPPERCASE OR LOWERCASE? SERIF OR SANS SERIF? EXPERIMENTAL LETTERFORMS THAT HAVE THE IRRITATING FAMILIARITY OF A PLAYED-TO-DEATH POP SONG. PROTOTYPE TRIES TO BE ALL THINGS TO ALL PEOPLE.

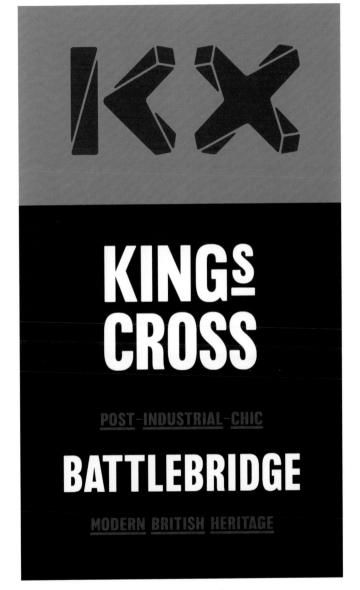

MUNICIPAL DEVELOP-MENT BRANDING
SOMEONE / UK

To capture both the heritage and future of an iconic London neighborhood—King's Cross—as part of a promotional branding system, a decidedly contemporary letter-sign is paired with an updated, 19th-century grotesque sans serif characteristic of the neighborhood's industrial background.

BROWNSTONE
ORNAMENTAL TEXT FONT
SUDTIPOS / ARGENTINA

This text face integrates script-like details in its characters' joints, along with swash elements and decorative flourishes.

OBSIDIAN FAMILY
HOEFLER & CO. / USA

This display family is the exciting result of an exercise in balancing 19th-century decorative engraving with object-oriented programming that defined the characters as volumes affected by the play of light. The design process was iterative: the tools revealed opportunities for code enhancements and unexpected qualities that were allowed to reshape the design brief itself. It escapes the limitations of its historical style while honoring its best traditions.

**EMILY-IN-WHITE
SCRIPT FACE**
JULIASYS STUDIO / GERMANY

This delicate, ephemeral script, like all of the designer's complementary work, capitalizes on the intuitive algorithms of the OpenType format to create a stunningly fluid and natural hand.

TITLING TREATMENT
FAITH / CANADA

Medieval blackletter and decorative interlace forms provide inspiration.

**LAUNDRY SERVICES
BRANDING** ANAGRAMA /
MEXICO

Precise stenciling, extreme contrast, and slickly formed ligatures elicit feelings of reliability and quality in this logotype.

EVITA FAMILY
SEALSTUDIO / USA

This typographic celebration of an iconic political leader evokes vernacular protest sign lettering from the relevant era.

DON'T CRY FOR ME, ARGENTINA!

EVITA

7 MAY 1919 — 26 JULY 1952

PERÓN

CASSANET FAMILY
ATIPO FOUNDRY / SPAIN

A multiweight family in two widths captures the aesthetic essence of French advertising posters from the period between the two World Wars.

BRIOCHE

THE 1934 PACKARD QX2 COUPE

VEUVE CLICQUOT

FRISCH!

LOS ZAPATOS DE CUERO PARA NIÑOS MÁS BELLOS

SANT AMBROGIO BOOK
Aa Bb Cc Dd Ee Ff Gg Hh Ii Ll Mm Nn
Oo Pp Qq Rr Ss Tt Uu Vv Xx Yy Zz
1 2 3 4 5 6 7 8 9 0

Sant Ambrogio Script
Aa Bb Cc Dd Ee Ff Gg Hh Ii Ll Mm Nn
Oo Pp Qq Rr Ss Tt Uu Vv Xx Yy Zz
1 2 3 4 5 6 7 8 9 0

RESTAURANT BRANDING
MUCCA DESIGN / USA

Vintage-inspired, complementary type families—one, a casually curly upright script, and the other, a geometric sans serif with echoes of the script's curves—set the tone for the visual identity of a New York City eatery opened by a Milanese restaurant outfit with a 1930s origin.

INKWELL FAMILY
HOEFLER & CO. / USA

This new superfamily is based on the idiosyncracies of writing, but is carefully systematized for the serious typographer. It incorporates the expressive aspects of scribbled notes (including reinking of important points), as well as more florid elements, like a blackletter and an outline version. Each variant offers a range of weights and alternate characters for compelling authenticity, and can be used interchangeably.

An American Diary
BUTTERSCOTCH
ABSTRACT PAINTING
Motorcycle Leathers
ROY LICHTENSTEIN
XANTHINE ORANGE
Imogen Cunningham

John White Alexander
SILVERSMITHING
Light Niagara Green
MACKINTOSH
Hangtag Instructions
INSTALLATION ART
NATIONAL FLAG BLUE

INTERSTELLAR ROCKETSHIP
POTATOE FARMS DEFEATED!
FLOPIES PROVE EXISTENCE
ROLLINGSTONE MAGAZINE"
MARYLAND INSTITUTE BALTO

JIMJAMS

CALCULA FAMILY
TYPOTHÈQUE / NETHERLANDS

An extensive range of ornamented, geometric sans serif faces that incorporate solid-stroke, inline, shadowed, and two-tone variants—along with idiosyncratic structural alternates to offer numerous expressive, stylish typesetting options.

FASHION HOUSE BRANDING ANAGRAMA / MEXICO

This wordmark for a sports-oriented fashion label alludes to the brush-drawn signage that is vernacular to California beachside concessions and the surf culture of the 1960s.

NEUBAU AKADEMIE FAMILY NEUBAU / GERMANY

This studiously drawn sans serif, inspired by Theinhardt's Royal Grotesque (which later became Berthold's Akzidenz), presents a comfortable, even rhythm and surprising warmth, given its rigorous construction.

Neubau Akademie™

L L R *I* M *M*

B *B* **B** *B*

M *M* **M** *M* **M** M *M*

M *M* M M

9702
3481
56

Neubau
Akademie™ Std
Bold

Ziffern
Numbres
Digits

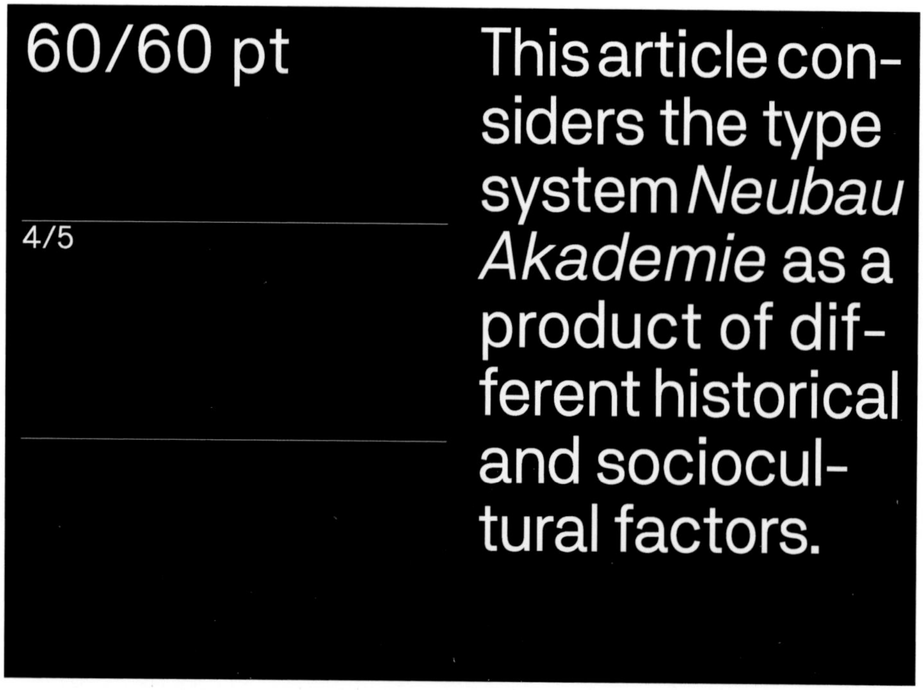

60/60 pt

4/5

This article considers the type system *Neubau Akademie* as a product of different historical and sociocultural factors.

TELECOM BRANDING
SOMEONE / UK

Straightforward circular terminals and transparent, overlapped stroke joints contribute feelings of directness and friendly sharing in the logo and house font developed for the client.

BARIOL & BARIOL SERIF FAMILIES
ATIPO FOUNDRY / SPAIN

These complementary families, each with a comprehensive range of weights and corresponding italics, provide a wealth of stylistic options that can support complex text hierarchies.

SAVOIR SAVOIR

A mouthful of velvety goodness: $4.50   A mouthful of velvety goodness: $4.50

Julieta! Que cosa?   *Julieta! Que cosa?*

SCHREIBST DU   **SCHREIBST DU**

0123456789?!&%@{0123456789?!&%@{   0123456789?!&%@{0123456789?!&%@{

AGMR

**PRIORI ACUTE
SERIF DISPLAY FACE**
BARNBROOK / UK

This face balances sturdy, classical serif construction with an inline component that produces an impossible spatial disconnect, similar to that of an optical illusion known as the Penrose Triangle. Some time after it was developed, the studio found an ideal use for it—in their design for a book on Surrealism in architecture.

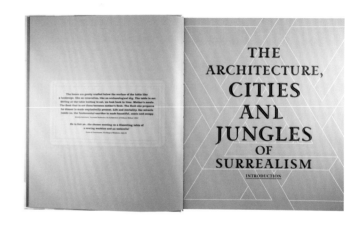

ABCDEFGHIJKLM NOPQRSTUVWXYZ

PHILADELPHIA YOUTH ORCHESTRA

**YOUTH ORCHESTRA
BRANDING**
PAONE DESIGN ASSOCIATES / USA

This reductive, monoline sans serif suggests musical notation by replacing crossbars with dots and enforcing a universal stroke angle for characters formed with diagonals. The face's near-Roman proportion lends it a classical quality while remaining contemporary in overall feel.

SPECIAL BENEFIT CONCERT CELEBRATING MAESTRO PRIMAVERA'S 50TH ANNIVERSARY

BRRR DISPLAY FACE
SWISS TYPEFACES / SWITZERLAND

An extended stance and a host of unusual details—brittle stroke joints, over-reaching arcs and extended tittles, diagonal elements in unexpected places, variable character widths, and the appearance of both italic and backslanted postures—give text set in this face a quirky rhythm. At a glance, it appears quite streamlined but, on closer inspection, reveals a cold, jumpy bounce across the line.

ABGM
RSQXJ
adefgn
prtxwz
01234
56789
X!?%("

ALPINE MEADOWS
Grace à Dieux! C'est Vendredi
Wunderschön
Schiaffeggiami la faccia e infornami una torta di carne tritata!

WIND FAMILY
TYPOTHÈQUE / NETHERLANDS

The first published typeface of Hansje van Halem, this experimental display face is intended for intriguing, layered optical effects in large-scale headlines. Four static styles are provided, but the font also enables full 360° rotation (clockwise or counterclockwise), offering unprecedented possibilities for exploring repetitive, textural patterns.

**MUSIC ENSEMBLE
BRANDING** THIRST / USA

The simple structure of
a geometric sans serif
capital set takes on new
life through exaggerated
top/bottom proportions,
partial, unjoined strokes,
and an inventive use of
circular forms to reenvision
several of its characters—
producing a serious, runic
quality, tempered with
a bit of whimsy.

ABCDEFGHI
JKLMNOPQ
RSTUVWXYZ
1234567890

**MUSAC BLACKLETTER
DISPLAY FONT** ESTUDIO
PONCE CONTRERAS / SPAIN

Bloated curves interact with
heavy, angular cuts, creating
a unique hybrid of blackletter
and sans serif structure.

**EDITORIAL TITLING
TREATMENT** FAITH / CANADA

Pure geometry constructs
this wordmark, cleverly
extending its diagonal language into the O (the only
circular character) to
better unify its four glyphs.

**EDITORIAL
TITLING TREATMENT**
FAITH / CANADA

This composition of forms draws from the language of Japanese *kawaii*-culture hiragana writing to give clear context to the subject of this headline's article without simply aping the style in a facile way.

POSTER TITLING
UN MUNDO FELIZ / SPAIN

Basic shapes combine to create simple, engaging letters in this detail of an exhibition poster.

22.04 — 02.07.2017

Palácio Calheta
Jardim Botânico Tropical
Rua General João de Almeida, 15
Belém

terça a domingo
10h às 18h
encerrado segunda
tuesday to sunday
10am to 6pm
closed monday

MUDE
Museu do Design
e da Moda, Coleção
Francisco Capelo

novo mundo — visões através da bienal iberoamericana de diseñ

exposição design exhibition MUDE Fora de Portas

NEWSPEAK IS BASED ON ARCHITECTURAL FORMS FROM STALINIST RUSSIA AND THE CYRILLIC ALPHABET LETTERFORMS PRESENTED WITH A DECADENT VISUAL LANGUAGE AND A SINISTER POLITICAL UNDERTONE

NEWSPEAK FAMILY
BARNBROOK / UK

Merging culturally appropriated forms in a sensitive way is a challenge, admirably accomplished in this display face that refers to period-specific architecture and a non-Roman alphabetic system.

CORE STENCIL FAMILY
SEALSTUDIO / USA

Both variants of this font family derive from type found on hand-drawn protest posters created during the American civil rights movement.

MEDGAR
HUEY
MALCOLM
ELBERT

ROSA
SOJOURNER
HARRIET
KATHLEEN

EDITORIAL TITLING TREATMENT FAITH / CANADA

Above, a florid homage to the typographic innovations of the French Art Nouveau era of the late 1800s.

WINE PRODUCER BRANDING
PARALLAX / AUSTRALIA

The flared strokes of this semiglyphic serif logotype, together with a sharp, partial outline shadow, impart a robust, elegant classicism in this updated branding program.

ESTD
HARDYS
1853

CORPORATE BRANDING
ANAGRAMA / MEXICO

This consulting firm's competent, buttoned-down integrity, willingness to look beyond convention, and meticulous attention to detail find expression in the combination of an industrial fat face and a quirky, cleverly integrated ampersand.

DRACULA FAMILY
STORM TYPE FOUNDRY /
CZECH REPUBLIC

Vintage blackletter types typically combine majuscules and miniscules of wildly different proportion. This new one unifies them in a slightly condensed drawing that also features a relatively large lowercase, designed for contemporary setting, and includes both solid and inline versions.

BOOK COVER TITLING
MUCCA DESIGN / USA

Custom characters inspired by the sleek types of the Art Déco period grace the cover of this book, devoted to the mixiology of a storied hotel's golden era.

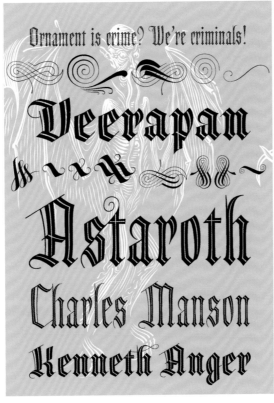

Ornament is crime? We're criminals!

Veerapan

Astaroth

Charles Manson

Kenneth Anger

Children of the night; what music they make!

Dracula Inline Regular and Light

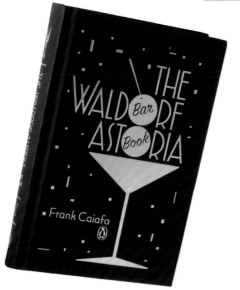

THE WALDORF ASTORIA Bar Book

• Frank Caiafa

RESTAURANT BRANDING
FAITH / CANADA

This comfortable, upright script mark for a pizzeria exudes casual accessibility in its rounded terminals and soft joints, but hints at a heritage of serious, Old World craftsmanship by slyly enforcing a subtle, strict repetition of angles among its verticals and in the directional axes of the curves.

MELANCHOLIA FAMILY
BARNBROOK / UK

A subtle sans serif that introduces a sense of wistfulness into the form through controlled, calligraphic gestures, a slight cracking of the curves, and the remnants of serifs. The family includes a set of true italics influenced by old-style serif italics, along with stylistic alternates and swash characters.

RUBÉN DISPLAY FACE
SEALSTUDIO / USA

This all-uppercase, irregularly-weighted sans serif with rectangular curved forms was inspired by banners carried during the National Chicano Moratorium march on August 29, 1970, and the death of renowned Latino activist Rubén Salazar.

Great
Pieces
NOTHING
VIOLENCE
What You Fear
no bystanding

Till your head is a stone

Her radiance scathes me

This is rain now, this big hush. And this is the fruit of it: tin-white, like arsenic

Diminished and flat, as after radical surgery
How your bad dreams possess and endow me

I have suffered the atrocity of sunsets. Scorched to the root. My red filaments burn and stand, a hand of wires. Now I break up in pieces that fly about like clubs. A wind of such violence Will tolerate no bystanding.

I am incapable of more knowledge. What is this, this face. So murderous in its strangle of branches? Its snaky acids hiss. It petrifies the will. These are the isolate, slow faults That kill, that kill, that kill.

NATIONAL CHICANO MORATORIUM AUG 29
EAST LA

WHO IS A CHICANO? AND WHAT IS IT THE CHICANOS WANT?

MEXICAN-AMERICAN'S DILEMMA: HE'S UNFIT IN EITHER LANGUAGE

CHICANO REMINDS BLACKS THEY ARE NOT THE ONLY MINORITY

AÀÁÂÃÄÅĀĂĄÆÆBRCCĆĈĊČĎĐEÉÉÉÈ
ÊĚĒÉĘFGĜĞĠĢĦĦĦĬÍÍÎÏĨĪĬ JĴKĶLĹ
ĻĽĿŁMMŃŇŇŅŊŊ OÒÓÔÕÖ OŌŎŐ Œ
ØÞPŔŘŖRSŚŜŞŠTŢŤTUÙÚÛÜŨŪŬŮŰŲVW
ŴÚWŴXYÝŶŸ ZŻŽŹ0123456789
$¢ƒ£¥€i!¿?----+=@&..:;""""

BEAUTY & LIFESTYLE BRANDING
MUCCA DESIGN / USA

A fresh, ownable typographic program for the Sephora cosmetics company retains an association with style genres typically associated with the fashion industry (high-contrast Didones) but alters the axis and thickens the thins to ensure robust reproduction across media platforms. The serif is joined by a complementary sans serif and two scripts that pay homage to the heyday of fashion editorial work.

Custom Sans

Custom Serif Display

Custom Serif *Text*

Custom Beauty Editor Script

Custom Collection Script

KAUTIVA FAMILY
SUDTIPOS / ARGENTINA

This modern sans serif retains a clean, rational quality, balanced by softly pinched curves and slight modulation in the strokes.

Awesome

Speakin**TOOSLANG**

bioactive

GLOBAL **CONCEPT**

add linguistic φπώφκ

Brandfobic

Regular CAPS & unicase

Augmented Reality

AWARENESS

COMPASSIONATE FLOW

GENTRIFIED

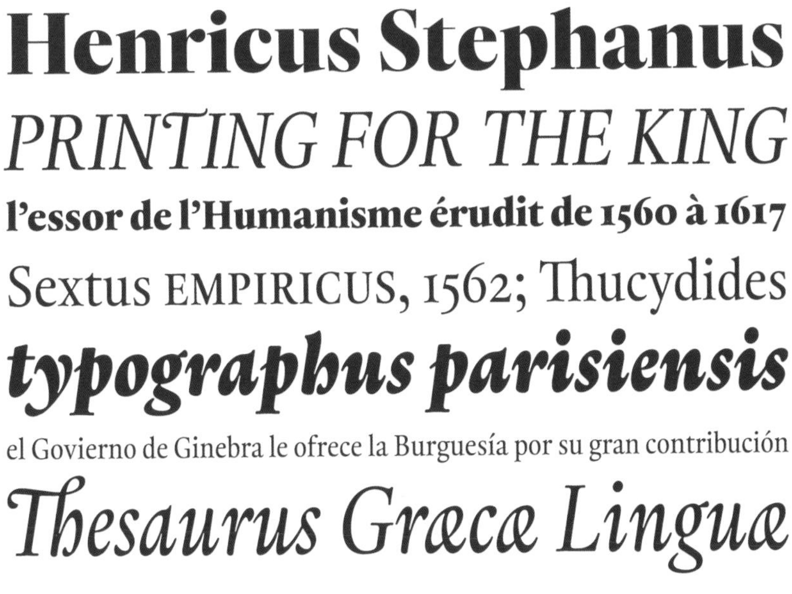

Henricus Stephanus

PRINTING FOR THE KING

l'essor de l'Humanisme érudit de 1560 à 1617

Sextus EMPIRICUS, 1562; Thucydides

typographus parisiensis

el Govierno de Ginebra le ofrece la Burguesía por su gran contribución

Thesaurus Græcæ Linguæ

THESAURUS FAMILY
TYPOTHÈQUE / NETHERLANDS

This new serif blends the vintage features of metal types used by the Estienne family in Paris and Geneva with contemporary ones: a large x-height, narrower forms, and increased modulation. The result is a versatile face that is both humanistic and rational, bridging the past and the present.

BEAUTY & LIFESTYLE BRANDING
MUCCA DESIGN / USA

The overall light weight, sharp terminals and joints, and exaggerated difference in proportion between condensed, upright characters and fully circular curved ones lends a sexy, somewhat retro flare to the identity of a cosmetics house.

EDITORIAL TITLING TREATMENT FAITH / CANADA

Swirling serifs and circular counters invade this bold wordmark to evoke the music scene of the 1970s with a syncopated, percussive arrangement of dots.

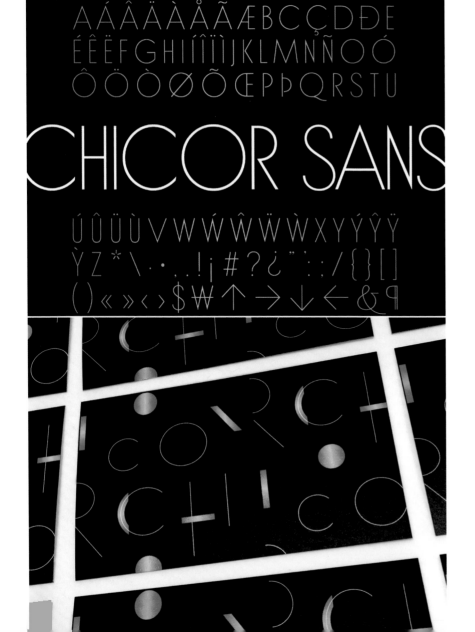

KLIMAX FAMILY
TYPOTHÈQUE / NETHERLANDS

This family's two variants, Plus and Minus (the heaviest and lightest possible styles) are optical opposites, but they share similar metrics and spacing, so they can be easily interchanged in a body of text. The counter-measures of the heavy variant are equivalent to the stroke weight of the light variant.

KENWOOD DISTRICT

Ludwig Bemelmans

HITCHCOCK HOUSE

Geomorphological

CAMERA OBSCURA

Huntington Beach

MOUNTAINEERING

Typolithographic

HYDROGEN BOND

Double Negative

TRADING HOURS

Concrete Block

PERISTYLE FAMILY
HOEFLER & CO. / USA

Carefully translating the formal characteristics of historical styles that inspired this super condensed, high-contrast sans serif family resulted in a face full of drama that is very much of the present, neither old fashioned nor eccentrically futuristic.

ARCHIA FAMILY
ATIPO FOUNDRY / SPAIN

This reserved, geometric sans serif incorporates unexpected details—the spur on the lowercase a, a squared-off descender on the g (among others)—that help it maintain the style's characteristic purity without becoming cold and mechanical or stuffy.

**AGMRSQ
adefgktx
01234567890?!&@**

AGMRSQ
adefgktx
01234567890?!&@

WINE PRODUCER BRANDING PARALLAX / AUSTRALIA

Hyper condensed and extreme in contrast, this wordmark brings an Art Déco heritage into the realm of bar codes and binary programming language—old and new in one delicious eyeful.

FURNITURE DESIGN BRANDING FAITH / CANADA

A striking, variable logotype for Ranbir Sidhu's design studio organizes geometrically abstracted letterforms under a modular system in a range of options, sometimes supporting—and at others, challenging—legibility. The designer worked in collaboration with the client and Denise Cole of Juliet Creative.

SALOMÉ FAMILY
ATIPO FOUNDRY / SPAIN

This bold, robust, serif family includes options with differing degrees of stroke information (all of extreme contrast), along with alternate display capitals that incorporate decorative swash junctures.

A A A A
a a a a
ABDGHO
PQRSU
ABCDEFGHIJKLMNO
PQRSTUVWXYZ
abcdefghijklmno
pqrstuvwxyz
0123456789 0123456789

MUSHROOMS
TOMATO
HAM
CAPSICUM
CHEESE
ANCHOVIES

MORDI SPECIAL
ABIGAIL HAWKINS / AUSTRALIA
OLD SCHOOL NEW SCHOOL
Victoria Grow, instructor

Inspired to create a face for a local Melbourne pizza shop, the designer of this monoline sans serif brings a sleek, engaging quality to the characters through an elegantly extended body, rounded terminals, and slightly tilted crossbars.

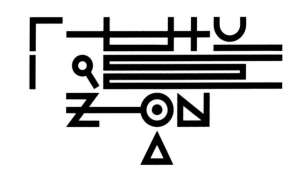

Marian 1554 Roman
Marian 1554 Italic

Marian 1565 Roman
Marian 1565 Italic

Marian 1571 Roman
Marian 1571 Italic

Marian 1680 Roman
Marian 1680 Italic

Marian 1740 Roman
Marian 1740 Italic

Marian 1742 Roman
Marian 1742 Italic

Marian 1757 Roman
Marian 1757 Italic

Marian 1800 Roman
Marian 1800 Italic

Marian 1812 Roman
Marian 1812 Italic

𝔐𝔞𝔯𝔦𝔞𝔫 𝔅𝔩𝔞𝔠𝔨

MARIAN FAMILY
COMMERCIAL TYPE / UK

Classics of the typographic canon—forms created by Austin, Baskerville, Bodoni, Garamond, Granjon, Fournier, van den Keere, and Kiš—are reduced to their skeletal essences. The family includes nine serifs (accompanied by their respective italics) and a blackletter variant.

MUSEUM BRANDING
SOMEONE / UK

The removal of selected strokes creates an alphabet of code-like glyphs for the identity of a spy museum.

DESIGN FESTIVAL BRANDING PARALLAX / AUSTRALIA

This densely constructed modular alphabet expresses its grid with units of various sizes, creating tension between mass and texture at differing scales.

ARCHITECTURE BIENNIAL BRANDING
THONIK / NETHERLANDS

The theme of the 6th Urbanism/Architecture Bi-City Biennale in Shenzhen was "re-living the city" and advocated a new kind of urbanism in need of a hunter–gatherer mentality. A woven bag inspired by the theme (and used as the basis for campaign images) gave rise to a modular alphabet; walls of woven type were used to mark the different sections in the exhibition.

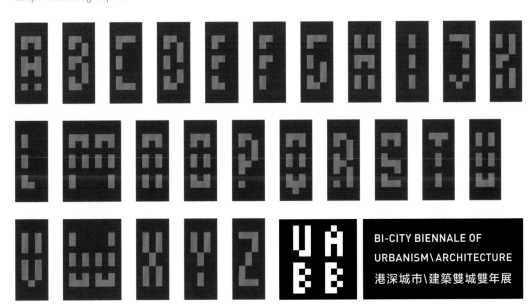

BI-CITY BIENNALE OF URBANISM\ARCHITECTURE
港深城市\建築雙城雙年展

RE-LIVING THE CITY
城市原点

2015 深港城市\建筑双城双年展
2015.12.04 - 2016.02.28
www.szhkbiennale.org

The images in this
group are in the public
domain, all made
available by the Metro-
politan Museum of Art
in New York through

Creative Commons
through a deeded do-
nation. The Museum's
acquisition credits
accompany each image.

The images in this group
are also in the public domain,
acquired from various sources
via Creative Commons. Credits
are provided as available.

Rogers Fund, 1923

Theodore M. Davis Collection,
Bequest of Theodore M. Davis,
1915

Fletcher Fund, 1926

Source unidentified

Rogers Fund, 1923

Rogers Fund, 1923

Museum Accession

Source unidentified

Rogers Fund, 1923

Fletcher Fund, 1924

The Cloisters Collection, 1999

Source unidentified

PICTURE INDEX
HISTORICAL PHOTOGRAPHS

Purchase, Raymond and
Beverly Sackler Gift, 1988

Fletcher Fund, 1926

Harris Brisbane Dick Fund, 1926

Austrian Gallery Belvedere

Rogers Fund, 1959

Fletcher Fund, 1926

Bequest of Phyllis Massar, 2011

Rijksmuseum / Van Moorsel
donation, 1981

Rogers Fund, 1958

Fletcher Fund, 1926

Harris Brisbane Dick Fund, 1917

Archivo General de la Nación,
Argentina

The images in this group were acquired from Wikimedia Commons and are licensed for use pursuant to conditions defined by the Creative Commons Attribution-Share Alike 3.0 Unported license or (where noted) are in the public domain.

Credits are provided as available.

These images were acquired from the Library of Congress online catalog and are assumed to be in the public domain. The Library of Congress notes no known restrictions for reproduction due to inapplicable, expired, or unrenewed copyright. Credits are provided as available.

Peter van der Sluijs

Source unidentified

Source unidentified

Source unidentified

Jacob Haehnlen / Philadelphia, 1869

Source unidentified

Bibliothèque Nationale de Paris

Reinraum (photographer)

Swiss Federal Council
Public domain

Mac Repository
Public domain

Source unidentified

Source unidentified

Source unidentified

Source unidentified

Marcin Wichary (photographer)

Source unidentified

United States Government / Works Progress Administration

Source unidentified

Source unidentified

Teddychen81 (photographer)

Source unidentified

Source unidentified

Source unidentified

Stefan Kühn (photographer)

Boffy B. (photographer)

National Library of Wales
Public domain

Etan J. Tal (photographer)

Source unidentified

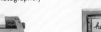

DIRECTORY OF CONTRIBUTORS

Anagrama
199/207/215/217/224
anagrama.com

Atipo Foundry
171/216/219/229/230
atipo.com

Barnbrook
42/212/213/220/223/226
barnbrook.net, virusfonts.net

Donald Brady
193
donaldbrady.com

Chermayeff & Geismar
& Haviv
204/208/209/212
cghnyc.com

Commercial Type
199/207/210/231
commercialtype.com

Jessica DeAngelis
195
jessrdeangelis@gmail.com

Madeline Deneys
167
madelinedeneys@gmail.com

Estudio Ponce Contreras
205/206/222
manuelponcecontreras.com

Faith
207/209/211/217/224/
226/227/228/230-231
faith.ca

Erika Fulton
167
erikafultondesign.com

Steff Geissbühler
37
geissbuhler.com

Kevin Harris
178–179/184
kevinstanleyharris@gmail.com

Abigail Hawkins
230
ahawkins320@gmail.com

Lance Hidy
43
hidystudio.com

Hoefler & Co.
135/201/202/216/219/229
typography.com

Rhiann Irvine
185
rhiannirvine.com

Juliasys Studio
202/217
juliasys.com

Jerry Kuyper
164–165
jerrykuyper.com

William Longhauser
40
longhauser.com

Moving Brands
170/203/209/210
movingbrands.com

Mucca Design
200/204/213/218/227/
229/230
mucca.com

Neubau
220
neubauberlin.com

Papo Letterpress
8–9/28
papoletterpress.com

Paone Design Assocs.
168/209/213/220
paonedesign.com

Parallax
204/212/224/229/232
parallaxdesign.com.au

Maximillian Pollio
167
maxpollio.com

Matthew Romanski
133
matthewromanski.com

Timothy Samara
133/140–143/165
timothysamara.com

Sealstudio
203/216/224/226
sealsbrand.co

Andrew Scheiderich
134/194
andrew.scheiderich@gmail.com

Ali Sciandra
78–79
alisciandra.com

SomeOne
201/207/215/221/232
someoneinlondon.com

Storm Type Foundry
203/206/227
stormtype.com

Students of Purchase
College/SUNY*
126/132/170/171/173/174/
176/177/193
c/o tsamara.designer@gmail.com

Sudtipos
45/216/229
sudtipos.com

Swiss Typefaces
209/211/213/223/231
swisstypefaces.com

Thirst
42/201/204/210/224/225
3st.com

Thonik
208/214/233
thonik.nl

Typothèque
169/200/205/219/223/
229/230
typotheque.com

Un Mundo Feliz
212/225
unmundofeliz2.blogspot.com

Danielle Weinberger
190
daniellwein@yahoo.com

Phillip Wong
193
phillipmw@gmail.com

ABOUT THE AUTHOR

Timothy Samara is a New York–based graphic designer who splits his time between professional practice and teaching; he is a frequent lecturer and contributor to design publications both in the U.S. and abroad. Samara has written eight books on design that have been translated into ten languages and are used by students and practitioners around the world. The second edition of his bestselling first book, *Making and Breaking the Grid*, was released in 2017.

ACKNOWLEDGMENTS

Assembling material for a book of this kind depends on the good will of so many busy people. My sincere thanks to all of the contributors who collected examples of their work for consideration, for their suggestions, and for their great encouragement. I would be remiss if I didn't acknowledge the efforts of the team at Rockport, whose diligence and patience can not be overstated: Thank you, Anne, Cora, John, Judith, Regina, and Renae. And last, but certainly not least, I would like to thank my partner Sean, my family, and all my friends for their support.

*
Sincere apologies to students of mine whose work is unattributed; the ravages of time made identification in my archive frustratingly difficult. If you recognize any of the projects included here as your own, please get in touch so that I may correct the omission in future reprintings.